Das große Übungsbuch

Mit Übungen fit in Englisch werden.

5. – 8. Klasse

Beatrix Pierce
Lorena Rautenberg
Alexander P. Saccaro
Quaid N. Williams

Bibliografische Information der Deutschen Nationalbibliothek
Die Deutsche Nationalbibliothek verzeichnet diese Publikation in der Deutschen Nationalbibliografie; detaillierte bibliografische Daten sind im Internet über http://dnb.d-nb.de abrufbar.

Auflage 5. 4. 3. 2. 1. | 2014 2013 2012 2011 2010
Die letzten Zahlen bezeichnen jeweils die Auflage und das Jahr des Druckes.

Dieses Werk folgt der reformierten Rechtschreibung und Zeichensetzung.

Umschlaggestaltung: Sabine Kaufmann, Stuttgart
Satz: Andrea Eckhardt, Göppingen / Klaus Bauer, Bondorf
Druck: Medienhaus Plump, Rheinbreitbach
ISBN 978-3-12-920035-3

9 783129 200353

Vorwort

Liebe Schülerinnen, liebe Schüler,

dieses Buch macht dich fit in Englisch. Vor dir liegt das gebündelte Wissen im fach Englisch vom 5. bis zum 8. Schuljahr – greif zu! Es bietet dir um deine Leistung in diesem Fach zu verbessern:

- Regeln (Seite 5 – 14)
- Übungen für die 5. und 6. Klasse (Seite 15 – 152)
- Übungen für die 7. und 8. Klasse (Seite 153 – 342)

Mit diesem Buch kannst du den aktuellen Unterrichtsstoff mitlernen oder Inhalte aus vorangegangenen Schuljahren nachschlagen und festigen. Nimm es einfach immer wieder zur Hand und bearbeite einen Abschnitt daraus.

Anhand der ausführlichen Lösungen kannst du überprüfen, ob du alles richtig gemacht hast. Die Lösungen zu jeder Aufgabe stehen auf dem Kopf unten auf jeder Seite.

Ob du nun Stoff wiederholen oder dich auf eine Klassenarbeit vorbereiten möchtest – dieser Band wird dich Schritt für Schritt zum Erfolg führen und bringt dir maximalen Durchblick, maximalen Erfolg und maximale Sicherheit.

Und jetzt kann's losgehen!

Das große Übungsbuch Englisch

Regeln

Teil 1 Seite 15 – 152
Teil 2 Seite 153 – 342

Der Plural

Bei Substantive, die den Plural regelmäßig bilden, wird an den Singular ein *-s* angehängt.
place → place**s** dog → dog**s**

Endet ein Substantiv auf *-s, -ss, -ch* oder *-x*, wird *-es* angehängt.
bus → bus**es** dish → dish**es**

Endet ein Substantiv auf *-y*, lautet die Pluralendung *-ies*:
baby → bab**ies** lady → lad**ies**

Ist der Endlaut eines Substantivs *-f* oder *-fe*, lautet die Pluralendung *-ves*:
scarf → scar**ves** shelf → shel**ves**

Achtung: Nicht alle Substantive auf *-f*, denn manche bilden Plural auch ganz regelmäßig:
belief → belief**s**

Einige wenige Wörter auf *-o* haben im Plural *-oes*:
potato → potat**oes**

Unregelmäßiger Plural

Zahlreiche Substantive bilden den Plural unregelmäßig. Hier hilft nur eines – gleich beim Vokabellernen mitlernen!
foot → **feet** mouse → **mice**

Bei einigen Substantiven, die den Plural unregelmäßig bilden, verändert sich auch die Aussprache.
child → **children** man → **men**

Einige Substantive haben in Singular und Plural dieselbe Form.
sheep → **sheep**

Schreibweise des Genitivs

Achte darauf, ob es sich um ein Wort im Singular oder im Plural handelt!
Denn im Singular steht immer ein Apostroph zwischen Substantiv und Genitivendung:
Susan**'s** book

Im Plural jedoch wird der Genitiv so geschrieben:
the girls' book

Ausnahme: unregelmäßig gebildete Pluralformen
women**'s** rights

Der unbestimmte Artikel

Der unbestimmte Artikel *a* verändert sich vor einem Substantiv, das mit einem Vokal beginnt, zu *an*:

a book	**an** exercise

Im Plural gibt es – wie im Deutschen – keinen unbestimmten Artikel.
Stattdessen wird z. B. *some/any – einige* verwendet:

a girl	**some** girls

Formen der Steigerung

Es gibt folgende Möglichkeiten, Adjektive zu steigern:
- einsilbige Adjektive mit *-er* und *-est*,
- zweisilbige Adjektive, die auf *-y* enden, mit *-ier* und *-iest*,
- zwei- oder mehrsilbige Adjektive mit *more* und *most*:

	1. Steigerung	*2. Steigerung*
fast	fast**er**	fast**est**
happy	happ**ier**	happ**iest**
nervous	**more** nervous	**most** nervous
horrible	**more** horrible	**most** horrible

Achtung Schreibweise! Ein stummes *-e* am Ende entfällt:

nice	nic**er**	nic**est**

Endet ein einsilbiges Adjektiv mit kurzer Silbe auf einen Konsonanten, wird dieser verdoppelt:

hot	ho**tter**	ho**ttest**

Adjektiv oder Adverb?

Adjektive stehen nach Verben der Sinneswahrnehmung, des Zustands und der Zustandsveränderung.
The soup smelt **awful**. – Die Suppe roch schrecklich.
The car didn't seem **perfect**. – Das Auto schien nicht perfekt (zu sein).
My father didn't become **rich**. – Mein Vater wurde nicht reich.

Adverbien stehen nach Verben der Tätigkeit.
The man walked **slowly**. – Der Mann ging langsam.

Adjektive beziehen sich immer auf ein Substantiv oder ein Pronomen.
Vor einem Substantiv steht daher nie ein Adverb.

Adverbien der Art und Weise geben an, wie etwas getan wird.
Sie beziehen sich daher immer auf ein Verb.

Ist das Verb eine Form von *to be*, steht immer ein Adjektiv
(Ausnahme: *progressive forms*).

Personal- und Possessivpronomen

Das **Personalpronomen** in der Subjektform *(I, you, he, she, it, we, you, they)* steht für das Subjekt des Satzes.

Peter is coming. – Peter kommt gerade.
He is coming. – Er kommt gerade.

Das **Possessivpronomen** *(my, your, his, her, ist, our, your, their)* gibt den Besitzer an und steht vor einem Substantiv.

This is **his** car. – Das ist sein Auto.

Stehen sie ohne Substantiv, werden folgende Formen verwendet.

mine – meiner/-e/-es	ours – unserer/-e/-es
yours – deiner/-e/-es	yours – euer/-re/-res
his – seiner/-e/-es	their – ihrer/-e/-es
hers – ihrer/-e/-es	

Das Stützwort *one*

Das Stützwort *one* (Plural *ones*) kann ein Substantiv, das schon einmal erwähnt wurde, ersetzen, um Wiederholungen zu vermeiden.

That's Peter's car. The red **one** over there. –
Das ist Peters Auto. Das rote dort drüben.

Tom has a lot of shirts. He only has blue **ones**. –
Tom hat viele Hemden. Er hat nur blaue.

Gebrauch des *simple present*

Das *simple present* wird zur Beschreibung von regelmäßigen Handlungen und Tätigkeiten verwendet. Signalwörter wie *always – immer, never – nie, every day – jeden Tag* usw. weisen darauf hin, dass es sich um gewohnheitsmäßige Tätigkeiten handelt.

Tom always **forgets** his homework. – Tom vergisst immer seine Hausaufgaben.

Fragen formulieren

Im *simple present* braucht die Frage das Hilfsverb *do/does*, wenn keine Form von *to be* im Satz vorkommt.

Bildung des *simple past*

Bei Verben, die das *simple past* regelmäßig bilden, wird an den Infinitiv *-ed* angehängt. Wo bereits ein *-e* vorhanden ist, entfällt dieses:
stay + -ed → **stayed**
dance + -ed → **danced**

Endet ein Verb auf ein gesprochenes *t* oder *d*, wird die Endung wie *id* ausgesprochen:
hate + -ed → **hated**

Endet ein Verb auf Konsonant + *-y*, wird dies im *simple past* zu *-i*:
try + -ed → **tried**

Verwendung des *simple past*

Das *simple past* beschreibt Handlungen, die in Vergangenheit geschehen und nun abgeschlossen sind. Es wird auch in Erzählungen, Geschichten und Aufzählungen verwendet.
Tom went home and drank a cup of tea. –
Tom ging nach Hause und trank eine Tasse Tee.
Once upon a time there was a little girl … –
Es war einmal ein kleines Mädchen …

Signalwörter für das *simple past* sind z. B.:

yesterday – gestern	last weekend – letztes Wochenende
on Monday – am Montag	two years ago – vor zwei Jahren

Simple past oder *past progressive*?

Das *past progressive* verwendet man für Handlungen, die in der Vergangenheit stattfinden und noch nicht abgeschlossen sind. Das *simple past* hingegen beschreibt plötzlich eintretende Handlungen.

Merke:
Das *past progressive* war im Verlauf und das *simple past* trat plötzlich auf.

While Simon was reading, the lights went out. – Während Simon las (→ *länger andauernder, nicht abgeschlossener Vorgang*), gingen die Lichter aus (→ *plötzlich eintretender Vorgang*).

When Chris arrived, a lot of people were already helping. – Als Chris ankam (→ *plötzlich eintretender Vorgang*), halfen bereits viele Menschen (→ *länger andauernder, nicht abgeschlossener Vorgang*).

Signalwörter

Signalwörter für das *present perfect* sind:
ever – jemals
yet – schon
not yet – noch nicht
already – schon
always – immer
never – noch nie, niemals
just – gerade

For – seit (Zeitspanne) und *since – seit* (Zeitpunkt) können sowohl mit dem *present perfect* als auch mit dem *present perfect progressive* verwendet werden.

Since und *for*

Mit *since – seit* und *for – seit* wird angegeben, wann eine Handlung begonnen hat. Während *since* den genauen Zeitpunkt bezeichnet, beschreibt *for* die Zeitspanne des Geschehens.

I have been waiting for you **since** 7 o'clock. – Ich warte auf dich seit sieben Uhr.
I have been waiting **for** two hours. – Ich warte seit zwei Stunden.

Das *past perfect*

Das *past perfect* wird mit *had* und dem *past participle* gebildet.
I had been you had been

Mit dem *past perfect* wird eine Handlung beschrieben, die vor einer anderen in der Vergangenheit stattfindenden Handlung geschieht.

Tom **had already** eaten when Peter called. –
Tom hatte schon gegessen, als Peter anrief.

Peter **had done** his homework before he called Tom. –
Peter hatte seine Hausaufgaben gemacht, bevor er Tom anrief.

Past perfect progressive

Das *past perfect progressive* beschreibt eine Handlung, die in der Vergangenheit noch andauerte, bis eine andere Handlung in der Vergangenheit einsetzte.

They **had been waiting** already for half an hour when Tom arrived. –
Sie hatten schon eine halbe Stunde gewartet, als Tom kam.

Gebrauch des *will-future*

Das *will-future* wird verwendet,
- um Vermutungen und Hoffnungen auszudrücken,
- um Handlungen oder Ereignisse in der Zukunft zu beschreiben, die der Sprecher nicht beeinflussen kann.

Das *going-to-future*

Mit dem *going-to-future* werden Pläne und Absichten formuliert. Es wird auch verwendet, wenn man ziemlich sicher ist, dass man etwas tun wird oder etwas geschehen wird.

I am going to France in April. – Ich werde im April nach Frankreich fahren.
It's going to rain soon. – Es wird bald regnen.

Das *simple present* im Passiv

Das Passiv des *simple present* wird mit dem *simple present* von *to be* und dem Partizip Perfekt gebildet.
A bus driver **is hired.** – Ein Busfahrer wird angestellt.
Soccer **is played** every day by many boys. – Fußball wird von vielen Jungen jeden Tag gespielt.

Das Passiv der Vergangenheitszeiten

Mit dem *simple past* von *to be* und dem Partizip Perfekt bildest du das *simple past passive.*

I **was called** last night at 3 o'clock. – Ich wurde gestern Nacht um drei Uhr angerufen.

Das *present perfect passive* setzt sich aus dem *present perfect* von *to be* und dem Partizip Perfekt zusammen, das *past perfect passive* entsprechend aus dem *past perfect* von *to be* und dem Partizip Perfekt.

The thief **has been caught** straightaway. – Der Dieb ist sofort gefasst worden.

The thief **had been caught** before the police arrived. – Der Dieb war gefasst worden, bevor die Polizei kam.

Der *by-agent*

Mit dem *by-agent* wird der Urheber der Handlung im Passiv genannt, aber nur wenn es wirklich wichtig ist. Ist nicht ganz klar oder unwichtig, wer etwas getan hat, steht das Passiv ohne *by-agent.*

Die *progressive form* im Passiv

Das *present progressive passive* wird mit dem *present progressive* von *to be* und dem Partizip Perfekt gebildet, das *past progressive passive* mit dem *past progressive* von *to be* und dem Partizip Perfekt.

They **are being entertained** by some actors. –
Sie werden gerade durch ein paar Schauspieler unterhalten.
The car **was being cleaned** by Tom. –
Das Auto wurde gerade von Tom gewaschen.

Das *present participle*

Das *present participle* wird mit dem Infinitiv und der Endung *-ing* gebildet:
to talk → talking to speak → speaking

Endet der Infinitiv auf einen Konsonanten, so wird dieser verdoppelt:
to swim → swi**mm**ing to cut → cu**tt**ing

Endet er auf ein stummes *-e*, entfällt dieses; endet er auf *-ie*, wird diese Silbe zu *-y*:
to slice → slicing to lie → l**y**ing

If-Sätze – Typ 1 und 2

Bei realistisch erscheinenden Bedingungen steht *simple present* im *if*-Satz, *will-future* im Hauptsatz. Tipp: *If* und *will* können nie im gleichen Satzteil stehen!
Bei nicht wahrscheinlichen, aber möglichen Bedingungen steht *simple past* im *if*-Satz, *conditional I* (*would* + Infinitiv) im Hauptsatz.

If-Sätze – Typ 3

Bei unrealistischen Bedingungen steht *past perfect* im *if*-Satz, *conditional II* (*would have* + Partizip Perfekt) im Hauptsatz.

Nicht-notwendige Relativsätze

Relativsätze, die zusätzliche Informationen liefern, werden nicht-notwendige Relativsätze genannt. Sie können auch weggelassen werden, ohne dass sich die Aussage des Hauptsatzes verändert. Sie werden – im Unterschied zu den notwendigen Relativsätzen – mit Kommas abgetrennt.

Eton, which has a famous college, is a very old town. –
Eton, das ein sehr berühmtes College hat, ist eine sehr alte Stadt.

Das große Übungsbuch Englisch

Teil 1 (5. – 6. Klasse)

1

Bilde den Plural der folgenden Substantive.

book ____________	plan ____________
plane ____________	minute ____________
answer ____________	apple ____________
face ____________	chair ____________
box ____________	dress ____________
table ____________	page ____________
sandwich ____________	pencil case ____________
bridge ____________	desk ____________
hour ____________	brush ____________
teacher ____________	pupil ____________

2

Bei welchen der folgenden Substantive wird die Pluralendung wie /iz/ ausgesprochen? Unterstreiche diese Substantive.

pages	exercises	churches	clothes	houses
faces	roles	stages	theatres	buses
titles	languages	phrases	pieces	centres
bridges	cornflakes	messages	places	brochures
voices	noises	noses	horses	scenes
brushes	cakes	classes	glasses	tables

1 books, planes, answers, faces, boxes, tables, sandwiches, bridges, hours, teachers, plans, minutes, apples, chairs, dresses, pages, pencil cases, desks, brushes, pupils

2 pages, exercises, churches, clothes, houses, faces, roles, stages, theatres, buses, titles, languages, phrases, pieces, centres, bridges, cornflakes, messages, places, brochures, voices, noises, noses, horses, scenes, brushes, cakes, classes, glasses, tables

3

Bilde den Singular der folgenden Substantive.

days ____________	boys ____________
babies ____________	families ____________
thieves ____________	plays ____________
wives ____________	knives ____________
shelves ____________	countries ____________
parties ____________	lives ____________
halves ____________	hobbies ____________

4

Setze die folgenden Substantive in den Plural.

a boy and a girl ____________

a brother and a sister ____________

a book on a shelf ____________

a pupil and a teacher ____________

a cat and a dog ____________

a short life ____________

a baby and a toy ____________

a night and a day ____________

a diary and a pen ____________

a house and a flat ____________

a bus and a lorry* ____________

* lorry = LKW (American English: truck = trucks)

3 day, baby, thief, wife, shelf, party, half, boy, family, play, knife, country, life, hobby
4 boys and girls, brothers and sisters, books on shelves, pupils and teachers, cats and dogs, short lives, babies and toys, nights and days, diaries and pens, houses and flats, buses and lorries

5

Wie lautet der Plural?

man ______________________ woman ______________________

child ______________________ tooth ______________________

foot ______________________ goose ______________________

mouse ______________________

6

Bilde den Plural der folgenden Substantive.

a lady and a gentleman ______________________

a woman and a child ______________________

a bad tooth ______________________

the foot of a man ______________________

a cat and a mouse ______________________

7

Ergänze die fehlenden Buchstaben.

You can stand on one f ______________________.

What you eat, is your f ______________________.

For most people the first meal in the morning is b ______________________.

Your father and mother are your p ______________________.

Father, mother and children are a f ______________________.

The people who live next door are your n ______________________.

5 men, women, children, teeth, feet, geese, mice
6 ladies and gentlemen, women and children, bad teeth, the feet of men, cats and mice
7 foot, food, breakfast, parents, family, neighbours

8

Einige der folgenden Substantive sehen wie Singulare, andere wie Plurale aus. Wie musst du sie gebrauchen? Trage die folgenden Substantive bitte in die entsprechenden Rubriken ein.

news	information	people
mathematics	police	homework

nur im Singular	**nur im Plural**
____________________	____________________
____________________	____________________
____________________	____________________
____________________	____________________

9

Vervollständige die Sätze, indem du die richtige Form von *to be* einträgst.

a) There __________ too much homework. We really can't do it.

b) There are some people who think that homework __________ fun.

c) These people __________ completely wrong, I can tell you.

d) What's the homework for today? Well, there __________ some maths homework,

and there ______ homework in English, German and Biology.

e) That __________ bad news again. But thanks for the information though* it _______

not very good.

* though = obwohl

8 Nur im Singular werden gebraucht: *news, mathematics, information, homework*. Als Plurale werden im Englischen immer *police* und *people* (= Leute, Menschen) gebraucht. Mit einem Plural -s bedeutet *peoples* im übrigen „Völker".

9 a) There is too much homework … **b)** … who think that homework is fun. **c)** These people are completely wrong … **d)** … there is some maths homework, and there is homework in … **e)** That is bad news again. But thanks for the information though it is not very good.

10

Welche der folgenden Substantive kannst du nur im Plural gebrauchen?

glasses	socks	shoes	trousers	jeans
skirts	pyjamas	shorts	boots	shirts

Nur als Pluralform

11

Debbies Schrank ist voller Kleider. Setze *a pair of, two pairs of …* ein, wo dies sinnvoll ist.

4 jeans	3 trousers	5 pyjamas
1 shorts	1 sunglasses	3 blouses
5 shoes	2 skirts	5 pullovers
7 socks	3 boots	1 coat

Debbie has got a lot of cothes. She has got

10 Nur als Pluralform möglich sind *glasses, trousers, jeans, pyjamas, shorts.*
11 She has got four pairs of jeans, three pairs of trousers, five pairs of pyjamas, a pair of shorts, a pair of sunglasses, three blouses, five pairs of shoes, two skirts, five pullovers, seven pairs of socks, three pairs of boots and one coat.

12

Verbinde die Substantive mit dem *s*-Genitiv.

Tom / house __________

Mr Benson / car __________

Mr Benson / wife __________

the Bensons / hobbies __________

my parents / bikes __________

my sisters / friends __________

my mother / brother __________

my brother / CDs __________

Mr Mason / lessons __________

the pupils / workbooks __________

my grandparents / radio __________

13

Setze die markierten Substantive in den Plural und verbinde sie mit dem *s*-Genitiv.

the baby / toys __________

the girl / mother __________

the boy / shoes __________

my uncle / brothers __________

my cousin / teacher __________

my aunt / letters __________

12 Tom's house, Mr Benson's car, Mr Benson's wife, the Bensons' hobbies, my parents' bikes, my sisters' friends, my mother's brother, my brother's CDs, Mr Mason's lessons, the pupils' workbooks, my grandparents' radio
13 the babies' toys, the girls' mother, the boys' shoes, my uncles' brothers, my cousins' teacher, my aunts' letters

14

Gebrauche den *s*-Genitiv.

a man / world ________________________

women / magazines ________________________

a woman / job ________________________

men / hobbies ________________________

children / playground ________________________

a child / toys ________________________

people / ideas ________________________

girls / day ________________________

15

Verbinde die Substantive mit dem *s*-Genitiv.

Are these your **teeth**? No, they are ________________________ (grandpa)

Is this your **baby**, Alice? No, it's my ________________________ (sister)

Are these your **parents**? No, they are ________________________ (Tom)

Are these your **jeans**? No, they are ________________________ (that girl)

Are these your **children**, Mrs Benson? No, they are ________________________ (Mr Owen)

Is that your **mum**, Ken? No, it's ________________________ (that boy)

Is this your hamster's **cage**? No, it's ________________________ (my parrot)

Is this your sister's **doll**? No, it's the ________________________ (twins)

Is this your child's **food**? No, it's ________________________ (the cat)

14 a man's world, women's magazines, a woman's job, men's hobbies, children's playground, a child's toys, people's ideas, girls' day
15 They are grandpa's teeth, … my sister's baby, …Tom's parents, … that girl's jeans, … Mr Owen's children, … that boy's mum, … my parrot's cage, … twins' doll, … the cat's food

16

Bilde den Singular der folgenden Substantive.
Antworte bitte.

Whose car is this?	(Mr Benson)	______
Whose house is this?	(my parents)	______
Whose books are these?	(the girls)	______
Whose bike is this?	(Mike)	______
Whose pencils are these?	(Sue)	______
Whose wife is this?	(Mr Mason)	______
Whose girlfriend is this?	(Tom)	______
Whose trousers are these?	(my uncle)	______
Whose hat is this?	(grandma)	______

17

Bilde Fragen mit *whose*.

______ ? This is Tom's girlfriend.

______ ? These are my toys.

______ ? That is your pen.

______ ? Those are the children's bikes.

______ ? This is her family.

______ ? This is my teacher's car.

______ ? These are my friends' friends.

______ ? This is Debbie's plate.

16 It's Mr Benson's car. It's my parents' house. These are the girls' books. This is Mike's bike. They are Sue's pencils. This is Mr Mason's wife. This is Tom's girlfriend. These are my uncle's trousers. This is my grandma's hat.
17 Whose girlfriend is this? Whose toys are these? Whose pen is that? Whose bikes are those? Whose family is this? Whose car is this? Whose friends are these? Whose plate is this?

18

Verbinde die folgenden Substantive mit dem *of*-Genitiv. Pass aber auf, welches Substantiv zuerst kommen muss.

the table / the legs ______

the book / the month ______

your eyes / the colour ______

this book / the pages ______

the apple / my eye ______

the photos / my sister ______

the room / the walls ______

this house / the roof ______

the girl / my dreams ______

this word / the plural ______

this exercise / the end ______

19

a) Unterstreiche das Genitiv-*s* mit einer anderen Farbe als das Apostroph-*s* der Kurzformen.

Tom's got a new friend. He's the new boy in Tom's class. Ken's family is new here, too. Ken's very good at maths. He can be very helpful, so most pupils in Tom's class like him. Ken's got a pet, too. It's a hamster. He must look after it, clean its cage and buy the hamster's food.

b) Schreibe die Kurzformen aus.

______

______

18 the legs of the table, the book of the month, the colour of your eyes, the pages of this book, the apple of my eye, the photos of my sister, the walls of the room, the roof of this house, the girl of my dreams, the plural of this word, the end of this exercise.
19 a) Tom**'s** got a new friend. He**'s** the new boy in Tom's class. Ken's family is new here, too. Ken**'s** very good at maths. He can be very helpful, so most pupils in Tom's class like him. Ken**'s** got a pet, too. It**'s** a hamster. He must look after it, clean its cage and buy the hamster's food.
b) Tom has got … He is the new boy … Ken is very good … Ken has got … It is a hamster.

20

Setze *a / an* vor die folgenden Substantive.

________ name	________ friend	________ aunt
________ year	________ invitation	________ game
________ school	________ example	________ uncle
________ teacher	________ song	________ exercise
________ pupil	________ unit	________ pencil
________ number	________ question	________ ruler
________ uniform	________ answer	________ evening
________ eye	________ island	________ library

21

Setze den unbestimmten Artikel ein. Entscheide dich zwischen *a* oder *an*.

________ useful exercise	________ funny exercise	________ beautiful exercise
________ interesting exercise	________ long exercise	________ intelligent exercise
________ complicated exercise	________ short exercise	________ important exercise
________ difficult exercise	________ good exercise	________ bad exercise
________ easy exercise	________ German exercise	________ awful exercise
________ English exercise	________ terrible exercise	________ terrible exercise
________ boring exercise	________ silly exercise	________ old exercise

20 a name, a year, a school, a teacher, a pupil, a number, a uniform, an eye; a friend, an invitation, an example, a song, a unit, a question, an answer, an island; an aunt, a game, an uncle, an exercise, a pencil, a ruler, an evening, a library

21 a useful exercise, an interesting exercise, a complicated exercise, a difficult exercise, an easy exercise, an English exercise, a boring exercise; a funny exercise, a long exercise, a short exercise, a good exercise, a German exercise, a terrible exercise, a silly exercise; a beautiful exercise, an intelligent exercise, an important exercise, a bad exercise, an awful exercise, an exciting exercise, an old exercise

22

Finde das Gegenteil der hervorgehobenen Adjektive und setze die richtige Form des unbestimmten Artikels ein.

a **stupid** girl — an *intelligent* girl

a **difficult** question — ____________

a **boring** lesson — ____________

a **nice** boy — ____________

a **happy** teacher — ____________

a **cheap** pullover — ____________

an **ugly** voice — ____________

an **old** book — ____________

a **terrible** boy — ____________

23

Setze die Formen des unbestimmten Artikels ein und erkläre, wann du *a* oder *an* einsetzen musst.

Das nächste Wort beginnt mit:

______ girl — ____________

______ bad girl — ____________

______ interesting girl — ____________

______ English girl — ____________

______ uniform — ____________

______ uncle — ____________

22 an intelligent girl, an easy question, an interesting lesson, a terrible / silly / boy, an unhappy / a sad teacher, an expensive pullover, a beautiful voice, a new book, a nice boy
23 a, a, an, an, a, an. Das nächste Wort beginnt mit einem Konsonant, Konsonant , Vokal, Vokal, einem so genannten Halbvokal /ju/, Vokal.

24

**a) Sprich die folgenden Beispielsätze laut aus.
Wann musst du den bestimmten Artikel / ðə /, wann / ði / aussprechen?**

the English lesson

the boring biology lesson

the teachers at my school

the difficult questions

the interesting subjects

the easy tests

the exciting exercises

the unhappy pupils

the uniforms of English pupils

the old churches

b) Worauf kommt es bei dem bestimmten Artikel an? Gibt es Unterschiede zu den Regeln für den Gebrauch von *a* / *an*?

____

____

25

Setze den richtigen Artikel ein.

Today Ken is ill.

He has got ________ temperature.

He has got ________ sore throat.

He has got ________ headache, too.

Has he got ________ cold?

Well, I think he has got ________ bad cold, or he has got ________ flu.

It's ________ pity he can't come to our party.

24 a) Mit / ði / werden ausgesprochen: the English lesson, the easy tests, the exciting exercises, the unhappy pupils, the interesting subjects, the old churches.
Vor Vokal wird *the* wie / ði /, vor Konsonant und Halbvokal wie / ðə / ausgesprochen.
b) Es gelten dieselben Regeln wie für den Gebrauch von a / an.
25 He has got a temperature. He has got a sore throat. He has got a headache, too. Has he got a cold? Well, I think he has got a bad cold or he has got the flu. It's a pity he can't come to our party.

26

Setze in den Plural.

this family ______________________

that boy ______________________

this man ______________________

that lady ______________________

this class ______________________

that page ______________________

this foot ______________________

this child ______________________

this policewoman ______________________

that adult ______________________

this house ______________________

27

Setze die entsprechenden Formen von *this* ein.

__________ is a man and __________ are women.

__________ is a child and __________ are children, too.

__________ is a teacher and __________ are teachers, too.

__________ is a mouse and __________ are mice, too.

__________ is my friend and __________ are your friends.

26 these families, those boys, these men, those ladies, these classes, those pages, these feet, these children, these policewomen, those adults, these houses
27 This is a man and these are women. This is a child and these are children, too. This is a teacher and these are teachers, too. This is a mouse and these are mice, too. This is my friend and these are your friends.

28

Setze die entsprechenden Formen von *this* und *that* ein.

______________ is my schoolbag and ______________ is your schoolbag.

______________ is my seat and ______________ is your seat.

______________ is my sandwich and ______________ is your sandwich.

______________ are my books and ______________ are your books.

______________ are my pencils and ______________ are your pencils.

______________ are my CDs and ______________ are your CDs.

______________ is my iPod and ______________ is your iPod.

______________ are my things and ______________ are your things.

______________ is my mobile and ______________ is her mobile.

And ____________ is my girlfriend; *don't think she is yours!*

29

Setze die entsprechenden Formen von *this* und *that* ein.

Look at __________ pullover. It's really nice and ______________ pullover is very nice, too.

Which pullover is nicer, ______________ pullover or ______________ pullover over there?

Look! Aren't they lovely? ______________ t-shirts right in front of you?

And what about ______________ t-shirts right here?

I like ______________ t-shirts here better. Can we go in and buy one?

Okay, but let's have a look at ______________ shirts in the shop window, too.

28 This is my schoolbag and that is your schoolbag. This is my seat and that is your seat. This is my sandwich and that is your sandwich. These are my books and those are your books. These are my pencils and those are your pencils. These are my CDs and those are your CDs. This is my iPod and that is your iPod. These are my things and those are your things. This is my mobile and that is her mobile. And this is my girlfriend; don't think she is yours!

29 Look at this pullover. It's really nice and that pullover is very nice, too. Which pullover is nicer, this pullover or that pullover over there? Look! Aren't they lovely? Those t-shirts right in front of you? And what about these t-shirts right here? I like these t-shirts here better. Can we go in and buy one?
Okay, but let's have a look at those shirts in the shop window, too.

30

Setze die passenden Possessivbegleiter ein.

This is *my* friend. These are __________ friends. (1. Person Plural)

This is *your* bike. These are __________ bikes. (2. Person Plural)

This is *his* car. These are __________ cars. (3. Person Plural)

This is *her* room. These are __________ rooms. (3. Person Plural)

This is *its* bone. These are __________ bones. (3. Person Plural)

31

Was kann *your* alles bedeuten? Übersetze bitte.

What's *your* telephone number, Mrs Benson? __________

When is *your* birthday, Tom? __________

Where is *your* homework, Tom and Ken? __________

Where's *your* car, Mr and Mrs Benson? __________

Where's *your* workbook, Alice? __________

32

Setze die richtigen Formen ein.

How old are __________, Alice?

Where are __________ from?

Where is __________ friend from?

Is she also in __________ class?

Are Tom and Ken __________ friends, too?

30 our friends, your bikes, their cars, their rooms, their bones
31 Ihre, dein, eure, Ihr, dein
32 How old are you? Where are you from? Where is your friend from? Is she also in your class? Are Tom and Ken your friends, too?

33

Setze die richtigen Formen des Possessivbegleiters ein.

1. I've got a bike. This is ____________ bike.
2. Sue has got a bike, too. That's ________________ bike.
3. Have you got a bike, Mrs Benson? Is that _____________ bike over there?
4. The saddle of the bike is new. ________________ saddle is new.
5. The Bensons have got a car. That's _________________ car.
6. We have got a new English book. This is ______________ new book.

34

Da hat doch jemand *its* mit *it's* verwechselt ... Korrigiere den Text. Ersetze *its* durch *it's*, wo *its* falsch ist.

Ken goes to a comprehensive school. **Its** a big school. **Its** a new school, too, but not everything is new. **Its** desks are old and a lot of **its** chairs are old, too. But many of **its** teachers are young. Ken likes it there. He thinks **its** a good school and that **its** fun to go there.

35

Wann ist *their* und wann ist *there* richtig? Setze die entsprechenden Formen ein.

Look, that's Tom's house over _____________.

Where? _________________, on your left.

That's ______________ house? Well, it's a big house.

Yes, and _________________ is a big garden behind it.

We often play _________________.

Oh, can we go _______________, too?

33 1. This is **my** bike. **2.** That's **her** bike. **3.** Is that **your** bike over there? **4. Its** saddle is new. **5.** That's **their** car. **6.** This is **our** new book.
34 ... It's a big school. It's a new school, too ... He thinks it's a good school and that it's fun to go there.
35 Look, that Tom's house over there. Where? There, on your left. That's their house? ...There is a big garden behind it. We often play there. Oh, can we go there, too?

36

Schaue dir die folgenden Sätze genau an und beantworte dann die folgenden Fragen:

Debbie is a **nice girl**. She is **nice**.

There are many **clever boys** in my class. **They** aren't all **stupid**.

	Richtig	Falsch
1. Adjektive beziehen sich immer nur auf Substantive.		
2. Substantive können Sachen oder Personen sein.		
3. Bei *to be* und einigen anderen Verben können Adjektive sich auch auf Pronomen beziehen.		
4. Adjektive sind im Englischen unveränderlich.		
5. Adjektive geben Eigenschaften der Personen oder der Sachen an, auf die sie sich beziehen.		

37

Wähle unter den folgenden Adjektiven drei aus, die die folgenden Personen charakterisieren.

nice, beautiful, good-looking, clever, crazy, exciting, fat, poor, rich, tall, short, strong, funny, interesting, boring, loud, difficult, old, young , sad, happy, loud, calm, stupid, intelligent, wonderful, uninteresting, aggressive, greedy, nervous, thin, funny

Beispiel: My favourite teacher: He / she is old and loud, but very funny.

My English teacher ____________________

My maths teacher ____________________

My mother ____________________

My friend ____________________

My __________ ____________________

36 1. falsch (Sie beziehen sich auch auf Pronomen, wie *she*), **2.** richtig, **3.** richtig, **4.** richtig, **5.** richtig
37 Mögliche Antworten: He / she is nice and young, but not very funny. He / she is young and clever, but not very exciting. She is good-looking and funny, but sometimes a bit loud. He is loud and strong, but very intelligent etc.

38

Schreibe auf, was dir dazu einfällt. Zwei Adjektive genügen.

Football? ______________________

Computers? ______________________

Boys? ______________________

Shopping? ww______________________

Comics? ______________________

Pop stars? ______________________

Girls? ______________________

Casting shows? ______________________

English lessons? ______________________

39

Setze bitte das entsprechende Adjektiv ein, um das Gegenteil zu bilden.

a new town ______________	a tall man ______________
a thin boy ______ an *old* town ______	a large house ______________
a stupid girl ______________	an empty stomach ______________
a nervous boy ______________	a cheap ticket ______________
a fast learner ______________	a long lesson ______________
a poor man ______________	an old woman ______________
an easy exercise ______________	a good girl ______________

38 Mögliche Antworten: Football is wonderful and exciting. Computers are useful and fast. Boys are loud and stupid. Shopping is boring and expensive. Comics are cheap and funny. Pop stars are crazy and often very loud. Girls are nice and good-looking. Casting shows are stupid and boring. English lessons are great, fantastic, exciting, wonderful!

39 an old town, a fat boy, an intelligent girl, a calm boy, a slow learner, a rich man, a difficult exercise; a short man, a small house, a full stomach, an expensive ticket, a short lesson, a young woman, a bad girl

40

Bilde den Komparativ und den Superlativ der folgenden Adjektive.

rich ________ ________

cheap ________ ________

long ________ ________

loud ________ ________

41

Bilde, wie in Kurztest 40, den Komparativ und den Superlativ.

nice ________ ________

large ________ ________

big ________ ________

thin ________ ________

hot ________ ________

fat ________ ________

42

Wie lauten der Komparativ und der Superlativ hier?

funny ________ ________

noisy ________ ________

busy ________ ________

easy ________ ________

lucky ________ ________

40 rich, richer, the richest; cheap, cheaper, the cheapest; long, longer, the longest; loud, louder, the loudest
41 nice, nicer, the nicest; large, larger, the largest; big, bigger, the biggest; thin, thinner, the thinnest; hot, hotter, the hottest; fat, fatter, the fattest
42 funny, funnier, the funniest; noisy, noisier, the noisiest; busy, busier, the busiest; easy, easier, the easiest; lucky, luckier, the luckiest

43

Wie lauten der Komparativ und der Superlativ hier?

famous ______________ ______________

boring ______________ ______________

expensive ______________ ______________

beautiful ______________ ______________

terrible ______________ ______________

44

Bilde die Steigerungsformen der folgenden Adjektive.

good ______________ ______________

bad ______________ ______________

much / many ______________ ______________

45

Setze *most* oder *the most* ein.

__________ pupils think that homework is useless.

This is a mistake __________ pupils make.

__________ mistakes are silly, but this mistake is __________ idiotic.

Sheila is __________ beautiful girl in our class. __________ pupils like her.

Ben thinks that __________ girls are stupid.

He only forgets that he is __________ stupid boy in our class.

43 famous, more famous, the most famous; boring, more boring, the most boring; expensive, more expensive, the most expensive; beautiful, more beautiful, the most beautiful; terrible, more terrible, the most terrible
44 good, better, the best; bad, worse, the worst; much / many, more, the most
45 Most pupils think … This is a mistake most pupils make. Most mistakes … the most idiotic. Sheila is the most beautiful girl … Most pupils … Ben thinks that most girls … He only forgets that he is the most stupid boy in our class.

46

Fülle die Lücken bitte entsprechend aus.

1. Adjektive mit einer Silbe und Adjektive mit zwei Silben, die auf *-y* und *-le* enden, bilden den Komparativ und den Superlativ mit *-er*, *-est*:

   cold ______________ ______________

   funny ______________ ______________

   simple ______________ ______________

2. Ein stummes *-e* am Ende des Adjektivs entfällt; nach Konsonant wird das *y* zu *i*:

   nice ______________ ______________

   easy ______________ ______________

3. Mit ganz wenigen Ausnahmen bilden alle anderen Adjektiven den Komparativ und den Superlativ mit *more*, *the most*:

   expensive ______________ ______________

   beautiful ______________ ______________

4. Einige ganz wenige Adjektive haben unregelmäßige Formen:

   good ______________ ______________

   bad ______________ ______________

47

Finde die Steigerungsformen der Adjektive.

dangerous ______________ ______________

dirty ______________ ______________

interesting ______________ ______________

careful ______________ ______________

quick ______________ ______________

46. 1. cold, colder, the coldest; funny, funnier, the funniest; simple, simpler, the simplest **2.** nice, nicer, the nicest; easy, easier, the easiest **3.** expensive, more expensive, the most expensive; beautiful, more beautiful, the most beautiful **4.** good, better, the best; bad, worse, the worst
47 dangerous, more dangerous, the most dangerous; dirty, dirtier, the dirtiest; interesting, more interesting, the most interesting; careful, more careful, the most careful; quick, quicker, the quickest

48

Bilde Sätze mit den folgenden Angaben:

1. Bob / terrible boy / Danny / terrible + / John terrible ++

   Bob is a terrible boy, but Danny is more terrible. John is the most terrible boy of all.

2. This mistake / bad / that mistake + / those mistakes ++

   ____

3. Sue / smart girl / Alice + / Debbie ++

   ____

4. This test / difficult / the English test + / the maths test ++

   ____

5. Bob / noisy / his neighbour + / John ++

   ____

49

Wähle ein Adjektiv aus und vergleiche. Gebrauche dabei *as ... as* oder *not as ... as.*

boring   interesting   difficult   bad   intelligent

football – tennis ______________________________

swimming – running ______________________________

English – German ______________________________

morning lessons – afternoon lessons ______________________________

books – comics ______________________________

I – my neighbour ______________________________

dolls – toy cars ______________________________

48 2. This mistake is bad. That mistake is worse, but those mistakes are the worst. **3.** Sue is a smart girl, but Alice is smarter. Debbie is the smartest girl of the three. **4.** This test is difficult, but the English test is more difficult. The maths test is the most difficult. **5.** Bob is noisy, but his neighbour is noisier. John is the noisiest of all.
49 Mögliche Antworten: Football is (not) as interesting as tennis. Swimming is (not) as boring as running. English is (not) as difficult as German. Morning lessons are (not) as bad as afternoon lessons. Books are (not) as interesting as comics. I am (not) as intelligent as my neighbour. Dolls are (not) as interesting as toy cars.

50

Mache den vorigen Kurztest noch einmal, gebrauche aber *than*.

51

Ersetze not *as ... as* durch *than*, pass dabei aber auf den Sinn des Satzes auf.

Girls aren't as strong as boys.

Girls aren't as noisy as boys.

Boys aren't as good at learning languages as girls.

Boys aren't as difficult as girls.

Girls aren't as tough as boys.

50 Mögliche Antworten: Football is more interesting than tennis. Swimming is more boring than running. German is more difficult than English. Afternoon lessons are worse than morning lessons. Books are more interesting than comics. I am more intelligent than my neighbour. Dolls are more interesting than toy cars.
51 Boys are stronger than girls. Boys are noisier than girls. Boys are worse at learning languages than girls. Girls are more difficult than boys. Boys are tougher than girls.

52

Setze *as (as … as)* oder *than* ein.

Are girls ________ intelligent ________ boys? Many people think girls are ________ intelligent, but others think that boys are more intelligent ________ girls. Just ask the boys in your class. They will tell you that boys aren't any better ________ girls, but secretly they think that they are the best. They can run faster ________ girls, they are stronger ________ girls, they are louder ________ girls and they are better at maths. Girls, they will say, are perhaps better in English ________ boys, but they are much worse in sports. What's your opinion? Do you think that girls are ________ clever ________ boys? Are they better or worse ________ boys?

53

Fülle die Lücken aus. Tipp: Denke dabei daran, dass *then* „dann, damals" heißt. Im Gegensatz dazu entspricht *than* dem deutschen „als" oder „wie" und kann nur im Vergleich gebraucht werden.

I tried to phone you yesterday, but you didn't answer the phone. What were you doing ________? I was reading a book ________. Reading a book? Was it so interesting? More interesting ________ the other one? Yes, it was. What was it about? It was about human intelligence, about the differences between men and women. Are there any? Aren't women ________ intelligent ________ men? Yes, they are. But in some fields men are better ________ women, in some fields they are ________ good ________ women and in some fields they are worse ________ women. Fine, ________ you seem to know everything about this problem …

52 Are girls as intelligent as boys? Many people think girls are as intelligent, … that boys are more intelligent than girls. … that boys aren't any better than girls, … They can run faster than girls, they are stronger than girls, they are louder than girls … Girls, they will say, are perhaps better in English than boys, … Do you think that girls are as clever as boys? Are they better or worse than boys?
53 What were you doing then? I was reading a book then. More interesting than the other one? Aren't women as intelligent as men? … men are better than women… they are as good as women … worse than women. Fine, then you seem to know …

Mengenangaben mit much / many

54

a) Setze *much* oder *many* vor die folgenden Substantive.

______	food	______	people	______	water
______	wood	______	stories	______	countries
______	families	______	children	______	women
______	sugar	______	information	______	lemonade
______	years	______	tea	______	milk
______	courage*	______	pictures	______	coffee

b) Erkläre, weshalb du bei einigen Substantiven *much*, bei anderen *many* eingesetzt hast.

____

____

* courage = Mut

55

Übersetze bitte. Gebrauche *much / many*.

viele Freunde ______________________________

viel Zeit ______________________________

viel Geld ______________________________

viele Partys ______________________________

viel Musik ______________________________

viel Spaß ______________________________

54 a) much food, much wood, many families, much sugar, many years, much courage; many people, many stories, many children, much information, much tea, many pictures; much water, many countries, many women, much lemonade, much milk, much coffee
b) *Many* steht bei Substantiven im Plural (zählbare Substantive z. B. *children*); *much* bei Substantiven, die im Englischen keinen Plural haben oder haben können (unzählbare Substantive z. B. *information*).
55 many friends, much time, much money, many parties, much music, much fun

56

Setze die entsprechenden Formen von *much / many / a lot of* ein.

Today there is a big party at Tom's school. ___________ people are there. There are _____________ pupils of Tom's class, too. There are _____________ stalls there, too, where the pupils present their work. There is the photo club, for example. You can see __________ photos at their stall. Then there is the rock club; they play __________ music and have ___________ fun. They also have a chess club, where you can meet __________ chess players and play against them. Then there is the bike club. There are __________ bikes at their stall. The pupils there show you how to repair your bike, so __________ pupils visit their stall.

57

a) Setze *much / many / a lot of / lots of* richtig ein.

How ________________ is this bike? It costs too _______________ money!

How ________________ bikes have you got here?

How ________________ bikes can you repair in a day?

How ________________ money does it cost to repair a bike?

Are there any girls in the club, too? How ________________ girls are in your club?

How ________________ time do spend there? I spend so ________________ time there!

How ________________ pupils are in the club?

b) Wann kannst du *much* und *many* nicht durch *a lot of* ersetzen?

____

56 … Many / a lot of people are there, including many / a lot of pupils in Tom's class. There are many / a lot of stalls there, too … You can see a many / lot of photos at their stall. … they play a lot of music and have a lot of fun. They also have a chess club, where you can meet many / a lot of chess players … There are many / a lot of bikes at their stall. … so many / a lot pupils visit their stall.

57 a) How much is this bike? It costs too much money! How many bikes have you got here? How many bikes can you repair …? How much money does it cost …? How many girls …? How much time …? I spend so much time there! How many pupils …? **b)** Nach dem Fragewort *how*, und nach den Adverbien *so* und *too*, ist nur *much* oder *many* möglich.

58

Übersetze die hervorgehobenen Begleiter.

I've got very **little** time today. ____________________

But I can find **a little** time for you. ____________________

I've got **a few** things to tell you. ____________________

Very **few** people know about this! ____________________

59

Antworte, bitte.

Vor welchen Substantiven muß du **a little / little** und vor welchen Substantiven musst du **a few / few** gebrauchen?

a little / little steht vor Substantiven, die ____________________

a few / few steht vor Substantiven, die ____________________

Und was bedeutet **little** vor einem Substantiv, das einen Plural haben kann wie zum

Beispiel *girl*: *She's my little girl* ____________________

Handelt es sich hier auch um eine Mengenangabe? ○ Ja ○ Nein

60

Übersetze bitte.

ein paar Freunde ____________________

einige Sachen ____________________

sehr wenig Worte ____________________

ein bisschen Zeit ____________________

sehr wenig Hausaufgaben ____________________

58 wenig, ein bisschen, ein paar / einige, wenig(e)
59 … im Englischen keinen Plural haben (unzählbar sind); einen Plural haben (zählbar sind); mein kleines Mädchen; bei *my little girl* handelt es sich natürlich nicht um eine Mengenangabe.
60 a few / some friends, a few / some things, very few words, a little time, very little homework

61

Sam, 3 Jahre alt, hat den Tisch gedeckt. Übersetze die hervorgehobenen Mengenwörter und das folgende Substantiv.

There are **some glasses** and **some spoons**, but there are**n't any knives** and forks on the table. There also is**n't any tea**, and there is**n't any sugar**. I can't see **any plates** either. Is there **any milk** on the table? Are there **any cups**? There is **some milk** on the table, but there is **no tea** and there are **no saucers**.

62

Entscheide, ob die folgenden Aussagen richtig oder falsch sind.

a) Die Bedeutung von **some** hängt davon ab, ob es vor einem Substantiv im Singular oder im Plural steht.

○ richtig ○ falsch

b) Vor einem Substantiv im Singular bedeutet **some** *etwas*, vor einem Substantiv im Plural *ein paar* oder *einige*.

○ richtig ○ falsch

c) Für **some** in der Bedeutung *ein paar / einige* kann ich auch **few** gebrauchen.

○ richtig ○ falsch

d) **Some** steht in nicht verneinten Aussagesätzen.

○ richtig ○ falsch

e) **not . . . any** bedeutet immer *kein(e)*.

○ richtig ○ falsch

f) Für **not . . . any** kann ich auch **no** gebrauchen.

○ richtig ○ falsch

g) Ein Satz kann auch mit **not . . . any** beginnen.

○ richtig ○ falsch

61 einige / ein paar Gläser, ein paar / einige Löffel, keine Messer, kein Tee, kein Zucker, keine Teller, (etwas) Milch, (irgendwelche) Tassen, (etwas) Milch, kein Tee, keine Untertassen.
62 a) richtig, **b)** richtig, **c)** falsch (richtig ist *a few*), **d)** richtig, **e)** richtig, **f)** richtig, **g)** falsch (mit *not … any* darfst du nie einen Satz beginnen).

63

Ersetze *no* durch *not ... any*.

	no friends.	______________________
	no money.	______________________
Mike has got	no parents.	______________________
	no brothers and sisters.	______________________
	no family.	______________________
	no food at home.	______________________
	no fun.	______________________

64

Setze bitte die passenden Mengenwörter ein.

Is there ____________ good film on tonight?

Yes, there is. There's a good film in the Rex.

Okay, let's go there. Oh, but there's a problem. I haven't got ________ money on me.

I hope you have got ____________.

Sorry, I haven't. I haven't got ____________ money on me either.

What can we do then? Have you got ___________ ideas?

Let me think. Oh yes, let's ring up Alice. Perhaps she has got __________ money and can lend us ____________. Perhaps she can even come with us.

But Alice has got ___________ time and _________ money. She must do some babysitting because her parents are out. Poor Tom and Ken! They're not having ____________ luck tonight!

63 Mike hasn't got any friends / any money / any parents / any brothers and sisters / any family / any food at home / any fun.
64 Is there any good film on tonight? ... I haven't got any money on me. I hope you have got some ... I haven't got any money on me either. ... Have you got any ideas? ... Perhaps she has got some money and can lend us some ... But Alice has got no time and no money. ... Poor Tom and Ken! They're not having any luck tonight!

65

Setze die folgenden Begleiter so ein, dass der Text einen Sinn ergibt. Bei manchen Sätzen hast du mehrere Möglichkeiten.

many *a few* *some* *any* *a little* *much*

Sam is still a small boy. He can speak, but ________________ of his sentences are not correct. He makes ____________ mistakes. You need ____________ time to understand him. His real problem, however, is food. He only likes _________ things. ____________ vegetables are a real horror to him and he doesn't eat _________ meat. He also doesn't drink ________________ milk. What he likes, are sweets, but too _____________ sweets aren't good for him.

66

Fülle die Tabelle richtig aus.

viel(e)		
wenig(e)		
ein paar / einige		
ein bisschen		
etwas		
kein(e)		

65 … but many / a lot of / some / a few of his sentences are not correct. He makes many / a lot of / some / a few mistakes. You need a little / a lot of / some time to understand him. … He only likes a few / some things. Some / Many vegetables are a real horror to him and he doesn't eat any / a lot of meat. He also doesn't drink any / much milk. What he likes, are sweets, but too many sweets aren't good for him.

66

viel(e)	much / a lot of	many / a lot of
wenig(e)	little	few
ein paar / einige	–	a few / some
ein bisschen	little	–
etwas	some	–
kein(e)	no / not … any	no / not … any

67

Setze die entsprechenden Begleiter ein.

There are ______________ children in the room. (viele)

______________ adults are there, too. (ein paar)

How ______________ children are there? (viele)

There is ______________ room left. (kein)

There are ______________ chairs left. (keine)

Most children are sitting on chairs, only __________ are standing. (einige wenige)

Why is there so ______________ noise? (viel)

______________ children are shouting. (einige)

Why are so ______________ children there? (viele)

I have ________ got ______________ idea. (keine)

But wait, isn't it Sam's birthday? Yes, it is.

68

Ergänze bitte die entsprechenden Mengenangaben.

a lot of homework → ______________ time

no work → ______________ money

many friends → ______________ fun

no friends → ______________ fun

a lot of money → ______________ friends

a lot of work → ______________ time

many sick teachers → ______________ school

67 There are many children in …, Some / a few adults …, How many children …?, … no room left, … no chairs left, … only a few are standing, … so much noise?, Some / a few children …, Why are so many …, I haven't got any idea.

68 a lot of homework = no / little time, no work = no money, many friends = a lot of fun, no friends = no fun, a lot of money = many friends, a lot of work = no / little time, many sick teachers = no school

69

Verbinde die folgenden Mengenangaben mit einem passenden Substantiv.

a cup	of	shoes
a glass	of	bread
a bowl	of	cake
a plate	of	names
a piece	of	soup
a bag	of	lemonade
a slice	of	peas
a bar	of	chocolate
a tin	of	crisps*
a box	of	coffee
a bottle	of	butter
a pound	of	milk
a pair	of	oranges
a list	of	sausages

* crisps = Kartoffelchips (AmE: chips)

70

Korrigiere, was falsch ist. Verwende dabei andere Mengenangaben.

a box of water	a pound of milk
a glass of apples	a slice of toast
a tin of crisps	a box of cornflakes
a piece of tea	a bottle of chocolate

69 Mögliche Lösungen: a cup of coffee, a glass of milk, a bowl of soup, a plate of sausages, a piece of cake, a bag of crisps, a slice of bread, a bar of chocolate, a tin of peas, a box of oranges, a bottle of lemonade, a pound of butter, a pair of shoes, a list of names

70 a glass / cup / bottle of water; a box / pound of apples; a bowl / a bag of crisps; a cup / pot of tea; a bottle / glass of milk; a bar / piece of chocolate

71

**Stelle die Fragen und beantworte sie. Beginne mit *there is / there are* . . .
Schreibe insgesamt 7 Sätze.**

Beispiel: There are thirty-two pupils in my classroom.

How many	boys	are there	in your school?	
	girls		in your class?	
	desks		in your classroom?	
	pupils			
	teachers			
	windows			
	posters			

72

Am Endes des Schuljahres werden die Sachen ausgelegt, die die Schüler während des Jahres vergessen haben . . . Schreibe auf, was sie liegen gelassen haben.

There are	15 pairs of trainers	in the caretaker's room.	
There is	2 right shoes		
	7 left shoes		
	4 shirts		
	6 anoraks		
	1 schoolbag		
	8 socks		
	5 English textbooks		

71 How many boys / girls / desks etc. are there in your school / class / classroom? There are ______ boys / girls / desks etc. in my school / in my class / in my classroom.
72 There are 15 pairs of trainers, two right shoes, seven left shoes, four shirts, six anoraks, eight socks and five English textbooks in the caretaker's room. There is also one schoolbag.

73

Übersetze bitte.

a) **Nobody** likes him. ________________

b) He likes **nobody**. ________________

c) He does**n't** like **anyone**. ________________

d) He does**n't** like **anything**. ________________

e) He likes **nothing**. ________________

f) He goes **nowhere**. ________________

g) He does**n't** go **anywhere**. ________________

h) You wo**n't** see him **anywhere**. ________________

i) He does**n't** want to see **anything**. ________________

74

Ersetze *nobody*, *nothing*, *nowhere*, wo dies möglich ist.

a) He likes nothing. ________________

b) He likes nobody. ________________

c) He does nothing. ________________

d) He goes nowhere. ________________

e) He is making nothing out of his life. ________________

f) Nobody can help him. ________________

g) Nothing can make him feel better. ________________

h) You can do nothing about him. ________________

73 a) niemand, **b)** niemanden, **c)** niemanden, **d)** nichts, **e)** nichts, **f)** nirgends, **g)** nirgends, **h)** nirgends, **i)** nichts
74 a) He doesn't like anything. **b)** He doesn't like anybody. **c)** He doesn't do anything. **d)** He doesn't go anywhere. **e)** He isn't making anything out of his life. **f)** nicht möglich **g)** nicht möglich. (Als Subjekt kann *nobody*, *nothing* nicht ersetzt werden.) **h)** You can't do anything about him.

75

Setze bitte die Zusammensetzungen von *any* ein.

Does ______________________ know him? No, nobody knows him.

Has ______________________ seen him? No, nobody has seen him.

Did he go ______________________? No, he went nowhere.

Can you see him ______________________? No, I can't see him anywhere.

Did he do ______________________? No, he didn't do anything.

Did he talk to ______________________? No, he didn't talk to anybody.

76

Setze *jemand*, *etwas* etc. ein.

______________________ must talk to him.	(jemand)
We must do ______________ about him.	(etwas)
But what can we do? Can we really do ______________?	(etwas)
We must find some help ______________________.	(irgendwo)
We must find ______________ to help him.	(jemanden)
If we don't, ______________ terrible will happen.	(etwas)

77

Ergänze bitte.

Wann musst du *some*, wann *any* gebrauchen? ______________________________________

Wann musst du *not* … *any* gebrauchen? ______________________________________

75 Does anybody/anyone know him? Has anybody/anyone seen him? Did he go anywhere? Can you see him anywhere? Did he do anything? No, he didn't do anything. Did he talk to anybody/anyone?
76 Somebody/Someone must talk to him. We must do something about him. But what can we do? Can we really do anything? We must find some help somewhere. We must find somebody to help him. If we don't, something terrible will happen.
77 *Some* in bejahten Sätzen, *any* in Fragen; *not* … *any* in verneinten Sätzen.

78

a) Lies diese Sätze genau durch. Welche Antwort wird wohl erwartet?

Would you like something to drink?

Do you need some help in the kitchen?

Can I have some more coffee, please?

____

b) Trage *some* und die entsprechenden Zusammensetzungen ein.

Can I have ____________ money, please? You know, it's time for my pocket money. Didn't I give you ____________ money yesterday? I really think I did. I hope you have got ____________ left.

Let's clean the car. Can ____________ come and help me? I really need ____________ help. Well, here's your chance. I'll give you ____________ extra money if you help me.

79

Setze *everybody*, *everything* und *everywhere* ein.

____________ liked the food. There were lots of things: sausages, chips, peas, beans, just ____________! John, who was also at the party, looked at the food and liked ____________ he saw. As he was very hungry, he ate ____________ he could lay his hands on. When the party was over, all the plates were empty. But there was a lot of food on the floor. There were chips ____________. John was on the floor, too. He was sick. ____________ laughed at him.

78 a) Hier wird eine positive Antwort erwartet. **b)** Can I have some money, please? … Didn't I give you some money yesterday? I really think I did. I hope you have got some left. Let's clean the car. Can somebody / someone come and help me? I really need some help. Well, here's your chance. I'll give you some extra money if you help me.

79 Everybody / Everyone liked the food. There were lots of things: sausages, chips, peas, beans, just everything! John … liked everything he saw. As he was very hungry, he ate everything he could lay his hands on. When the party was over, all the plates were empty. But there was a lot of food on the floor. There were chips everywhere. John was on the floor, too. He was sick. Everybody laughed at him.

80

Wie lautet deine Telefonnummer? Kannst du sie auf Englisch sagen? Kannst du auch die folgenden Telefonnummern lesen?
(Tipp: BrE: 0 = oh, 00 = double oh; AmE: 0 = zero / oh, 00 = zero, zero / oh, oh)

Here's a list of the telephone numbers of Tom's friends:

Mike	57 97 91	
Debbie	30 06 90	mobile 0170 354 507 45
Alice	98 76 30	mobile 0510 809 607 543
Ken	24 39 19	
Kevin	92 95 28	
Ben	19 85 43	
Sue	70 08 03	

81

Bring die Buchstaben in die richtige Reihenfolge.

fniefet ____________________

nttwey ____________________

eeetinnn ____________________

veenle ____________________

yeight ____________________

ddernuh ____________________

sadnuoht ____________________

eierntth ____________________

thtyir ____________________

80 five seven nine seven nine one, three double oh six nine oh; mobile oh one seven oh three five four five oh seven four five; nine eight seven six three oh; mobile oh five one oh eight oh nine six oh seven five four three; two four three nine one nine; nine two nine five two eight; one nine eight five four three; seven double oh eight oh three.

81 fifteen, twenty, nineteen, eleven, eighty, hundred, thousand, thirteen, thirty

82

Lies die folgenden Zahlen laut. Welche Zahlen passen nicht zu den anderen? Schreibe sie auf.

a)	7	14	21	29	35
b)	9	18	27	37	45
c)	99	90	81	75	63
d)	77	71	63	56	49
e)	63	60	58	54	51
f)	12	18	25	30	36

83

Lies die folgenden Zahlen laut und schreibe sie aus.

3	13	33
4	14	44
5	15	55
8	18	88
9	19	99

82 a) 29 – twenty-nine; **b)** 37 – thirty-seven; **c)** 75 – seventy-five; **d)** 71 – seventy-one; **e)** 58 – fifty-eight; **f)** 25 – twenty-five
83 three, thirteen, thirty-three; four, fourteen, forty-four; five, fifteen, fifty-five; eight, eighteen, eighty-eight; nine, nineteen, ninety-nine

84

What time is it? **Schreibe die folgenden Uhrzeitangaben aus.**

6.00 ______________________ 9.35 ______________________

6.30 ______________________ 10.20 ______________________

6.45 ______________________ 10.30 ______________________

7.15 ______________________ 11.40 ______________________

8.50 ______________________ 11.55 ______________________

85

Schreibe ihn bitte aus.

English	PE	break	Maths
Geography	lunch	Music	Art

Tom's first lesson is from ______________________ to ______________________.

PE is from ______________________ to ______________________.

Break is from ______________________ to ______________________.

Maths is from ______________________ to ______________________.

Geography is from ______________________ to ______________________.

Lunch break is from ______________________ to ______________________.

Music is from ______________________ to ______________________.

84 It's six o'clock; half past six (AmE = six thirty); a quarter to seven (AmE = six forty-five); a quarter past seven (AmE = seven fifteen); ten to nine (AmE = eight fifty); twenty-five to ten, thirty-five past nine (AmE = nine thirty-five); twenty past ten (AmE = ten twenty); half past ten (AmE = ten thirty); twenty to twelve (AmE = eleven forty); five to twelve (AmE = eleven fifty-five).

85 Tom's first lesson is from ten to nine to twenty to ten. PE is from a quarter to ten to twenty-five to eleven. Break is from twenty-five to eleven to ten to eleven. Maths is from five to eleven to a quarter to twelve. Geography is from ten to twelve to twenty to one. Lunch is from twenty to one to twenty to two. Music is from a quarter to two to half past two.

86

Lies den folgenden Busfahrplan laut und schreibe ihn dann aus.

Bristol, Bus Station	Wraxall	Nailsea	Tickenham Primary School	Clevedon, Kenn Road	Millcross	Clevedon, Cambridge Road

Beispiel: The bus leaves Bristol Bus Station *at ten thirty-one.*

It leaves Wraxhall ____________________.

It leaves Nailsea ____________________.

It leaves Twickenham Primary School ____________________.

It leaves Clevedon, Kenn Road ____________________.

It leaves Millcross ____________________.

It arrives in Clevedon, Cambridge Road, ____________________.

87

Schreibe die folgenden Uhrzeiten aus. Setze *minutes* ein, wo dies notwendig ist.

5.35 ____________________

6.41 ____________________

7.25 ____________________

8.45 ____________________

8.46 ____________________

9.59 ____________________

11.19 ____________________

86 It leaves Wraxhall at ten forty-eight. It leaves Nailsea at ten fifty-three. It leaves Tickenham Primary School at eleven oh two. It leaves Clevedon, Kenn Road at eleven oh eight. It leaves Millcross at eleven thirteen. It arrives in Clevedon, Cambridge Road at eleven twenty-four.

87 It's twenty-five to six (AmE = five thirty-five). It's nineteen minutes to seven (AmE = six forty-one). It's twenty-five minutes past seven (AmE = seven twenty-five). It's a quarter to nine (AmE = eight forty-five). It's fourteen minutes to nine (AmE = eight forty-six). It's one minute to ten (AmE = nine fifty-nine). It's nineteen minutes past eleven (AmE = eleven nineteen).

88

Schreibe die folgenden Zahlen aus.

100 ______________________________

200 ______________________________

345 ______________________________

888 ______________________________

1,000 ______________________________

2,000 ______________________________

100,000 ______________________________

1,000,000 ______________________________

89

Weißt du noch, wie man Jahreszahlen liest? Es ist ganz einfach:

1492 *fourteen (hundred and) ninety-two* **1900** *nineteen hundred*

1648 *sixteen (hundred and) forty-eight* **2001** *two thousand one*

Lies und schreibe die folgenden Daten aus:

1776 ______________________________

2008 ______________________________

1888 ______________________________

1066 ______________________________

1668 ______________________________

1096 ______________________________

2049 ______________________________

88 a / one hundred, two hundred, three hundred and forty-five, eight hundred and eighty-eight, a / one thousand, two thousand, one hundred thousand, one million

89 seventeen hundred and seventy-six, two thousand eight, eighteen hundred and eighty-eight, ten hundred and sixty-six, sixteen hundred and sixty-eight, ten hundred and ninety-six, two thousand forty-nine

90

Lies die folgenden Ordnungszahlen laut und schreibe sie aus.

1st the ______________________ 12th ______________________

2nd the ______________________ 14th ______________________

3rd ______________________ 15th ______________________

4th ______________________ 19th ______________________

5th ______________________ 20th ______________________

8th ______________________ 31st ______________________

9th ______________________ 44th ______________________

11th ______________________ 67th ______________________

91

Beantworte die Fragen.

Which is the second month of the year? ______________________

What about December? Which month is it? ______________________

When is Christmas in English-speaking countries? On the ______________ of December.

And which is the fifth month? ______________________

Which is the eighth month? ______________________

And what about Tuesday? Which day of the week is it? ______________________

Which is the fifth day of the week? ______________________

Which is the first day of the week? ______________________

Look at Tom's timetable. Which lesson is Art? ______________________

And which lesson is Maths? ______________________

90 the first, the second, the third, the fourth, the fifth, the eighth, the ninth, the eleventh; the twelfth, the fourteenth, the fifteenth, the nineteenth, the twentieth, the thirty-first, the forty-fourth, the sixty-seventh
91 February, the twelfth month, twenty-fifth, May, August, the second day, Friday, Monday, the sixth lesson, the third lesson

92

Schreibe sie bitte richtig aus.

senadydwe ______________________

yrefabur ______________________

robetoc ______________________

thydrusa ______________________

omnyda ______________________

yuanajr ______________________

tugsua ______________________

syatruda ______________________

amcrh ______________________

ysetuda ______________________

93

An welchem Wochentag ist Toms Geburtstag dieses Jahr?

It's on a F ______________________.

And when is his father's? It's on a W ______________________.

And when is his mother's? It's on a Tu ______________________.

And when is his cousin's? It's on a Sa ______________________.

And when is his friend's? It's on a Th ______________________.

And when is Debbie's birthday? It's on a Su ______________________.

And when is your birthday this year? It's on ______________________.

92 Wednesday, February, October, Thursday, Monday, January, August, Saturday, March, Tuesday
93 It's on a Friday. It's on a Wednesday. It's on a Tuesday. It's on a Saturday. It's on a Thursday. It's on a Sunday.
It's on a ______________.

94

Schreibe die Geburtstage wie in dem folgenden Beispiel aus:

Tom, 12: *Tom is twelve. It's his twelfth birthday.*

His father, 39 His mother, 37 His uncle, 44

His aunt, 51 His grandma, 72 His grandpa, 78

His father ______________________________

His mother ______________________________

His uncle ______________________________

His aunt ______________________________

His grandma ______________________________

His grandpa ______________________________

95

Lies den Geburtstagskalender laut und schreibe ihn entsprechend aus.

Tom, 2nd April: *Tom's birthday is on the second of April.*

His father, 11th August His grandpa, 21st March His uncle, 13th January

His mother, 14th July His grandma, 19th May

His father's birthday is ______________________________

His mother's birthday is ______________________________

His uncle's birthday is ______________________________

His grandpa's birthday is ______________________________

His grandma's birthday is ______________________________

94 His father is thirty-nine; it's his thirty-ninth birthday. His mother is thirty-seven; it's her thirty-seventh birthday. His uncle is forty-four; it's his forty-fourth birthday. His aunt is fifty-one; it's her fifty-first birthday. His grandma is seventy-two; it's her seventy-second birthday. His grandpa is seventy-eight; it's his seventy-eighth birthday.

95 His father's birthday is on the eleventh of August. His mother's birthday is on the fourteenth of July. His uncle's birthday is on the thirteenth of January. His grandpa's birthday is on the twenty-first of March. His grandma's birthday is on the nineteenth of May.

96

Lies und schreibe die folgenden Daten aus.

17/12/1956

____

28/06/1940

____

25/07/2008

____

19/04/1913

____

03/12/2001

____

97

Kannst du die Feiertage den Daten zuordnen? Schreibe auf, was du gefunden hast.

27/08	1/5	1/1	25/12	26/12

New Year's Day is ______________________________

Boxing Day is ______________________________

Christmas Day is ______________________________

May Day is ______________________________

Summer Bank Holiday is ______________________________

96 The seventeenth of December, nineteen fifty-six; the twenty-eighth of June, nineteen forty; the twenty-fifth of July, two thousand eight; the nineteenth of April, nineteen thirteen; the third of December, two thousand one.

97 New Year's Day is on the first of January; Boxing Day is on the twenty-sixth of December; Christmas Day is on the twenty-fifth of December; May Day is on the first of May; Summer Bank Holiday is on the twenty-seventh of August.

98

Zeit- und Ortsangaben enthalten oft Präpositionen. Eine kleine Liste solcher Zeitangaben findest du hier. Setzte die richtige Präposition ein.

______ the morning
______ the evening
______ the afternoon
______ three o'clock
______ night
______ Christmas
______ three o'clock (vor)
______ three o'clock (bis)
______ my birthday
______ the morning of my birthday
______ February, 3rd
______ December
______ June
______ 2008
______ three o'clock (nach)
______ morning ______ night

99

Setze die richtigen Präpositionen ein.

I usually don't go to bed ______ 11 o'clock (vor).

I often go to bed ______ midnight (nach).

I usually wake up ______ 7 o'clock ______ morning.

I leave the house ______ breakfast (nach).

I have lunch ______ about 1 o'clock.

I come home ______ the late afternoon.

______ the evening I often watch TV or read a book.

Things are different ______ Sundays, of course.

98 in the morning, in the evening, in the afternoon, at three o'clock, at night, at Christmas, before three o'clock, until three o' clock (kann *by three o'clock* heißen, wenn man „bis spätestens" meint); on my birthday, on the morning of my birthday, on February, 3rd, in December, in June, in 2008, after three o'clock, from mornig to night

99 I usually don't go to bed before 11 o'clock. I often go to bed after midnight. I usually wake up at 7 o'clock in the morning. I leave the house after breakfast. I have lunch at about 1 o'clock. I come home in the late afternoon. In the evening I often watch TV or read a book. Things are different on Sundays, of course.

100

Setze die richtigen Präpositionen ein.

I've got a friend who likes work very much. He works __________ morning ________ night. He works _________ the morning, _________ the afternoon, __________ the evening, even _________ Saturdays and ________ Sundays. He seldom goes to bed _________________ midnight (vor). He gets up very early, ______ about 6. ___________________ a short breakfast (nach) he settles down to work. Nothing can stop him. Last year he even worked _______________ his birthday and even _______________ December 25th, Christmas Day. Let's wish him a Merry Christmas this year!

101

Setze bitte die richtige Präpositionen ein.

Tom was born _________ 1997.

His birthday is _________ April.

It is __________ April 2nd. His friend's birthday is __________ the same day.

It's ______________ a Friday this year.

__________ Saturday they are going to have a big party.

It's always fun to have parties __________ the weekend!

It will begin _____________ 3 o'clock and end ________ 11.

They'll prepare for the party ___________ morning ___________ night (von / bis) on Friday.

100 … He works from morning to night. He works in the morning, in the afternoon, in the evening, even on Saturdays and on Sundays. He seldom goes to bed before midnight. He gets up very early, at about 6. After a short breakfast he settles down to work. Nothing can stop him. Last year he even worked on his birthday and even on December, 25th, Christmas Day. Let's wish him a Merry Christmas this year!
101 Tom was born in 1997. His birthday is in April. It's on April 2nd. His friend's birthday is on the same day. It's on a Friday this year. On Saturday they are going to have a big party. It's always fun to have parties at the week-end! (AmE = on the weekend). It will begin at 3 o'clock and end at 11. They'll prepare for the party from morning to night on Friday.

102

Was ist das Gegenteil von ...

on the left	__________
in front of the house	__________ the house
on the table	__________
into the room	__________ the room
over the house	__________ the house
near the station	far __________ the station

103

Setze die folgenden Präpositionen ein. Manche kannst du mehrmals verwenden.

at *on* *above* *in* *in front of* *under* *next to* *behind*

Let's have a look __________ Tom's room. __________ the left there is his bed with a lamp __________ it. __________ the right there is a wardrobe. __________ the middle of the room there is a table and some chairs. There is one window __________ his room. __________ the window (vor) there is a desk with his schoolbooks __________ it. There is a computer __________ his desk, too. There are posters __________ the wall. But Tom's room is a mess. His socks are __________ his bed (unter) and his pullover is __________ the floor, too. There is an empty bottle of Coke __________ one corner of the room and there are many CDs __________ his bed (auf). Look! And what's that __________ the computer (hinter)? There is an old sandwich __________ an empty bag of chips (neben)!

102 on the right, behind the house, under the table, out of the room, under the house, far from the station.
103 Let's have a look at Tom's room. On the left there is his bed with a lamp above it. On the right there is a wardrobe. In the middle of the room ... There is one window in his room. In front of the window there is a desk with his schoolbooks on it. There is a computer on his desk, too. There are posters on the wall ... His socks are under his bed and his pullover is on the floor, too. There is an empty bottle of Coke in one corner of the room and there are many CDs on his bed. Look! And what's that behind the computer? There is an old sandwich next to an empty bag of chips.

104

Antworte bitte. Gebrauche eine der angegebenen Präpositionen.

Where is your bed?	(rechts / links / in der Mitte)
Where are your clothes?	(auf / unter / in).
Where are your posters?	(an) the wall.
Where is your desk?	(in der Mitte, links von, rechts von, vor)
What is ______ your desk?	(auf)
What is ______ your bed?	(hinter)

105

Setze die fehlenden Präpositionen ein.

Where are the children? They are not ______________. They	zu Hause
are not ________ their room.	in
___________ the house there is a field. Are they playing	in der Nähe
____________ the field? It's not very _________ _________ the	auf / weit weg von
house.	
Or are they ______________ the street? There is a garden	auf
_________ the house. Are they there? No, they aren't.	um … herum
Where are they then? Oh, here they are. They are _______ the	in
living-room. Yes, they are. They are in the living room __________	vor
the telly. What film are they watching? It's a western. Look, here it is.	
It's ________ page 12 of the TV guide.	auf

104 It's on the right / on the left / in the middle. They are on / under / in the wardrobe. They are on the wall. It's in the middle, on the left, on the right, in front of … What is on your desk? What's behind your bed?
105 They are not at home. They are not in their room. Near the house there is a field. Are they playing in the field? It's not very far from the house. Or are they in the street? There is a garden round (AmE = around) the house … They are in the living-room in front of the telly …Oh, look, here it is, on page 12 of the TV guide.

106

Setze die folgenden Präpositionen ein.

near *on* *at* *to* *into* *in front of* *out of* *under* *in*

It's already 8 o'clock. Tom's still ________ his room. He's packing his things for school. His English textbook is still ________ his desk. Some other books are lying ________ the floor ________ his bed. His pencil-case is also ________ the desk, ________ his computer. He's putting everything ________ his schoolbag. The bus is already waiting ________ the bus stop. Tom runs ________ the bus stop, but doesn't make it. So he has to go ________ school by bike. When he gets there, he rushes ________ the classroom, but he's late. His teacher is already there. He's standing ________ board with the register ________ his hands. A bit late, aren't you, Tom? You couldn't get ________ bed this morning, could you?

107

Ordne die Erklärungen den richtigen Präpositionen zu.

1. **to**	a) ist das Gegenteil von *into*
2. **in**	b) gibt an, dass sich etwas oder jemand auf ein Ziel hinbewegt
3. **into**	c) ist das Gegenteil von *above* und von *over*
4. **out of**	d) bedeutet immer *von irgendwo her* oder *weg von*
5. **from**	e) gibt an, dass jemand oder etwas in einem Raum ist
6. **at**	f) gibt an, dass jemand oder etwas in einen Raum hineingeht
7. **on**	g) jemand oder etwas befindet sich auf einer Oberfläche
8. **under**	h) gibt an, wo jemand oder etwas ist

106 … Tom's still in his room … His English textbook is still on his desk. … books are lying on the floor near / under his bed. His pencil-case is also on the desk in front of / near his computer. …everything into / in his schoolbag. The bus is already waiting at the bus stop. Tom runs to the bus stop, but he doesn't make it. So he has to go to school by bike. … he rushes into the classroom … He's standing in front of / near / at the board with the register in his hands … You couldn't get out of bed this morning, could you?

107 **1** b), **2** e), **3** f), **4** a), **5** d), **6** h), **7** g), **8** c)

108

Übersetze die hervorgehobenen Formen.

I am Tom. ______________________

You are my sister. ______________________

You are right, Mr Owen. ______________________

You are right, Mr and Mrs Owen. ______________________

He is here. ______________________

She is at home. ______________________

It is on my desk. ______________________

We are at school. ______________________

You are wrong, Tim and Danny. ______________________

You don't like her, do you, John? ______________________

They are here. ______________________

109

Beantworte die folgenden Fragen.

a) Wann gebrauchst du diese Pronomen? Als Objekt oder als Subjekt eines Satzes?

____

b) Was musst du dir bei **I** merken?

____

c) Wie viele unterschiedliche Bedeutungen hat **you**? Nenne sie!

____

d) Welche Substantive kannst du durch **it** ersetzen? Unterstreiche sie.

food, cats, house, sister, girl, ball, desks, school, teacher, pupil, pages, door

108 ich, du, Sie, Sie, er, sie, es, wir, ihr, du, sie
109 a) als Subjekt eines Satzes; **b) I** wird immer großgeschrieben. **c)** drei Formen (du, ihr, Sie); **d)** food, house, ball, school, door

110

Setze die richtigen Pronomen ein.

It's really nice to see ________, Mrs Owen.

How are ____________, Mrs Owen?

Are ____________ all right?

And how is Alice? Is _______ all right?

How old is ________ now?

Is ________ here, too?

Where are your bags? Are _________ still in the car?

111

Tom sucht nach seinen Sachen ...
Ersetze das hervorgehobene Substantiv durch ein Pronomen.

Where is **my schoolbag**? ____________ is here.

Where are **my pencils**? _____________ are over there.

Where is **my paper**? ________________ is here on the table.

Where are **my pen and my ruler**? _________ are over there.

Where are **my books**? ________ are on the shelf.

Where is **my English exercise-book**? ________ is in your schoolbag.

Where is **my biro***? ___________________ is on your desk.

Where is **my German textbook**? _____________ is on your desk, too.

Where is **my money**? Is ___________ on my desk, too?

Can _____________ have it?

* AmE = ballpoint pen

110 It's nice to see you, Mrs Owen. How are you, Mrs Owen? Are you all right? ... Is she all right? How old is she now? Is she here, too? ... Are they still in the car?
111 It ..., They ..., It ..., They ..., They ..., It ..., It ..., It ..., Is it ...?, Can I have it?

112

Setze das richtige Pronomen ein.

Hello, ______ am Tom.

Are ________ new here?

Where are __________ from?

What about your parents? Are _________ from Bristol, too?

Is that your bike? Is _________ new?

Have ______ got a sister?

How old is ______ ?

Is _________ in your class?

Is _________ nice?

Can __________ meet her?

113

Setze die richtigen Pronomen ein.

Where is your homework, Tom?

_______ is not here. _______ can't find it. ______ must still be on my desk.

And where is your homework, Danny? Is ________ at home, too?

No, Sir, _______ think ______ is on the bus.

What are ________ doing, Alice and Sue? Are ________ doing your homework now?

No, sir, _________ are just writing a letter.

What! ________ are writing a letter during the English lesson?

Yes, Sir, __________ are.

112 I am Tom. Are you new here? Where are you from? … Are they from Bristol, too? … Is it new? Have you got a sister? How old is she? Is she in your class? Is she nice? Can I meet her?
113 It is not here. I can't find it. It must still be … Is it …? I think it is on the bus. What are you doing …? Are you doing …? No, sir, we are … What! You are … Yes, sir, we are.

114

Trage die entsprechenden Objektformen des Personalpronomens ein.

Singular:			Plural:	
I	______	→	we	______
you	______	→	you	______
he	______	→	my uncles/they	______
she	______	→	my aunts/they	______
it	______	→	my cats/they	______

115

Welche Bedeutung hat *you* in diesen Sätzen?

a) **You** are right, Tom. ______

You are right, Tom and Jerry. ______

You are right, Mr Owen. ______

You are right, Mr and Mrs Owen. ______

b) I can't help **you**, Tom. ______

I can't see **you**, Tom. ______

I can't help **you**, Tom and Jerry. ______

I can't see **you**, Mr Owen. ______

I can't help **you**, Mr. Owen. ______

I can't see **you**, Mr and Mrs Owen. ______

I can't help **you**, Mr and Mrs Owen. ______

114 me, you, him, her, it; us, you, them, them, them

115 a) du, ihr, Sie, Sie; **b)** dir, dich, euch, Sie, Ihnen, Sie, Ihnen

116

Wie heißen sie auf Deutsch? Schaue dir die folgenden Sätze an.

He can see **me / him / her / it.**　　He can see **us / them.**

He can help **me / him / her / it.**　　He can help **us / them.**

me ________ / ________　　us ________ / ________

him ________ / ________　　them ________ / ________

her ________ / ________

it ________ / ________

117

Tom ist wieder auf der Suche. Beantworte Toms Fragen.

I can't see …　　*I can't find …*

Where is **my schoolbag**? ________________________________

Where is **my chewing-gum**? ________________________________

Where are **my sandwiches**? ________________________________

Where is **my money**? ________________________________

Where is **Alice**? ________________________________

Where is **that new boy**? ________________________________

Where are **the others**? ________________________________

Where is **my anorak**? ________________________________

Where are **my glasses**? ________________________________

Where is **my scarf**? ________________________________

And where are **my shoes**? ________________________________

116 mich / mir; ihn / ihm; sie / ihr; es / ihm; uns / uns; sie / ihnen
117 I can't see / find it, it, them, it, her, him, them, it, them, it, they

118

Setze die richtigen Pronomen ein.

Let ______ play together. What game can _____ play? We can play football!

Oh, but then _____ need two more people.

Then let _____ look for Tom and Danny.

Where are __________ ? I can't see ___________ .

Oh, look, __________ are over there.

Let _______ go and talk to _______________ .

Hey, Tom and Dan, can you play with _____ ?

No, _____ can't. Can't __________ see that ________ are busy?

What are ___________ doing?

Well, can ___________ see those girls over there? _____ are watching _______ .

119

Setze die richtigen Pronomen ein.

I've got a problem, Dad. Can _____ help ______ ?

Sorry, son. _____ have got no time. Ask your mother. Perhaps _____ can help _______ .

But Tom's mother is busy, too. So ____________ says to Tom: Oh, sorry, Tom. _____ really can't. __________ must go shopping. Ask your sister.

But Tom's sister is not at home. So __________ can't ask ___________ .

Poor Tom! What can _____ do? Can ______ ask his teacher? His teacher will perhaps be angry with __________ .

118 Let us / let's play together / What game can we play? … But then we need two more people. Then let us look for Tom and Danny. Where are they? I can't see them. Oh, look, they are over there. Let us / let's go and talk to them. Hey, Tom and Dan, can you play with us? No, we can't. Can't you see that we are busy? What are you doing? Well, can you see those girls over there? We are watching them.

119 Can you help me? Sorry, son. I have got no time … Perhaps she can help you. But Tom's mother is busy. So she says to Tom: … I really can't. I must go shopping. … So he can't ask her. … What can he do? Can he ask his teacher? His teacher will perhaps be angry with him.

120

Übersetze die folgenden Fragen und beantworte dann die Frage zur Grammatik.

a) Can you help **me**? ______________________________

b) Can you see **me**? ______________________________

c) Can you go **with me**? ______________________________

Wann musst du den Objektfall des Personalpronomens gebrauchen?

a) für ein Substantiv im ______________________________

b) für ein Substantiv im ______________________________

c) für ein Substantiv nach einer ______________________________

121

Setze die entsprechenden Pronomen ein.

Where are Alice and Ken? Everybody is looking for ________, but nobody can find ________. Where are ________ hiding? The children are looking for Alice first. Where is ________? Is ________ in Tom's room? No, ________ isn't in the room. ________ is empty. There is no trace of* ________ there. Is ________ under Tom's bed? No, ________ isn't. Is ________ behind the door? No, ________ isn't. ________ isn't behind ________. Where is ________ then? ________ is in the wardrobe, with Ken! ________ are hiding behind some clothes, so nobody can find ________. But ______ are laughing, so the children can hear ____________.

* There is no trace of … = Da ist keine Spur von …

120 a) im Wem-Fall (= Dativ); **b)** im Wen-Fall (= Akkusativ); **c)** nach einer Präposition
121 … Everybody is looking for them, but nobody can find them. Where are they hiding? The children are looking for Alice first. Where is she? Is she in Tom's room? No, she isn't in the room. It is empty. There is no trace of her there. Is she under Tom's bed? No, she isn't. Is she behind the door? No, she isn't. She isn't behind it. Where is she then? She is in the wardrobe, with Ken! They are hiding behind some clothes, so nobody can find them. But they are laughing, so the children can hear them.

122

Ersetze die Substantive mit dem Possessivbegleiter durch das entsprechende Pronomen.

This is **my pen**. It's ________________.

Is this **your pen**? Is it ________________?

That's **her bag**. That's ________________.

That's **his book**. That's ________________.

This is **our dog**. It's ________________.

Is this **your car**? Is this ________________?

Are these **their bikes**? Are these ________________?

123

Setze die entsprechenden Possessivpronomen ein.

This is not your table. We are sitting here. This table is ________________,

You sit over there! ____________ is over there.

Hey, that's my chair, Ben. It isn't ________________.

Those aren't your seats, Ken und Sam. ____________ are over there.

Is this your glass? No, it isn't. It belongs to Alice. It's ____________.

And this plate? Is it yours, Debbie? Yes, it's ________________.

And what about this plate? Is it Tom's? Yes, it is. It's ____________.

Don't eat those chocolate puddings! Mike and Ken put them on the table.

They are ____________.

Is that your purse? I don't think it's ____________. It must be Debbie's.

Yes, it's ____________.

122 mine, yours, hers, his, ours, yours, theirs

123 … This table is ours. Yours is over there. … Ben. It isn't yours. Those aren't your seats, Ken und Sam. Yours are over there. Is this your glass? No, … It's hers. … Debbie? Yes, it's mine. … Yes, it is. It's his. …They are theirs. … I don't think it's mine. … Yes, it's hers.

124

Setze die Possessivpronomen ein.

a) Look at these shoes! I don't think they are ___________; they aren't my size.

But, perhaps they are ___________, Tom. They really look as if they could be ___________.

No, they aren't. I never forget my trainers. I always keep __________ in my locker.

b) Debbie, look here. Isn't Alice missing a blouse? Couldn't that be hers? I don't really think

that blouse is _________. It's too small.

c) Oh look, Betty. Aren't Sue and Mary looking for their English books? The books over

there could be ____________________. Let's see if we find their names in them. Oh no,

they aren't _________________. They're ours!

d) And what about those socks over there? Oh, they smell rather bad. Then they are

Bob's socks. We should tell him that the socks over here are _______________.

125

Kennst du die richtige Form?

Er ist ein Freund **von mir***.	He's a friend ________________________________.
Sie ist eine Kollegin **von dir**, oder?	She's a colleague ____________________, isn't she?
Ist Tom ein Freund **von ihm**?	Is Tom a friend ______________________________?
Nein, Tom ist ein Freund **von ihr**.	No, Tom's a friend ____________________________.
Sie sind Kollegen **von uns** ...	They are colleagues ___________________________.
... und auch Kollegen **von euch**!	... and colleagues _______________________, too!
Seid ihr auch Freunde **von ihnen**?	Are you also friends __________________________?

Typischer Fehler: "a friend from me" würde heißen, dass er ein Freund ist, den ich jemandem geschenkt habe!

124 a) … they aren't mine. … perhaps they are yours, Tom. … as if they could be yours. … I always keep mine in my locker. **b)** … that blouse is hers. **c)** … could be theirs. … they aren't theirs. **d)** … the socks over there are his.
125 of mine, of yours, of his, of hers, of ours, of yours, of theirs.

126

Ersetze die hervorgehobenen Substantive.

Look at these pullovers. Do you like them? Which **pullovers**? ____________________

The green **pullover** and the blue **pullover** over there. ____________________

No, I don't like them, but look at that red **pullover**. I like that one a lot! ________________

I know that red is your favourite colour.

But why don't you like that **pullover** over there? ____________________

You mean the yellow **pullover**? ____________________

Yes, that **pullover**. The **pullover** with Big Ben on it. ________________________

Okay, it's not too bad.

Okay, then let's go in and try on that yellow **pullover**. ____________________

127

Unterstreiche die Substantive, bei denen das Ersetzen sinnvoll ist.

Excuse me, could I try on that yellow pullover?

Which pullover?

The pullover over there with Ben Big on it.

Here you are. Try it on, if you like.

I like it, but it's a bit too small. Haven't you got a bigger pullover?

No, I'm afraid not*. That's the only pullover left.

Okay, could you show me the red pullover over there?

Sure I can. Just try it on.

Oh, I like this pullover very much. And how much is it? I'll take it. I love red pullovers.

* I'm afraid not = Leider nicht

126 Which ones? The green one and the blue one … Look at the red one. … that one over there? … the yellow one. Yes, that one. The one with Beg Ben on it. … that yellow one.

127 Excuse me, could I try on that yellow pullover? Which one? The one over there with Ben Big on it. … a bigger one? … the only one left. … show me the red one over there? … Oh, I like this one very much.

128

Setze die fehlenden Formen von *to be* ein.

We ________ happy
We ________ proud.
Our teachers ________ too loud.

We ________ late
That ________ all right.
School can wait!

Girls ____________ nice,
or cold as ice.
And Sally has got a dirty face!

You ________ right,
and I __________ wrong.
But my brother ________ very strong!

129

Schreibe die Kurzformen in Langformen um.

Hi, I'm Danny. ______________________________

I'm from Sheffield. ______________________________

My parents? They're from Sheffield, too. ______________________________

We're new here. ______________________________

And who's that in that photo? ______________________________

That's my sister. ______________________________

She's ten. ______________________________

128 We are happy
We are proud.
Our teachers are too loud.
We are late
That's all right.
School can wait

Girls are nice,
or cold as ice.
And Sally has got a dirty face!
You are right,
and I am wrong.
But my brother is very strong!

129 I am Danny. I am from Sheffield. They are from Sheffield, too. We are new here. And who is that in that photo? That is my sister. She is ten.

130

Setze die richtigen Formen von *to be* ein.

_________ you new here?

What _____ your name?

How old ___________ you?

Where _________ you from?

What about your parents? __________ they from Sheffield, too?

_________ that your bike? __________ it new?

__________ that your sister? __________ she in your class?

What about her friends? They __________ very nice.

_________ I right?

131

Setze die richtigen Formen von *to be* ein. Einige Formen werden verneint.

Sorry, I ____________ not Ken, I _________ Tom.

You're from Bristol, right? We ______________ from Bristol, we _________ from York.

_______ you new here? Yes, we ____________.

______ the girl over there your sister? No, she _________. She ___________ my sister.

_________ she in your class? No, she _______________ in my class. She _________ in my sister's class.

What about the boys over there? _______ they in your class? They ___________ in my class either.

And the man over there? He _________ our teacher. He __________ our caretaker.

130 Are you new here? What is your name? How old are you? Where are you from? Are they from Sheffield, too? Is that your bike? Is it new? Is that your sister? Is she in your class? They are very nice. Am I right?
131 Sorry, I am not Ken, I am Tom. … We aren't from Bristol. We are from York. Are you new here? Yes, we are. Is the girl over there your sister? No, she isn't. She isn't my sister. Is Tanya in your class? No, she isn't in my class. She is in my sister's class. … Are they in your class? No, they aren't in my class either. … He is our teacher. He is our caretaker.

132

Danny ist total durcheinander. Stelle seine Fragen.

you / Excuse me / Tom / are? ______________________________?

you / are / from Bristol? ______________________________?

that / your sister / is? ______________________________?

she / in your class / is? ______________________________?

what / her name / is? ______________________________?

how / is / she / old? ______________________________?

these boys / in your class / are / too? ______________________________?

your classroom / is / that? ______________________________?

the man over there / a teacher / is? ______________________________?

133

Gib Kurzantworten.

a) Are you often late? No, ______________________.

b) Are your teachers always late? No, ______________________.

c) Are your friends happy? Yes, ______________________.

d) Are you and your friends happy? Yes, ______________________.

e) Are you a nice and friendly person? Yes, ______________________.

f) Are you a good pupil? Yes, ______________________.

g) Are your marks always good? Yes, ______________________.

h) Is this exercise difficult? No, ______________________.

i) And your school reports? Are they good? Yes, of course ______________________!

132 Excuse me, are you Tom? Are you from Bristol? Is that your sister? Is she in your class? What is her name? How old is she? Are these boys in your class, too? Is that your classroom? Is the man over there a teacher?
133 a) No, I'm not. **b)** No, they aren't. **c)** Yes, they are. **d)** Yes, we are. **e)** Yes, I am. **f)** Yes, I am. **g)** No, they aren't. **h)** No, it isn't. **i)** Yes, of course they are!

134

Entscheide, ob diese Sätze mit *there is* oder *there are* gebildet werden.

__________________ lamps

__________________ a lot of desks

__________________ windows in the classroom.

__________________ a lot of chairs

__________________ a board

__________________ a mirror

__________________ posters

135

Gib eine Kurzantwort, beantworte aber anschließend die Frage mit der Information in Klammern in einem ganzen Satz.

Beispiel: Is there a bed in your room? (ja, 2) *Yes, there is. There are two beds in my room.*

Is there a wardrobe in your room? (ja, 1) ______________________________

Are there books in your room? (nein) ______________________________

Is there a computer in your room? (ja, 1) ______________________________

Are there chairs in your room? (ja, 3) ______________________________

Is there a toilet in your room? (nein) ______________________________

Is there a lamp in your room? (ja, 2) ______________________________

Is there a TV set in your room? (ja, 1) ______________________________

134 There are lamps / There are a lot of desks / There are windows / There are a lot of chairs / There is a board / There is a mirror / There are posters in the classroom.
135 Yes, there is. There is one / a wardrobe in my room.; No, there aren't. There aren't any books in my room.; Yes, there is. There is one / a computer in my room.; Yes, there are. There are three chairs in my room.; No, there isn't. There isn't a toilet / There is no toilet in my room.; Yes, there is. There are two lamps in my room.; Yes, there is. There is one / a TV set in my room.

136

Gib Kurzantworten auf Fragen mit *there is / there are*.

Are there many pupils at your school? ______________________

Are there many boys in your class? ______________________

Are there any nice girls / boys in your class? ______________________

Is there a cafeteria at your school? ______________________

Is there a gym, too? ______________________

Is there an outdoor swimming pool, too? ______________________

Are there many activities at your school? ______________________

Is there a theatre group or a photo club? ______________________

137

Gib Kurzantworten.

Is that an English book? Yes, ______________________.

Is that an interesting book? No, ______________________.

Is that your teacher? Yes, ______________________.

Is that Mr Mason? Yes, ______________________.

Is that your school? No, ______________________.

Is that your boyfriend? Yes, ______________________.

Is that your girlfriend? No, ______________________.

Is that a silly question? Yes, ______________________.

136 Mögliche Antworten: Yes, there are. / No, there aren't; Yes, there are. / No, there aren't.; Yes, there are. / No, there aren't.; Yes, there is. / No, there isn't.; Yes, there is. / No, there isn't.; Yes, there is. / No, there isn't.; Yes, there are. / No, there aren't.; Yes, there is. / No, there isn't.

137 Yes, it is.; No, it isn't.; Yes, it is.; Yes, it is.; No, it isn't.; Yes, it is.; No, it isn't.; Yes, it is.

138

Gib Kurzantworten.

Isn't that Mr Mason? Yes, ______.

Isn't he your English teacher? Yes, ______.

Aren't you happy to see him? No, ______.

Is that your school cafeteria? Yes, ______.

What about the food there? Is it good? No, ______.

Are there any good restaurants here? No, ______.

Is that a good restaurant? No, ______.

Are you hungry? Yes, ______.

139

Stelle Fragen und gib Kurzantworten.

Frag deinen Freund,

1. ob er ein guter Schüler ist: *Are you a good pupil? Yes, I am. / No, I'm not.*
2. ob er glücklich ist: ______
3. ob seine Lehrer nett sind: ______
4. ob seine Schule groß ist: ______
5. ob sein Englischlehrer gut ist: ______
6. ob sein Unterricht (= lessons) langweilig ist: ______
7. ob viele Jungen in seiner Klasse sind: ______

138 Yes, it is.; Yes, he is.; No, I'm not.; Yes, it is.; No, it isn't.; No, there aren't.; No, it isn't.; Yes, I am.
139 2. Are you happy? Yes, I am. / No, I'm not. **3.** Are your teachers nice? Yes, they are. / No, they aren't. **4.** Is your school large/big? Yes, it is. / No, it isn't. **5.** Is your English teacher good? Yes, he is. / No, he isn't. **6.** Are his lessons boring? Yes, they are. / No, they aren't. **7.** Are there many boys in your class? Yes, there are. / No, there aren't.

140

Stelle Fragen mit den Fragewörter *who, how, what, where*.

________ are you?	I'm Tom.
________ are you?	Fine, thanks. And you?
________ is his name?	His name is Ken.
________ is your friend?	Danny is my friend.
________ old are you?	I'm twelve.
________ are the other boys?	They are at school.
________ is your bike?	It's right there.
________ is your sister?	She's at home.
________ is your English teacher?	Mr Mason is my English teacher.
________ is that on your chair?	It's a book.
________ kind of book is it?	It's an English book.

141

Übersetze die folgenden Sätze!

Wo bist du? ________________________

Wie heißt du? ________________________

Wo bist du her? ________________________

Wie heißt dein Vater? ________________________

Wie alt bist du? ________________________

Wo sind deine Eltern? ________________________

Wer ist dein Freund? ________________________

140 Who are you? How are you? What is his name? Who is your friend? How old are you? Where are the other boys? Where is your bike? Where is your sister? Who is your English teacher? What is that on your chair? What kind of book is it?

141 Where are you? What's your name? Where are you from? What's your father's name? How old are you? Where are your parents? Who is your friend?

142

Setze die richtigen Langformen von *have got* ein.

Mr and Mrs Benson ________________ a son.

They ____________ a daughter, too.

Mr Benson ______________ an interesting job.

The Bensons ______________ a house.

They ________________ a car, too.

Mrs Benson ____________________ got a sister.

She _________________ a nice house in the country.

She ____________________ two children, too.

143

Schreibe über deine Familie. Gebrauche die Kurzformen.

I ____.

My mother / father ____.

She / he ____, too.

My sister / brother ____.

He / she ____, too.

We ____.

My uncle and my aunt ____.

My cousin / cousins ____.

142 Mr and Mrs Benson have got a son. They have got a daughter, too.; Mr Benson has got an interesting job. The Bensons have got a house. They have got a car, too. Mrs Benson has got a sister. She has got a nice house in the country. She has got two children, too.

143 I've got …; My mother's got … / My father's got …; She's got … / He's got …; My sister's got … / My brother's got …; He's got … / She's got …; We've got …; My uncle and my aunt have got …; My cousin has got … / My cousins have got …

144

Schreibe auf, was sie haben und was nicht.

~~brother~~	~~sister~~	~~flat~~	bike	mobile
aunt	brother	house	~~car~~	~~computer~~

Sam ______________ a brother, but ______________________ an aunt.

Ken ______________________, but ______________________________.

The Bensons ______________________. They ______________________.

Emma ______________________. She ______________________.

Alice ______________________, but she ______________________.

145

Stelle Fragen und antworte.

a) ______________ you ________ a sister, Sam?

No, I ____________ a sister, but I ____________________ an aunt.

b) ____________ you ______________ a sister, Ken?

No, I ________________ a sister, but ________________ a brother.

c) ______________________________ a flat, Mr and Mrs Benson?

No, we ________________ a flat. We ________________ a house.

d) ______________ Emma ______________ a bike?

Yes, ________________ a bike, but she ________________

a car.

144 Sam hasn't got a brother, but he's got an aunt.; Ken hasn't got a sister, but he's got a brother.; The Bensons haven't got a flat. They've got a house.; Emma has got a bike. She hasn't got a car.; Alice has got a mobile phone, but she hasn't got a computer.
145 a) Have you got a sister, Sam? No, I haven't got a sister, but I've got an aunt.; **b)** Have you got a sister, Ken? No, I haven't got a sister, but I've got a brother.; **c)** Have you got a flat, Mr and Mrs Benson? No, we haven't got a flat. We've got a house.; **d)** Has Emma got a bike? Yes, she has got a bike, but she hasn't got a car.

146

Schaue dir den Kurztest 144 noch einmal an und gib dann die richtigen Kurzantworten.

Have you got a brother, Sam? ____________________

Has Sam got an aunt? ____________________

Has Ken got a brother? ____________________

Have Mr and Mrs Benson got a house? ____________________

Have you got a flat, Mr and Mrs Benson? ____________________

Has Emma got a bike? ____________________

147

Gib Kurzantworten.

1. Have you got a sister? ____________________
2. Has your mother got a CD player? ____________________
3. Has she got many CDs? ____________________
4. Have your parents got a computer? ____________________
5. Have you got a mobile phone? ____________________
6. Have your friends got a mobile? ____________________
7. Have you got a pet? ____________________
8. Has it got a cage? ____________________
9. Has your mother got a car? ____________________
10. Has she got an iPod? ____________________
11. Have you and your family got a house? ____________________

146 No, I haven't.; Yes, he has.; Yes, he has.; Yes, they have.; No, we haven't.; Yes, she has.

147 Mögliche Antworten: **1.** Yes, I have. / No, I haven't.; **2.** Yes, she has. / No, she hasn't.; **3.** Yes, she has. / No, she hasn't.; **4.** Yes, they have. / No, they haven't.; **5.** Yes, I have. / No, I haven't.; **6.** Yes, they have. / No, they haven't.; **7.** Yes, I have. / No, I haven't.; **8.** Yes, it has. / No, it hasn't.; **9.** Yes, she has. / No, she hasn't.; **10.** Yes, she has. / No, she hasn't.; **11.** Yes, we have. / No, we haven't.

148

Gib Kurzantworten mit *to be* und *have got*.

Is your school a big school? ______________________

Are there many pupils in your class? ______________________

Have you got any friends in your class? ______________________

Have you got a boyfriend / girlfriend? ______________________

What about your teachers? Are they nice? ______________________

Have your teachers got time for you? ______________________

Have you got many lessons in the afternoon? ______________________

Are you happy with your school reports? ______________________

Are your parents happy with your school reports? ______________________

Are you nervous before a test? ______________________

Is English your favourite subject? ______________________

149

Wo muss, wo darf kein *e* stehen?

My parents **hav__n't** got a flat. They **hav__** got a house.

Our house **is____n't** a big house, but it is big enough for us.

The rooms **ar__n't** very big, and the garden is small, too.

But I **hav_____** got my own room, and my sister **has__** got her own room, too.

We **ar_____** very happy about that. We **hav______** got enough room for our things.

148 Mögliche Antworten: Yes, it is. / No, it isn't.; Yes, there are. / No, there aren't.; Yes, I have. / No, I haven't.; Yes, I have. / No, I haven't.; Yes, they are. / No, they aren't.; Yes, they have. / No, they haven't.; Yes, I have. / No, I haven't.; Yes, I am. / No, I'm not.; Yes, they are. / No, they aren't.; Yes, I am. / No, I'm not.; Yes, it is. / No, it isn't.; Yes, I am. / No, I'm not.

149 haven't; have; isn't; aren't; have; has; are; have.

150

a) Setze die entsprechenden Formen von *can* und *may* ein.

I ________________ speak English, but I ________________ speak Spanish.

______________ we see each other tomorrow, Alice? No, I ______________. I'm busy.

________________ I smoke here, sir? No, you ____________________.

________________ I do my homework here? Yes, you ________________.

b) Wo liegen die Unterschiede zwischen *can* und *may*?

____

____

151

Setze die Formen von *can* und *may* ein.

_______________ I ask you a question, sir?

Yes, you ______________________.

_______________ I leave the classroom, sir?

Okay, but first tell me why you want to leave.

I must go to the toilet, sir. _________________ I leave the classroom now?

John, just have a look at your watch. _______________ you tell me the time?

Yes, I _________________. It's three minutes to twelve.

Well, John, then you certainly _________________ wait another three minutes.

Oh sir, I hope I ________________.

150 a) I can speak English, but I can't speak Spanish. Can we see each other tomorrow, Alice? No, I can't. I'm busy. May I smoke here, sir? No, you may not. May I do my homework here? Yes, you may.
b) *can* bedeutet, dass man etwas tun kann oder auch (umgangssprachlich) tun darf. *May* bedeutet ebenfalls „dürfen", ist aber förmlicher als *can*.
151 May I ask you a question, sir? Yes, you may. May I leave the classroom, sir? Okay, but first tell me why you want to leave. I must go to the toilet, sir. May I leave the classroom now? John, just have a look at your watch. Can you tell me the time? Yes, I can. It's three minutes to twelve. Well, John, then you certainly can wait another three minutes. Oh sir, I hope I can.

152

Übersetze die folgenden Sätze und Fragen.

Muss ich kommen? ______________________________.

Du darfst nicht kommen. ______________________________.

Muss er kommen? ______________________________.

Er muss nicht kommen. ______________________________.

Er braucht nicht zu kommen. ______________________________.

153

Setze bitte die entsprechenden Hilfsverben ein.

1.	1.	1. 2.	1. 2. 3.	1.	1.

154

Stelle dir vor, du wärst krank und müsstest zuhause bleiben. Was dürftest du und was nicht? Setze die richtigen Hilfsverben ein (müssen, dürfen, brauchen).

I ____________ stay in bed. I ____________ take my medicine.

I ____________ do my homework. I ____________ go to school.

I ____________ play football. I ____________ see a doctor.

152 Must I come? You mustn't come. Must he come? He needn't come. He needn't come.
153 können – can; nicht können – can't; dürfen – can / may; nicht dürfen – can't, may not, mustn't; müssen – must; nicht müssen, nicht brauchen – needn't
154 I must stay in bed. I must take my medicine. I needn't do my homework. I needn't go to school. I mustn't play football. I must see a doctor.

155

Setze die richtigen Hilfsverben ein. Es gibt mehrere Möglichkeiten.

I ____________ clean the classroom.

I ____________ kiss my teacher.

I ____________ talk to my neighbour.

I ____________ smoke at school.

I ____________ call my teacher names.

I ____________ listen to my teacher.

I ____________ do my homework.

I ____________ fight with my neighbour.

156

Übersetze die folgenden Sätze. Gib auf die Wortstellung acht!

Was kann ich für dich tun? ____?

Wie kann ich dir helfen? ____?

Warum kannst du mir nicht helfen? ____?

Was musst du tun? ____?

Wohin musst du gehen? ____?

157

Korrigiere bitte die Wortstellung.

I / always do / must / what others tell me. ____?

Get up early / must / I. ____?

I / the bus / mustn't / miss. ____?

My homework / do / I / must. ____?

I / at school / stay / must / all day long. ____?

155 Mögliche Antworten: I needn't clean the classroom.; I needn't / mustn't kiss my teacher.; I mustn't talk to my neighbour.; I mustn't smoke at school.; I mustn't call my teacher names.; I must listen to my teacher.; I must do my homework.; I mustn't fight with my neighbour.
156 What can I do for you?; How can I help you?; Why can't you help me?; What must you do?; Where must you go?
157 I must always do what others tell me.; I must get up early.; I mustn't miss the bus.; I must do my homework.; I must stay at school all day long.

158

Stelle Fragen.

You / must / your mother / help? ______________________________ ?

When / her / help / you / must? ______________________________ ?

How long / her / must / help / you? ______________________________ ?

Why / you / help / her / must? ______________________________ ?

What / do / you / must? ______________________________ ?

Clean / you / the bathroom / must? ______________________________ ?

The cooking / do / you / must / too? ______________________________ ?

159

Gib Kurzantworten.

Can I watch this film? Yes, ______________________________ .

Can I have a party here tomorrow? Yes, ______________________________ .

Can I invite all my friends? Yes, ______________________________ .

Can we stay up late? Yes, ______________________________ .

Can we go to bed after midnight? Yes, ______________________________ .

Can you give me some extra pocket money? Yes, ______________________________ .

Can you make us a cake? Yes, ______________________________ .

Can I stay home from school the next day? No, ______________________________ .

Can I borrow* your CD player? Yes, ______________________________ .

Can we smoke in the living room? No, ______________________________ .

* to borrow something from someone = sich von jemandem etwas ausleihen

158 Must you help your mother?; When must you help her?; How long must you help her?; Why must you help her?; What must you do?; Must you clean the bathroom?; Must you do the cooking, too?
159 Yes, you can.; Yes, you can.; Yes, you can.; Yes, you can.; Yes, you can.; Yes, I can.; Yes, I can.; No, you cannot / can't.; Yes, you can.; No, you can't.

160

Übersetze bitte.

Come here, Tom. ______________________

Come here, Tom and Mike. ______________________

Come here, Mr Benson. ______________________

Come over to our place, Mrs Benson. ______________________

Come with us, Mr and Mrs Benson. ______________________

161

Welche Verben könntest du hier einsetzen?

C ______________________ back soon.

B ______________________ here at seven.

P ______________________ up your socks.

E ______________________ your soup.

T ______________________ up your room.

H ______________________ a bath or a shower.

W ______________________ your hands.

B ______________________ your teeth.

D ______________________ your homework.

H ______________________ me now.

S ______________________ the table.

D ______________________ the dishes.

G ______________________ to bed now.

160 Komm ..., Kommt ..., Kommen Sie ..., Kommen Sie ..., Kommen Sie ...
161 Come back soon.; Be here at seven.; Pull/Pick up your socks.; Eat up your soup.; Tidy up your room.; Have a bath or a shower.; Wash your hands.; Brush your teeth.; Do your homework.; Help me now.; Set the table.; Do the dishes.; Go to bed now.

162

Gebrauche verneinte Formen, wo sie sinnvoll sind.

forget your homework ____________________

talk to your neighbour ____________________

listen to me ____________________

fall asleep ____________________

speak German in English lessons ____________________

kick your neighbour ____________________

leave him alone ____________________

run around in the classroom ____________________

be late ____________________

do your homework now, do it later ____________________

be so loud ____________________

163

Wandle die folgenden Sätze um. Gebrauche Imperative.

You must watch out for cars. ____________________

You must stop at red traffic lights. ____________________

You mustn't cross the street when the lights are red. ____________________

You mustn't play football in a busy street. ____________________

You mustn't ride your bike on the pavement. ____________________

You mustn't hurt anybody. ____________________

You mustn't stop in the middle of the street. ____________________

162 Don't forget your homework.; Don't talk to your neighbour.; Listen to me.; Don't fall asleep.; Don't speak German in English lessons.; Don't kick your neighbour.; Leave him alone.; Don't run around in the classroom.; Don't be late.; Don't do your homework now, do it later.; Don't be so loud.

163 Watch out for cars.; Stop at red traffic lights.; Don't cross the street when the lights are red.; Don't play football in a busy street.; Don't ride your bike on the pavement.; Don't hurt anybody.; Don't stop in the middle of the street.

164

Bilde das Partizip Präsens der folgenden Verben.

clean ______	wash ______	sing ______
laugh ______	talk ______	fight ______
drink ______	eat ______	listen ______
shout ______	knock ______	do ______
watch ______	fix ______	go ______
buy ______	play ______	say ______
cry ______	try ______	carry ______

165

Beachte die Bildung des Partizip Präsens bei den folgenden Verben.

write ______	choose ______	lose ______
come ______	ride ______	take ______
change ______	have ______	drive ______
trip ______	plan ______	put ______
sit ______	clap ______	run ______
drop ______	stop ______	swim ______
cut ______	get ______	forget ______
lie ______	die ______	tie ______

164 cleaning, laughing, drinking, shouting, watching, buying, crying; washing, talking, eating, knocking, fixing, playing, trying; singing , fighting, listening, doing, going, saying, carrying.

165 writing, coming, changing, tripping, sitting, dropping, cutting, lying; choosing, riding, having, planning, clapping, stopping, getting, dying; losing, taking, driving, putting, running, swimming, forgetting, tying

166

Was machen die Kinder gerade im Pausenhof? Bilde Sätze mit den folgenden Angaben.

They / eat their sandwiches ____________________

Many / stand together in groups ____________________

They / talk ____________________

Somebody / shout ____________________

Some children / play ____________________

Two pupils / fight ____________________

Somebody / call a teacher ____________________

167

Bilde Sätze im *present progressive*.

The pupils / leave the schoolyard. ____________________

They / go into the school building. ____________________

Some / run. ____________________

A pupil / lie / on the floor. ____________________

He / cry. ____________________

A teacher / come. ____________________

The teacher / carry him into the office. ____________________

He put / him on a stretcher*. ____________________

The secretary / get him a glass of water. ____________________

She / call an ambulance. ____________________

* stretcher = Bahre

166 They are eating their sandwiches.; They are standing together in groups.; They are talking.; Somebody is shouting.; Some children are playing.; Two pupils are fighting.; Somebody is calling a teacher.
167 The pupils are leaving the schoolyard.; They are going into the school building.; Some are running.; A pupil is lying on the floor.; He is crying.; A teacher is coming.; The teacher is carrying him into the office.; He is putting him on a stretcher.; The secretary is getting him a glass of water.; She is calling an ambulance.

168

Lies die Regeln und fülle die Lücken aus.

a) Das present progressive besteht immer aus zwei Teilen:

(1) aus einer Form von *to be* und (2) aus dem *Partizip Präsens*.

Shh! Be quiet! We ____________ (to be) ____________________ (listen) to the teacher!

b) Das Partizip des Präsens bildest du, indem du *-ing* an den Infinitiv ohne *to* anhängst:

to go = __________________, to do = _________________, to try = __________________

c) Bei vielen einsilbigen Verben, die auf einen Konsonant enden, wird der Konsonant verdoppelt. Bei Verben wie *to take*, die auf ein *-e* enden, das nicht ausgesprochen wird, entfällt das *-e*. Bei Verben, die wie *to lie* auf *-ie* enden, wird das *-ie* zu *-y*:

to stop = _________________, to take = _______________, to die = __________________

169

Die Schüler sind wieder im Klassenzimmer, aber ihr Lehrer ist noch nicht da.
Schreibe auf, was sie nicht tun.

The pupils (not sit) in their chairs. ______________________________

They (not do) their exercises. ______________________________

They (not take) notes. ______________________________

They (not look) at their exercise books. ______________________________

They (not work). ______________________________

Tom (not sleep). ______________________________

Mike (not flirt) with Alice. ______________________________

Alice (not write) letters to her neighbours. ______________________________

Kevin and Ken (not throw) things at the girls. ______________________________

168 a) Shh! Be quiet! We are listening to the teacher! **b)** going, doing, trying **c)** stopping, taking, dying.
169 The pupils aren't sitting in their chairs.; They are not doing their exercises.; They aren't taking notes.; They aren't looking at their exercise books.; They aren't working.; Tom isn't sleeping.; Mike isn't flirting with Alice.; Alice isn't writing letters to her neighbours.; Kevin and Ken aren't throwing things at the girls.

170

Was tun sie gerade? Bilde Fragen.

Tom / sit / in* his chair? ______________________________?

He / do / an exercise? ______________________________?

Kevin and Ken / make / girls angry? ______________________________?

Alice / flirt / with Mike? ______________________________?

Robert / lie / on the floor? ______________________________?

Bob, Ben and John / play / cards? ______________________________?

Debbie / read / a magazine? ______________________________?

Fiona / run / around the classroom? ______________________________?

Tim / play / football in the classroom? ______________________________?

* Man kann sowohl *to sit in a chair* als auch *to sit on a chair* sagen. Beides ist richtig.

171

Schaue dir den vorigen Kurztest noch einmal an und gib dann Kurzantworten.

Is Debbie reading a magazine? Yes, ______________________________.

Is Robert running around the classroom? No, ______________________________.

Are Kevin and Ken doing exercises? No, ______________________________.

Is Alice flirting with Tom? No, ______________________________.

Are Fiona and Tom playing cards? No, ______________________________.

Is Tom doing his exercises? Yes, ______________________________.

Is Ben lying on the floor? No, ______________________________.

Is Debbie crying? No, ______________________________.

Are Kevin and Ken playing with the girls? No, ______________________________.

Is Tim drawing a picture? No, ______________________________.

170 Is Tom sitting in his chair?; Is he doing an exercise?; Are Kevin and Ken making the girls angry?; Is Alice flirting with Mike?; Is Robert lying on the floor?; Are Bob, Ben and John playing cards?; Is Debbie reading a magazine?; Is Fiona running around the classroom?; Is Tim playing football in the classroom?

171 Yes, she is.; No, he isn't.; No, they aren't.; No, she isn't.; No, they aren't.; Yes, he is.; No, he isn't.; No, she isn't.; No, they aren't.; No, he isn't.

172

Gib Kurzantworten.

Are you all sitting on your chairs? ____________________

Are you running around the classroom? ____________________

Are you still doing your homework? ____________________

Are you playing cards? ____________________

And what about the others?

Are they all waiting for their teacher? ____________________

Are they leaving the classroom? ____________________

Are they drawing pictures on the board? ____________________

173

Stelle Fragen mit Fragewörtern.

Where you / go? ____________________ ?

What you / do? ____________________ ?

Why / you / not listen? ____________________ ?

Who / talk? ____________________ ?

What / you / read? ____________________ ?

Why / you / leave the room? ____________________ ?

Why you / not take notes? ____________________ ?

Why / you / not / do this exercise? ____________________ ?

172 Mögliche Antworten: Yes, we are. / No, we aren't.; Yes, we are. / No, we aren't.; Yes, we are. / No, we aren't.; Yes, we are. / No, we aren't.; Yes, they are. / No, they aren't.; Yes, they are. / No, they aren't.; Yes, they are. / No, they aren't.

173 Where are you going?; What are you doing?; Why are you not listening? / Why aren't you listening?; Who is talking?; What are you reading?; Why are you leaving the room?; Why are you not taking notes? / Why aren't you taking notes?; Why aren't you doing this exercise? / Why are you not doing this exercise?

174

Füge bitte die entsprechende Präposition hinzu.

What are you looking ______________________? (suchen)

Who are you waiting ______________________? (warten)

Who are you looking ______________________? (ansehen)

What are you listening ______________________? (zuhören)

What are you talking ______________________? (reden über)

Who are you looking ______________________? (sich kümmern um)

Who are you thinking ______________________? (denken an)

Why are you running ______________________? (wegrennen)

What are you writing ______________________? (aufschreiben)

What word are you looking ______________________? (nachschlagen)

What are you putting ______________________ your bag? (hineintun)

What trousers are you trying ______________________? (anprobieren)

175

Setze die richtige Präposition ein.

to get on a bus	to get ______________ a bus
to turn a radio on	to turn it ______________
to put on a shirt	to take it ______________
to take off your clothes	to put them ______________
to fall asleep	to wake ______________
to stand up	to sit ______________

174 What are you looking for?; Who are you waiting for?; Who are you looking at?; What are you listening to?; What are you talking about?; Who are you looking after?; Who are you thinking of? *(think of = denken an; think about = nachdenken über)*; Why are you running away?; What are you writing down?; What word are you looking up?; What are you putting in your bag?; What trousers are you trying on?

175 to get off a bus, to turn it off, to take it off, to put them on, to wake up, to sit down

176

a) Setze die dritte Person Singular ein.

he ___	(play)	she ___	(do)
he ___	(carry)	she ___	(watch)
she ___	(go)	he ___	(die)
he ___	(say)	she ___	(kiss)
he ___	(try)	she ___	(have)
he ___	(buy)	she ___	(make)

b) Unterstreiche die Verben, die unregelmäßig sind und schreibe sie heraus.

___ ___

___ ___

177

Setze die 3. Person Singular ein.

His mother ___ him up at seven.	(wake)
He ___ to wake up.	(try)
He ___, then he ___.	(wash / get dressed)
After that he ___ breakfast.	(have)
He ___ goodbye to his mother.	(say)
Then he ___ his things and ___ the house.	(pack / leave)
He ___ to the bus station and ___ the bus.	(go / catch)
Sometimes he ___ his homework on the bus.	(do)
At half past eight he ___ at school.	(arrive)

176 a) plays, carries, goes, says, tries, buys; does, watches, dies, kisses, has, makes
b) to do, to go, to have, to say (nur in der Aussprache)
177 His mother wakes him up at seven.; He tries to wake up.; He washes, then he gets dressed.; After that he has breakfast.; He says goodbye to his mother.; Then he packs his things and leaves the house.; He goes to the bus station and catches the bus.; Sometimes he does his homework on the bus.; At half past eight he arrives at school.

178

Setze die richtigen Verbformen ein.

When the Bensons ____________ home, it's still very early.	come
Then they ____________ tea.	have
After tea, they ____________ up the dishes.	wash
Tom sometimes ____________ them.	help
Then Mrs Benson ____________ his newspaper.	read
Mrs Benson ____________ a magazine or a book.	read
Later they ____________ TV.	watch
Mr Benson ____________ films. His wife ____________ so, too.	like / do
At about eleven they ____________ to bed.	go

179

Gebrauche die verneinten Formen des *simple present*.

The Bensons / not get up / early.	They ____________.
Mrs Benson / not go / to work.	She ____________
They / not have / an early breakfast.	They ____________
They / not make / their beds.	They ____________
Tom / not do / any homework.	He ____________
He / not go / to school.	He ____________
Mr Benson / not do / the gardening.	He ____________
The Bensons / not stay / at home all day.	They ____________

178 When the Bensons come home …; Then they have tea.; After tea they wash up the dishes.; Tom sometimes helps them.; Then Mr Benson reads his newspaper.; Mrs Benson reads …; Later they watch TV.; Mr Benson likes films. His wife does so, too.; At about eleven they go to bed.
179 … don't get up early.; … doesn't go to work.; … don't have an early breakfast.; … don't make their beds.; … doesn't do any homework.; … doesn't go to school.; … doesn't do the gardening.; … don't stay at home all day.

180

Gebrauche verneinte Formen bei den Sätzen, die für dich nicht zutreffen.

On Sundays

I learn English. ______________________________.

I listen to music. ______________________________.

I go for a walk with my girlfriend / boyfriend. ______________________________.

I clean the windows in my room. ______________________________.

I write e-mails to my friends. ______________________________.

I make breakfast for my parents. ______________________________.

I go to school. ______________________________.

I watch TV. ______________________________.

181

Frage deinen Lehrer / deine Lehrerin, was er / sie am Wochenende normalerweise macht. Benutze dabei die folgenden Verben bzw. Angaben.

go out in the evening ______________________________.

correct tests ______________________________.

get up late ______________________________.

stay in bed all day ______________________________.

play computer games ______________________________.

go shopping ______________________________.

visit your parents ______________________________.

call your students' parents ______________________________.

go to the park with your family ______________________________.

180 Mögliche Antworten: On Sundays, I learn / don't learn English.; I listen / don't listen to music.; I go / don't go for a walk with my girlfriend / boyfriend.; I clean / don't clean the windows in my room.; I write / don't write emails to my friends.; I make / don't make breakfast for my parents.; I go / don't go to school.; I watch / don't watch TV.

181 Do you go out in the evening?; Do you correct tests?; Do you get up late?; Do you stay in bed all day?; Do you play computer games?; Do you go shopping?; Do you visit your parents?; Do you call your students' parents?; Do you go to the park with your family?

182

Gib Kurzantworten.

Do you like pets? Yes / No, ______

Do you like sports? ______

Do your parents like sports? ______

Does your father play football? ______

Does he watch football on TV? ______

Does your mother like boxing? ______

Do your parents smoke? ______

Do people like you? ______

Do your teachers like you? ______

Do you hate English? ______

183

Gib Kurzantworten.

Do you like people? ______

Are you afraid of people? ______

Are people afraid of you? ______

Do you often go out alone? ______

Have you got any friends? ______

Do you help other people? ______

Do people help you? ______

Are you laughing now? ______

182 Yes, I do. / No, I don't.; Yes, I do. / No, I don't.; Yes, they do. / No, they don't.; Yes, he does. / No, he doesn't.; Yes, he does / No, he doesn't.; Yes, she does. / No, she doesn't.; Yes, they do. / No, they don't.; Yes, they do. / No, they don't.; Yes, they do. / No, they don't.; Yes, I do. / No, I don't.

183 Yes, I do. / No, I don't.; Yes, I am. / No, I'm not.; Yes, they are. / No, they aren't.; Yes, I do. / No, I don't.; Yes, I have. / No, I haven't.; Yes, I do. / No, I don't.; Yes, they do. / No, they don't.; Yes, I am. / No, I'm not.

184

Mit welchen Fragewörtern fragst du nach dem Subjekt, Objekt usw.? Trage sie in die Tabelle ein.

Debbie	sees	Tom	in the classroom	at 9.
The shop	shows	its top cars	in its showrooms	this week.
Subjekt	**Verb**	**Objekt**	**Ort**	**Zeit**
a) ________ b) ________	________	a) ________ b) ________	________	________

185

Frage nach dem Subjekt, dem Verb, dem Objekt, dem Ort und der Zeit in den oben stehenden Sätzen.

a) Subjekt: ________________________

b) Verb ________________________

c) Objekt ________________________

d) Ort ________________________

e) Zeit: ________________________

184 Subjekt: **a), b)** *who / what*; Verb: *what*; Objekt: **a), b)** *who / what*; Ort: *where*; Zeit: *when*
185 a) Who sees Tom …? What shows its top cars …? **b)** What does Debbie do …? What does the shop do …? **c)** Who does Debbie see …? What does the shop show …? **d)** Where does Debbie see Tom at 9? Where does the shop show its top cars this week? **e)** When does Debbie see Tom in the classroom? When does the shop show its top cars?

186

Schaue dir die Fragen aus dem vorigen Kurztest noch einmal genau an und vergleiche sie mit der Lösung. Beantworte dann die folgenden Fragen.

a) Wann musst du *what*, wann *who* gebrauchen?

what: ○ Sachen ○ Personen ○ Zeiten

who: ○ Sachen ○ Personen ○ Orte

b) Welches Fragewort musst du gebrauchen, wenn du nach dem Verb fragst?

○ how ○ who ○ when ○ why ○ what ○ where

c) Wann gebrauchst du *to do* bei der Fragebildung nicht?

○ in Fragen nach dem Objekt ○ in Fragen nach dem Verb

○ in positiven Fragen nach dem Subjekt

d) Bei einer Frage nach dem Subjekt steht das Verb im Plural oder im Singular?
Kleiner Tipp: Im Deutschen ist es genauso!

○ Im Singular ○ Im Plural

187

Stelle jeweils zwei Fragen nach den hervorgehobenen Satzteilen.

Mr Hedges works as a caretaker **at Tom's school.**

____?

____?

He likes **his job.**

____?

____?

Children like **him.**

____?

____?

186 a) what für Sachen, who für Personen; **b)** what; **c)** nicht bei positiven Fragen nach dem Subjekt; **d)** Im Singular
187 Who works as a caretaker at Tom's school? Where does Mr Hedges work? Who likes his job? What does he like? Who likes him? Who do children like?

188

Stelle Fragen nach den hervorgehobenen Satzteilen.

a) **Mr Mason** is a teacher.
b) Mr Mason is **at home**.
c) He **corrects** his pupils' tests at home.
d) He always corrects them **on Saturday afternoon**.
e) He often finds **a lot of mistakes** in their tests.
f) He doesn't always like **what he sees**.
g) Sometimes **he** gets angry.

a) ____ ?

b) ____ ?

c) ____ ?

d) ____ ?

e) ____ ?

f) ____ ?

g) ____ ?

189

Stelle Fragen nach den hervorgehobenen Satzteilen.

a) He **gives** his pupils a lot of work.

____

b) He calls **his wife**.

____

c) He corrects **the mistakes**.

____

d) **Mr Mason** begins to cry when he sees the pupils' mistakes.

____

188 a) Who is Mr Mason? b) Where is Mr Mason? **c)** What is he doing? **d)** When does he correct them? **e)** What does he often find in their tests? **f)** What doesn't he always like? **g)** Who gets angry sometimes?
189 a) What does he do? **b)** Who does he call? **c)** What does he correct? **d)** Who begins to cry?

190

Setze *how, why, which, what* ein.

__________ many books do you read a year? About 50 books, I think.

__________ often do you go to the public library? Once a week.

__________ don't you buy them? They are too expensive.

__________ much does this book cost? It costs £10.

__________ book are you talking about? The green book over there.

__________ do you read so many books? I like books.

__________ kind of books do you like? I like all kinds of books.

191

Übersetze die folgenden Fragen.

Magst du Fernsehen? __________

Was schaust du normalerweise im Fernsehen an? __________

Was für Filme magst du? __________

Was sagen deine Eltern dazu? __________

Welche anderen Programme schaust du dir an? __________

Wie oft machst du das Fernsehen an? __________

Wie lange schaust du fern? __________

Wann machst du das Fernsehen aus? __________

Schläfst* du manchmal vor dem Fernseher ein? __________

Wann gehst du ins Bett? __________

* to fall asleep = einschlafen

190 how, how, why, how, which, why, what

191 Do you like (watching) TV?; What do you normally watch on TV?; What kind of films do you like?; What do your parents say about them / the films?; What other programmes do you watch?; How often do you turn on the TV?; How long do you watch TV?; When do you turn off the TV?; Do you sometimes fall asleep in front of the TV?; When do you go to bed?

192

Debbie hat sich Notizen über ihren Tagesablauf gemacht. Die Reihenfolge stimmt allerdings nicht. Nummeriere die Sätze in der richtigen Reihenfolge.

- go to bed and read a book
- wake up
- have supper
- leave the house
- wash / dress
- have lunch at school
- kiss her mother goodbye
- come home in the late afternoon
- do homework
- go to her first class, English
- fall asleep
- watch TV
- have breakfast
- run to the bus

193

Schreibe auf, was Debbie tut (s. Kurztest Nr. 192) und verbinde die einzelnen Sätze mit den folgenden Signalwörtern:

afterwards first then the next day after that after before

First she ____________________

192 1. wake up; **2.** wash / dress; **3.** have breakfast; **4.** kiss her mother goodbye; **5.** leave the house; **6.** run to the bus; **7.** go to her first class, English; **8.** have lunch at school; **9.** come home in the late afternoon; **10.** do her homework; **11.** have supper; **12.** watch TV; **13.** go to bed and read a book; **14.** fall asleep

193 Mögliche Antworten: First Debbie wakes up, then she washes, dresses and has breakfast. After that she goes to school. She kisses her mother good-bye, then she runs to the bus. When the morning lessons are over, she has lunch at school, too. After she comes home in the late afternoon, she does her homework. Afterwards she has supper. Then she watches TV or plays a game or two. After that she goes to bed and reads a book. The next day she goes to school again.

194

Schreibe, wie der Tag bei den Bensons verläuft. Gebrauche die folgenden Angaben. Die Verben und Signalwörter musst du allerdings ergänzen.

get up at seven / wash / dress / breakfast / leave the house at 8 / Mrs Benson bus / work in a hospital / look after patients / lunch there, too / Mr Benson work for a newspaper / write and correct articles / often Mr Benson lunch in town / the Bensons home in the early evening / tea or supper

____

____

____

____

____

195

Übersetze bitte die hervorgehobenen Signalwörter für das *simple present*.

They **often** play with their children. ______________

They **always** talk to them. ______________

They **often** help them with their homework. ______________

They **usually** watch TV or read a book. ______________

They **sometimes** go out. ______________

They **never** stay out all night. ______________

Sometimes their friends come to see them. ______________

They **always** have a good time. ______________

They are **seldom** bored. ______________

They **never** get angry. ______________

194 The Bensons get up at seven. They wash and dress. Then they have breakfast. At 8 they leave the house. Mrs Benson takes the bus. She works in a hospital. She looks after patients. She has lunch there, too. Mr Benson works for a newspaper. He writes and corrects articles. He often has lunch in town. The Bensons come home in the early evening. Then they have tea or supper.
195 oft, immer, oft, gewöhnlich / normalerweise, manchmal, nie/niemals, manchmal, immer, selten, nie.

196

Sieh dir den Kurztest Nr. 195 nochmals an und kreuze dann die richtigen Antworten an.

1. Wo stehen die Signalwörter bei den einfachen Formen von *to be*?

   - vor dem Verb
   - hinter dem Verb

2. Wo stehen die Signalwörter bei dem *simple present*?

   - vor dem Verb
   - hinter dem Verb?

3. Wo stehen die Signalwörter bei verneinten Formen des *simple present*?

   - vor dem Verb
   - hinter dem Verb

4. Wo kann *sometimes* noch stehen?

   - überall
   - am Satzanfang

197

Setze die Signalwörter ein.

He forgets his homework. ______________________ (nie)

He is late. ______________________ (niemals)

He is on time. ______________________ (immer)

He listens to his teacher. ______________________ (immer)

He doesn't talk in class. ______________________ (immer)

He is bored. ______________________ (niemals)

He knows everything. ______________________ (gewöhnlich)

He forgets things. ______________________ (selten)

We make fun of him. ______________________ (manchmal)

But it's not funny! ______________________ (manchmal)

196 1. Hinter dem Verb, **2.** Vor dem Verb, **3.** Vor dem Verb, **4.** Am Satzanfang

197 He never forgets his homework.; He is never late.; He is always on time.; He always listens to his teacher.; He doesn't always talk in class.; He is never bored.; He usually knows everything.; He seldom forgets things.; We sometimes make fun of him.; But sometimes it's not funny.

198

Beantworte die folgenden Fragen mit einer Kurzantwort und Signalwörten wie *never*, *always* etc.

1. Do you often drive your teachers crazy? (No / never)

   ____

2. Are you always a friendly person? (Yes / seldom unfriendly)

   ____

3. Are you always happy when you go to school? (Yes / always)

   ____

4. Do your teachers give you good marks*? (Yes / usually)

   ____

5. Do you listen to your teachers? (Yes / always)

   ____

* marks (AmE: grades) = Noten (Schule)

199

Schreibe auf, was du tust. Verwende die folgenden Angaben und Signalwörter:

play computer games with my friends *get older* *get a birthday present*
get pocket money from my parents *brush my teeth*

Every morning I ______________________________.

Every afternoon I ______________________________.

Every day I ______________________________.

Every week I ______________________________.

Every year I ______________________________.

198 1. No, I don't. I never drive my teachers crazy. **2.** Yes, I am. I am seldom unfriendly. **3.** Yes, I am. I'm always happy when I go to school. **4.** Yes, they do. They usually give me good marks. **5.** Yes, I do. I always listen to them.
199 Mögliche Antworten: Every morning I brush my teeth. Every afternoon I play computer games with friends. Every day I get older. Every week I get pocket money from my parents. Every year I get a birthday present.

200

a) Bilde Sätze mit den angegebenen Verben.

The sun ______________________________. (shine)

It's not ______________________________. (rain)

The birds ______________________________. (sing)

And we ______________________________ indoors! (sit)

We ______________________________ a test*. (do)

Look! Mike ______________________________. (dream)

He ______________________________ to the birds. (listen)

Our teacher ______________________________ to talk to Mike. (try)

b) Erkläre, warum du hier das *present progressive* gebrauchen musst.

____

____

* einen Test schreiben = to do a test (AmE: to take a test)

201

Welche Signalwörter kannst du nicht mit dem *present progressive* gebrauchen?

next year	listen!	this morning	then
at this moment	just	this afternoon	today
look!	now	this evening	the next day
every morning	after that	the next evening	seldom

200 a) The sun is shining.; It's not raining.; The birds are singing.; And we are sitting indoors!; We are doing a test.; Look! Mike is dreaming.; He is listening to the birds.; Our teacher is trying to talk to Mike.
b) Die Handlung läuft gerade ab, ist also noch nicht abgeschlossen.
201 *next year, then, the next day, every morning, after that, the next evening, seldom* sind **keine** Signalwörter für das *present progressive*.

202

Das *simple present* oder das *present progressive*? Was ist richtig?

Where is David?

He ______________________________ (clean) Debbie's bike.

What? Why ___________ he _________________ (clean) her bike during my English lesson?

That _______________ (be) his birthday present to her.

Okay, okay, I _______________ (see). He ________________ (know) we have English today, doesn't he?

I ______________________________ (think) so.

Well, maybe he ______________________________ (not know) that it's my birthday, too. He can clean my car too – as a birthday present to me!

203

Das *simple present* oder das *present progressive*? Antworte, bitte.

a) Doesn't Mr Brown live here? No, he doesn't. He ________________ in London now. (live)

b) Can I talk to Debbie? I'm afraid not*. She ___________________________ a bath. (have)

c) Can you talk to me, Bob? Sorry, not now, I ________________________ the football match on TV. (watch)

d) Look! That's Bobby's team. They ______________________ against another school. (play) ____________ you _________ football, too? (play)

e) Tom, where are you? In my room. What ____________ you _____________ there? (do) I _________________ very busy (be). I _______________________ my homework. (do)

* I'm afraid not. = Leider nicht.

202 … He is cleaning Debbie's bike. What? Why is he cleaning her bike during my English lesson? That is his birthday present to her. Okay, okay, I see. He knows we have English today, doesn't he? I think so. Well, maybe he doesn't know that …
203 a) He lives in London now. **b)** She is having a bath. **c)** I'm watching the football match on TV. **d)** They are playing against another school. Do you play football, too? **e)** What are you doing there? I'm very busy. I'm doing my homework.

204

Welche der hervorgehobenen Verben kannst du normalerweise nicht im *present progressive* verwenden? Unterstreiche sie.

Everybody **knows** me, but nobody **understands** me.

Nobody **comes** to see me. Nobody **talks** to me. I **am** all alone.

Nobody **likes** me, nobody **wants me** and nobody **loves** me. I **cry** all day.

Can you **hear** me? Can you **see** me?

205

***Present progressive* oder *simple present*?**

Alice often ____________________ TV, but this evening she ____________________ to watch anything. (watch / not want)

She ____________________ to go out. Today ____________________ her girlfriend's birthday, and there will be a party at her house. (want / be)

Alice ____________________ to be there, but her mother ____________________ her friends. (want / not like)

She ____________________ why Alice ____________________ such friends. (not understand / have)

What can Alice do? Look! She ____________________ (be) in her room.

She ____________________ in front of the mirror. She ____________________ on her new dress and a bit of make-up! (stand / put)

What ____________ she ____________________?! (do) She ____________________ out. (go)

____________________ she always ____________________ things like that? (do)

Yes. She always ____________________ what she wants! (do)

204 know, understand, be, like, want, love, hear, see

205 Alice often watches TV, but this evening she doesn't want to watch anything. She wants to go out. Today is her girlfriend's birthday, and there will be a party at her house. Alice wants to be there, but her mother doesn't like her friends. She doesn't understand why Alice has such friends. What can Alice do? Look! She is in her room. She is standing in front of the mirror. She is putting on her new dress and a bit of make-up! What is she doing?! She is going out. Does she always do things like that? Yes, she always does what she wants!

206

Setze die Formen des *simple past* von *to be* ein.

a) Last week Tom ____________________ ill.

b) He ____________________ at home.

c) His parents ____________________ also at home.

d) His friends ____________________ there, too.

e) I ____________________ there, too.

f) The room ____________________ full of people.

g) There ____________________ very little room in front of his bed.

h) Everybody ____________________ worried.

i) Only Tom ____________________ happy.

j) He ____________________ not at school, and he missed the English exam!

207

Setze die verneinten Vergangenheitsformen von *to be* ein.

Tom ____________________ well.

His friends ____________________ happy.

You ____________________ happy.

His mother ____________________ happy either.

His parents called the doctor, but he ____________________ there.

He ____________________ at home.

We ____________________ happy about that.

206 a) Last week Tom was ill. **b)** He was at home. **c)** His parents were also at home. **d)** His friends were there, too. **e)** I was there, too. **f)** The room was full of people. **g)** There was very little room in front of his bed. **h)** Everybody was worried. **i)** Only Tom was happy. **j)** He was not at school …

207 Tom wasn't well. His friends weren't happy. You weren't happy. His mother wasn't happy either. His parents called the doctor, but he wasn't there. He wasn't at home. We weren't happy about that.

208

Ergänze bitte die fehlenden Formen.

I	was	not	I ______
you	______	not	you ______
he,she, it	______	not	he, she, it ______
we	______	not	we ______
you	______	not	you ______
they	______	not	they ______

209

Schaue dir den Kurztest 206 noch einmal an und stelle dann die entsprechenden Fragen.

a) ______________________________ ?

b) ______________________________ ?

c) ______________________________ ?

d) ______________________________ ?

e) ______________________________ ?

f) ______________________________ ?

g) ______________________________ ?

h) ______________________________ ?

i) ______________________________ ?

j) ______________________________ ?

208 I was not; you were not; he, she, it was not; we were not; you were not; they were not; I wasn't; you weren't; he, she, it wasn't; we weren't; you weren't; they weren't.

209 a) Was Tom ill last week? **b)** Was he at home? **c)** Were his parents at home, too? **d)** Were his friends there, too. **e)** Was I / were you there, too? **f)** Was the room full of people? **g)** Was there little room in front of his bed? **h)** Was everybody worried? **i)** Was Tom happy? **j)** Was he at school?

210

Setze die Formen des *simple past* von *to be* ein und gib Kurzantworten.

a) ______________ you ill, Tom? Yes, ______________________________.

b) ______________ you worried? No, ______________________________.

c) ______________ your parents worried? Yes, ______________________________.

d) ______________ your friends there? Yes, ______________________________.

e) ______________ all of them there? No, ______________________________.

f) ______________ Alice there? No, ______________________________.

g) ______________ Debbie there? Yes, ______________________________.

h) ______________ she rude to you? No, ______________________________.

i) ______________ you happy? Yes, ______________________________.

211

Stelle Fragen mit Fragewörtern. Ergänze die fehlenden Formen von *to be*.

Why / not at school last week? ______________________________?

How long / ill? ______________________________?

Why / ill? ______________________________?

When / better again? ______________________________?

How many of your friends / there? ______________________________?

Who / missing? ______________________________?

Why / Debbie not there? ______________________________?

Where / the doctor? ______________________________?

210 a) Were … / Yes, I was. **b)** Were … / No, I wasn't. **c)** Were … / Yes, they were. **d)** Were … / Yes, they were. **e)** Were … / No, they weren't. **f)** Was … / No, she wasn't. **g)** Was … / Yes, she was. **h)** Was / No, she wasn't. **i)** Were / Yes, I was.
211 Why were you not at school last week? How long were you ill? Why were you ill? When were you better again? How many of your friends were there? Who was missing? Why was Debbie not there? Where was the doctor?

212

a) Wie wird das *present progressive* gebildet?

Mit dem ○ Präsens von *to be* ○ Präsens von *to do*

und dem ○ Partizip Präsens ○ Partizip Perfekt

b) Und wie steht es mit dem *past progressive*? Es wird gebildet

mit der ○ Vergangenheit von *to be* ○ Vergangenheit von *to do*

und dem ○ Partizip Perfekt ○ Partizip Präsens

c) Vervollständige die folgenden Sätze:

What ________________ you ________________ (do) right now?

What ________________ you ________________ (do) yesterday when I called you?

213

Bilde das Partizip Präsens der folgenden Verben.

watch	________________	fetch	________________
make	________________	take	________________
sit	________________	run	________________
go	________________	do	________________
lie	________________	die	________________
swim	________________	cry	________________
play	________________	try	________________
carry	________________	hurry	________________

212 a) Mit dem Präsens von **to be** und dem Partizip Präsens; **b)** mit der Vergangenheit von **to be** und dem Partizip Präsens; **c)** What are you doing right now? What were you doing yesterday when I called you?
213 watching, making, sitting, going, lying, swimming, playing, carrying; fetching, taking, running, doing, dying, crying, trying, hurrying

214

Bilde Sätze mit dem *past progressive*.

When the doorbell rang yesterday morning at seven o'clock, …

I / just get up ______________________________

my parents / have breakfast ______________________________

my father / read morning paper ______________________________

my sister / still sleep ______________________________

our neighbors / still lie in their beds ______________________________

my younger brother / still dream ______________________________

other people / have a good time ______________________________

215

Bilde Sätze im *past progressive* mit den folgenden Angaben.

Yesterday at 11 am …

most people / not lie in their beds anymore ______________________________

my parents / not have breakfast anymore ______________________________

most people / not sleep anymore ______________________________

I / not lie in my bed anymore either ______________________________

I / not sit at the breakfast table anymore ______________________________

I not play / football ______________________________

I / sit on a chair ______________________________

I / do an English test* ______________________________

* to do a test (AmE: to take a test) = einen Test schreiben

214 When the doorbell rang yesterday at seven o'clock … I was just getting up.; my parents were having breakfast.; my father was reading the morning paper.; my sister was still sleeping.; our neighbors were still lying in their beds.; my younger brother was still dreaming.; other people were having a good time.
215 Yesterday at 11 am … most people were not lying in their beds anymore.; my parents were not having breakfast anymore.; most people were not sleeping anymore.; I was not lying in my bed anymore either.; I was not sitting at the breakfast table anymore.; I was not playing football.; I was sitting on a chair.; I was doing an English test.

216

Vervollständige die Fragen und gib Kurzantworten. Pass beim Partizip Präsens auf die richtige Schreibung auf.

_______ you (do) _______________ a test? No, _______________

_______ your teachers (ask) _______________ questions? Yes, _______________

_______ you (talk) _______________ to your neighbour? No, _______________

_______ your neighbour (make) _______________ fun of you? Yes, _______________

_______ you (cry) _______________? No, _______________

217

Stelle bitte die entsprechenden Fragen.

I called you yesterday evening and couldn't reach you …

What / you / do when I called? You / watch a film? What film / you / watch?

What / your parents / do? You talk / someone / on the phone? You have / dinner / with your family? What / you eat?

____

____

____

____

____

____

____

____

____

216 Were you doing a test? No, I wasn't.; Were your teachers asking questions? Yes, they were.; Were you talking to your neighbour? No, I wasn't.; Was your neighbour making fun of you? Yes, he was.; Were you crying? No, I wasn't.

217 What were you doing when I called? Were you watching a film? What film were you watching? What were your parents doing? Were you talking to someone on the phone? Were you having dinner with your family? What were you eating?

218

Bilde das *simple past* der folgenden Verben.

a) happen, knock, pass, push; ______________________________

turn, watch, cheer, cook, talk; ______________________________

answer, ask, climb, finish; ______________________________

explain, guess, help, look; ______________________________

stay, play, enjoy ______________________________

b) love, dance, explore, agree ______________________________

c) invite, hate, point, end, fold ______________________________

d) hurry, cry, carry, tidy ______________________________

e) plan, drop, stop, clap ______________________________

219

Ergänze den Text.

1. Bei Verben, die das *simple past* regelmäßig bilden, wird ein __________ an den Infinitiv angehängt.
   Wo bereits ein -*e* vorhanden ist, entfällt dieses (z. B.: *dance* + *ed* = *danced*).
2. Die Endung -*ed* wird bei Verben, die auf ein gesprochenes / t / oder / d / enden, wie __________ ausgesprochen (z. B. *hate* + *ed* = *hated*).
3. Ein -*y* wird nach __________ zu *ie*; nach __________ bleibt es erhalten (z. B. *try* → *tried*, aber *play* → *played*).
4. Der letzte Konsonant bei einsilbigen Verben mit kurzem betonten Vokal wird __________ (z. B. *drop* → *dropped*).

218 a) happened, knocked, passed, pushed; turned, watched, cheered, cooked, talked; answered, asked, climbed, finished; explained, guessed, helped, looked; stayed, played, enjoyed; **b)** loved, danced, explored, agreed; **c)** invited, hated, pointed, ended, folded; **d)** hurried, cried, carried, tidied; **e)** planned, dropped, stopped, clapped
219 1. … wird ein -*ed* angehängt. **2.** … wie /id/ ausgesprochen. **3.** … nach Konsonant zu *ie*, nach Vokal bleibt es erhalten. **4.** … wird verdoppelt.

220

Bilde das *simple past* der folgenden Verben.

choose ______	eat ______	speak ______
come ______	fly ______	stand ______
do ______	fall ______	take ______
drive ______	feel ______	tell ______
keep ______	leave ______	throw ______
lose ______	make ______	know ______
meet ______	read ______	write ______
have ______	go ______	wear ______
hear ______	give ______	fight ______
hurt ______	hide ______	mean ______
sell ______	ride ______	find ______

221

Bilde das *simple past* der folgenden Verben. Ein Verb passt jedoch nicht in die jeweilige Reihe. Unterstreiche es!

1. cut ______	get ______	put ______	cost ______
2. know ______	fly ______	grow ______	show ______
3. drink ______	sing ______	begin ______	win ______
4. sleep ______	keep ______	feel ______	see ______
5. catch ______	think ______	bring ______	buy ______

220 chose, came, did, drove, kept, lost, met, had, heard, hurt, sold; ate, flew, fell, felt, left, made, read, went, gave, hid, rode; spoke, stood, took, told, threw, knew, wrote, wore, fought, meant, found

221 1. cut, got, put, cost; **2.** knew, flew, grew, showed; **3.** drank, sang, began, won; **4.** slept, kept, felt, saw; **5.** caught, thought, brought, bought

Das simple past (Verneinung)

222

Gebrauche das *simple past*.

Yesterday the Masons / come home late. ____________________

They / open the door. ____________________

They / switch on the light. ____________________

They / go into the living-room. ____________________

Something / be / wrong. ____________________

They / notice it immediately. ____________________

The cupboards / be / all open. ____________________

They / see / all their things on the floor. ____________________

They immediately / understand. ____________________

Mr Mason / call the police. ____________________

223

Setze die Verben in das *simple past*.

Half an hour later the police ____________________. (arrive)

They ____________ in front of the Masons' house. (park)

They ____________ out of the car. (get)

The Masons ____________ the door. (open)

Three policemen ____________ the house. (enter)

They ____________ hello to the Masons. (say)

They ____________ them a lot of questions. (ask)

Then they ____________ a lot of pictures. (take)*

* ein Foto machen = to take a picture (NICHT to make!)

222 came, opened, switched, went, was, noticed, were, saw, understood, call

223 arrived, parked, got, opened, entered, said, asked, took

224

Setze die verneinten Vergangenheitsformen ein.

The police examined the rooms,

but they ______________ anything. (not find)

There ______________ any finger prints. (not be)

They ______________ any tools. (not see)

There ______________ any shoe prints on the floor. (not be)

The burglar ______________ an amateur. (not be)

He ______________ many mistakes. (not make)

He ______________ the police to catch him. (not want)

The police ______________ happy. (not be)

225

Wie bildest du die Verneinung im *simple past*? Fülle die Lücken aus.

a) Du bildest die Verneinung mit ______________ oder __________ (Kurzform).

b) Danach folgt immer der ______________.

c) Bei *to be* steht keine Form von to ______________. Hier genügt ein __________.

d) Verneine die folgenden Sätze.

they saw ______________ they noticed ______________

they found ______________ they heard ______________

they listened ______________ this meant ______________

I understood ______________ they were ______________

I did ______________ we did ______________

224 they didn't find …; There weren't …; They didn't see …; There weren't …; The burglar was not …; He didn't make …; He didn't want …; The police were not…

225 a) *did not* oder *didn't*, **b)** Infinitiv, **c)** von *to do*. Hier genügt ein *not*. **d)** they didn't see, they didn't find, they didn't listen, I didn't understand, I didn't do; they didn't notice, they didn't hear, this didn't mean, they were not, we didn't do

226

Stelle die Fragen der Polizisten.

a) You call us half an hour ago? ______________________________?

b) You leave the window open? ______________________________?

c) Anybody know that you were out tonight? ______________________________?

d) You turn the lights on? ______________________________?

e) You notice anything out of the ordinary*? ______________________________?

f) Your neighbour notice** anything? ______________________________?

g) You be out all evening? ______________________________?

h) You shut that door? ______________________________?

i) The burglar*** steal anything? ______________________________?

j) He open that safe? ______________________________?

* anything out of the ordinary = irgendwas Außergewöhnliches
** to notice = erkennen, mitbekommen
*** burglar = Einbrecher, Dieb

227

Schaue dir die Fragen in Kurztest 226 noch einmal an. Gib dann die entsprechenden Kurzantworten.

a) Yes, ______________________

b) No, ______________________

c) No, nobody ______________________

d) Yes, ______________________

e) Yes, ______________________

f) No, ______________________

g) Yes, ______________________

h) No, ______________________

i) Yes, ______________________

j) Yes, ______________________

226 a) Did you call us …? **b)** Did you leave the window open? **c)** Did anybody know …? **d)** Did you turn the lights on? **e)** Did you notice anything …? **f)** Did your neighbour notice anything? **g)** Were you out all evening? **h)** Did you shut that door? **i)** Did the burglar steal anything? **j)** Did he open that safe?

227 a) Yes, we did. **b)** No, we didn't. **c)** No, nobody did. **d)** Yes, we did. **e)** Yes, we did. **f)** No, he / she didn't. **g)** Yes, we were. **h)** No, we didn't. **i)** Yes, he did. **j)** Yes, he did.

228

Fülle den Text aus.

Though* the burglar ____________ a beginner (not be), the police ____________ him and ____________ him (catch / arrest**). The next day they ____________ him to a particular room (take), ____________ him to sit down (tell) and ____________ to ask him a lot of questions (begin).

* though = obwohl
** to arrest = festnehmen

229

Stelle die entsprechenden Fragen.

They asked him:

- how get into the house
- what find in the house
- how open the safe
- what in the safe ?
- what take out of the safe
- how long stay in the house
- when leave the house

____

____

____

____

____

____

____

228 Though the burglar was not a beginner, they caught him and arrested him. The next day they took him to a particular room, told him to sit down and began to ask him a lot of questions.
229 How did you get into the house? What did you find in the house? How did you open the safe? What was in the safe? What did you take out of the safe? How long did you stay in the house? When did you leave the house?

230

Beantworte die folgenden Fragen.

1. Mit welchen Fragewörtern fragst du nach dem Subjekt und dem Objekt?

   ○ who ○ why ○ what ○ how

2. Bei welchen Fragen darfst du *to do* nicht gebrauchen? ______________________

   ____

3. Und wie ist es bei Fragen nach anderen Satzteilen? Was musst du dann gebrauchen?

   ____

   ____

231

Stelle Fragen nach den markierten Substantiven.

The burglar broke into the house.

____

The neighbours didn't see **him**.

____

The burglar opened **the safe**.

____

The burglar took the money out of the safe.

____

The burglar took **the money** out of the safe.

____

230 1. who / what; **2.** Bei nicht verneinten Fragen nach dem Subjekt. **3.** Bei Fragen nach allen anderen Satzteilen muss man *to do* gebrauchen.
231 Who broke into the house? Who didn't the neighbours see? What did he open? Who took the money out of the safe? What did he take out of the safe?

232

Stelle die Fragen der Reporter an die Polizei.

How be able / to find the burglar?

____ ?

What mistakes / he make?

____ ?

Anybody / help him?

____ ?

When / break into the house?

____ ?

What / he steal?

____ ?

233

Stelle die entsprechenden Fragen.

Why / you / break into that house? ____________________ ?

Who / tell you to break into that house? ____________________ ?

You / alone when you broke into the house? ____________________ ?

What / you hope to find there? ____________________ ?

You / spend all the money you stole? ____________________ ?

You / give the money back? ____________________ ?

What / you need the money for? ____________________ ?

232 How were you able to find the burglar? What mistake did he make? Did anybody help him? When did he break into the house? What did he steal?

233 Why did you break into that house? Who told you to break into the house? Were you alone when you broke into the house? What did you hope to find there? Did you spend all the money you stole? Did you give the money back? What did you need the money for?

234

Bilde das *past progressive* mit den folgenden Angaben (Achtung: einmal geht es nicht!).

Yesterday Tom and some others went to the swimming pool. When they arrived …

the sun / shine ____________________

the sun / not hide behind clouds ____________________

many people / be / there ____________________

many people / swim in the pool ____________________

others / talk to their friends ____________________

others / play football ____________________

some people / sleep ____________________

some / read a book or a magazine ____________________

some / lie in the sun and dream ____________________

235

Setze die Formen des *past progressive* ein.

Everything was peaceful.

People not shout ____________________

People not run around ____________________

People not fight ____________________

Mike lie peacefully in the grass ____________________

Ken not scream at the others ____________________

Only John tell silly stories ____________________

234 … the sun was shining.; … the sun was not hiding behind clouds.; … many people were there.; … many people were swimming in the pool.; … others were talking to their friends.; … others were playing football.; … some people were sleeping.; … some were reading a book or a magazine.; … some were lying in the sun and dreaming.

235 People were not shouting. People were not running around. People were not fighting. Mike was lying peacefully in the grass.; Ken was not screaming at the others. Only John was telling silly stories.

236

Ergänze die Fragen und gib Kurzantworten.

What __________ you doing at 5 o'clock yesterday afternoon?

a) __________ you having a swim? No, __________

b) __________ you still lying in the grass? No, __________

c) __________ you packing your things? Yes, __________

d) __________ Ken packing his things, too? Yes, __________

e) __________ Mike still listening to music? No, __________

f) __________ John still talking of Alice? Yes, __________

g) __________ the others listening? No, __________

237

Setze die entsprechenden Formen des *past progressive* ein.

While Tom __________ his things (pack), other people __________ their things, too (pack). Others __________ still __________ (swim). They __________ their friends (call) or __________ in the grass (lie). The sun __________ still __________ (shine). The sky was a bit cloudy, but it __________ (be / not rain).

While Tom __________ home (go), his mother __________ tea (make) and __________ the table (set). The water __________ nearly __________ (boil) when Tom finally got home.

236 What were you doing at 5 o'clock yesterday afternoon? **a)** Were … / No, I wasn't. **b)** Were … / No, I wasn't. **c)** Were … / Yes, I was. **d)** Was … / Yes, he was. **e)** Was … / No, he wasn't. **f)** Was … / Yes, he was. **g)** Were … / No, they weren't.

237 While Tom was packing his things, other people were packing their things, too. Others were still swimming. They were calling their friends or lying in the grass. The sun was still shining. The sky was a bit cloudy, but it wasn't raining. While Tom was going home, his mother was making tea and setting the table. The water was nearly boiling …

238

Gestern besuchte Toms Klasse den Zoo von Bristol. Hier ist Toms Bericht. Setze die Verben in das *simple past*.

Yesterday we ______________ to the zoo with Mr Winterbottom, our biology teacher (go). We ______________ to the bus stop (walk). We ______________________ on the bus (get). In the bus we ________________ for our seats (look). Everybody ______________________ happy (be). But soon the trouble _____________ (start). Mike ________________________ (not feel) very well. He ________________ sick (get). It _________________ terrible (be)!

239

Hier ist einiges durcheinandergeraten. Bringe die Sätze in die richtige Reihenfolge und setze die Verben in das *simple past*.

- The bus ___________________ at the zoo. (arrive)
- He ____________________ angry. (become)
- Some pupils _______________ to run around inside the bus. (start)
- Others _____________________ to eat their crisps. (begin)
- The bus driver ______________________ this. (see)
- He ____________________ to shout. (begin)
- There _______________ crisps everywhere. (be)
- We ________________ off the bus. (get)
- I ______________________ happy. (be)
- We ___________________ there. (be)
- Other pupils _____________ their feet on the seats. (put)

238 Yesterday we went to the zoo .... We walked to the bus stop. We got on the bus. In the bus we looked for our seats. Everybody was happy. But soon the trouble started. Mike didn't feel very well. He got sick. It was terrible!

239 Some pupils started to run around in the bus. Others began to eat their crisps. There were crisps everywhere. Other pupils put their feet on the seats. The bus driver saw this. He became angry. He began to shout. The bus arrived at the zoo. We got off the bus. I was happy. We were there.

240

Verbinde die Sätze in den Kurztests Nr. 238 und 239 mit den folgenden Signalwörtern:
first, then, the next moment, later, when, soon, finally, suddenly.

____

____

____

____

____

____

241

Bevor sie den Zoo betraten, erzählte ihnen Mr. Winterbottom, was er bei seinem letzten Zoobesuch gesehen hatte. Setze die Verben in die Vergangenheit und füge die entsprechenden Signalwörter ein.

There were people who …

a) ______________________ to feed the animals. (always try)

b) Others ______________________ to make the animals angry. (sometimes try)

c) They ______________________ on their cages. (sometimes knock)

d) Or they ______________________ loud noises. (often make)

e) They ______________________ things at them. (often throw)

f) They ______________________ fun of them. (usually make)

g) They ______________________ nice to them. (be seldom)

240 Yesterday we went to the zoo. First we walked to the bus stop. Then we got on the bus. In the bus we looked for our seats. Everybody was happy. But soon the trouble started. Mike suddenly didn't feel very well. The next moment he got sick. Suddenly some pupils started to run around inside the bus. Others began to eat their crisps. Soon there were crisps everywhere. Other pupils put their feet on the seats. When the bus driver saw this, he became angry. He began to shout. At last, the bus arrived at the zoo. When we got off the bus, I was happy that we were finally there.

241 a) always tried **b)** sometimes tried **c)** sometimes knocked **d)** often made **e)** often threw things **f)** usually made **g)** were seldom

242

Setze die Präpositionen ein und schreibe auf, wann sie geboren wurden.

_____ February	Dora _____ 2007	Dina _____ 2006

_____ 4th March	_____ Wednesday, 23rd May	_____ Tuesday last week

Beginne wie folgt:

The two young wolves ______________________________

____

____

____

243

Schaue dir die Kurztests 238 bis 242 noch einmal an. Sie sagen dir, wann du das *simple past* im Englischen benutzen musst.

1. In den Kurztests 238 und 239 berichtet oder erzählt jemand etwas, das:

   ● bereits vorbei ist. ● noch andauert. ● bis in die Zukunft noch andauert.

2. Ein solcher Bericht oder eine solche Erzählung besteht aus Handlungen oder Vorgängen, die aufeinanderfolgen. Solche Handlungen oder Vorgänge stehen im Englischen im:

   ______________________________.

3. Im Kurztest 241 wird das *simple past* für wiederholte und gewohnheitsmäßige Handlungen benutzt. Im Kurztest 242 steht das *simple past* für Handlungen oder Vorgänge, die ____________ sind. (Signalwörter: *yesterday*, *last*, *ago*, *in* + Datum …)

242 The two young wolves were born in February. The elephants were born in 2007 and in 2006. The zebra was born on 4th March. The polar bear was born on Wednesday, 23rd May. The gorilla was born on Tuesday last week.
243 1. bereits vorbei ist; **2.** simple past; **3.** vorüber.

244

Setze die richtigen Verbformen ein.

All the children ______________ to see the young polar bear, but Mr	want
Winterbottom ______________ them that the bear ______________	tell / be
still too young to leave its cage. So they ______________ over to see	go
the monkeys. When they ______________ there, feeding-time ________	get /be
over. But some of the monkeys ______________ still very hungry. They	be
______________ their bananas or ____________ on their carrots and	eat / nibble*
apples. Others ______________ so hungry anymore. Some ________	not be
______________ in a corner. Others ______________ some-	sit / hide
where in their cage and some ______________. Two gorillas	sleep
______________ each other. A young one ______________	chase / stand
near the window of his cage and ______________ at the visitors.	look

to nibble = (an)knabbern

245

Finde Beispiele für die folgenden Erklärungen in dem obigen Text.

1. Hast du das System kapiert? Du gebrauchst das *simple past* für Handlungen, die neu einsetzen, sich wiederholen oder – wie in einer Geschichte – aufeinander folgen.

____

2. Das *past progressive* gebrauchst du dagegen für Handlungen, die zu einem bestimmten Zeitpunkt der Vergangenheit noch nicht vorüber sind, sondern gerade ablaufen.

____

244 All the children wanted to see the young polar bear, but Mr Winterbottom told them that the bear was still too young to leave its cage. So they went over to see the monkeys. When they got there, feeding-time was over. But some of the monkeys were still very hungry. They were eating their bananas or nibbling on their carrots and apples. Others were not so hungry anymore. Some were sitting in a corner. Others were hiding somewhere in their cage, and some were sleeping. Two gorillas were chasing each other. A young one was standing near the window of his cage and looking at the visitors.

245 1. So they went over to ther monkeys' house. When they got there … **2.** They were eating their bananas, nibbling on their carrots, etc. Alles geschieht in dem Augenblick, wo die Kinder sie sehen.

246

Setze die richtigen Verbformen ein.

But where ________________ the baby gorilla (be)? ____________ he in the cage or somewhere else (be)? Then, suddenly, Mike ____________________ (see) him. The baby __________________________ (lie) beside its mother and ______________________ to get some milk (try). "Isn't he cute?", a girl _______________ (shout). "Look at him! He _____________ just _________________ there like my baby brother (lie)." Everybody _____________________ when she _______________________ that (laugh / say).

247

Setze das *simple past* oder das *past progressive* ein.

It __________ six o'clock (be), and the zoo ________________ its doors (close). "Come on," Mr Winterbottom ____________ (shout), "the bus is waiting for us." And indeed it _______ (be). It __________________ there (wait). Their bus driver ________ there, too (be). He _________________ angry anymore (not be), but before they ________________ on the bus (get), he ___________ (say) that he wanted to tell them a few things …

So they all ___________ in (get) and _____________ down in their seats (sit). Or at least most of them ____________ (do). Mr Winterbottom _____________ (tell) them again and again not to run around, but some of them __________________ (not listen). And so

And so it ___________________________ (happen).

246 But where was the baby gorilla? Was he in the cage or somewhere else? Then, suddenly, Mike saw him. The baby was lying beside its mother and was trying to get some milk. „Isn't he cute?", a girl shouted. „Look at him! He is just lying there like my baby brother." Everybody laughed when she said that.

247 It was six o'clock and the zoo was closing its doors. „Come on," Mr Winterbottom shouted, … And indeed it was. It was waiting there. Their bus driver was there, too. He wasn't angry anymore, but before they got on the bus, he said that he wanted to tell them … So they all got in and sat down in their seats. Or at least most of them did. Mr Winterbottom told them again and again not to run around, but some of them didn't listen. And so it happened.

248

Füge die richtigen Verbformen ein.

Suddenly the bus __________ to a stop (come). John __________ still __________ (stand), and he __________ (fall) onto the floor and __________ (hit) his head on a seat. One of the pupils __________ Mr Winterbottom at once (call). He __________ very angry (become) when he __________ (see) that John __________ (lie) on the floor. "Why don't you listen?" he __________ (shout). But when he __________ (see) that John's mouth __________ (bleed), he __________ (run) to the bus driver and __________ (ask) him to call a doctor. A few minutes later an ambulance __________ (arrive). Two paramedics* __________ (come) into the bus. They __________ (have) a look at the boy. Then they __________ (fetch) a stretcher. They __________ (put) John on it and __________ (load**) him onto the ambulance.

* paramedic (ambulance man) = Sanitäter, Rettungsassistent, Notarzt
** to load = befördern

249

Es waren viele Leute in der Notaufnahme. Einige unterhielten sich und erzählten, weshalb sie hier waren. Setze die richtigen Verbformen der folgenden Verben ein.

I __________ a shower when I __________. (have / slip)

I __________ the windows when one window __________, and the broken glass __________ my hands. (clean / break / cut)

And what did John tell them? ______________________________

____

248 Suddenly the bus came to a stop. John was still standing when it stopped, and he fell onto the floor and hit his head on a seat. One of the pupils called Mr Winterbottom at once. He became very angry when he saw that John was lying on the floor. „Why don't you listen?" he shouted. But when he saw that John's mouth was bleeding, he ran to the bus driver and asked him to call a doctor. A few minutes later an ambulance arrived. Two paramedics came into the bus. They had a look at the boy. Then they fetched a stretcher. They put John on it and loaded him onto the ambulance.

249 I was having a shower when I slipped. I crashed onto the floor. I was cleaning the windows when one window broke, and the broken glass cut my hands. John: I was running around on the bus when it suddenly stopped. I fell and hit my head on a seat.

250

Unterstreiche im Text die Hilfsverben. Setze dann den ganzen Text in das *simple past*.

The paramedics take John to the accident and emergency department*. He must wait for a doctor. He feels better, but he can't move. So he can only stay where he is. He can't walk around the room. When the nurse comes in, she tells him that he must stay where he is and that he mustn't stand up. But she also tells him that he needn't worry.

____

____

____

____

* Notaufnahme = accident and emergency department, A&E (AmE = emergency room, ER)

251

Setze bitte die Vergangenheitsform ein. Schaue dir dann die Lösungen an und korrigiere, was du eventuell falsch gemacht hast.

can	______________	(konnte)
can't	______________	(konnte nicht)
can / may	______________	(durfte)
can't / may not	______________	(durfte nicht)
mustn't	______________	(durfte nicht)
needn't	______________	(musste nicht, brauchte nicht)

Lerne dann diese Vergangenheitsformen auswendig!

250 must, can't, can, can't, must, mustn't; The paramedics took John to the accident and emergency department. He had to wait for a doctor. He felt better, but he couldn't move. So he could only stay where he was. He couldn't walk around the room. When the nurse came in, she told him that he had to stay where he was and that he was not allowed to stand up. But she also told him that he didn't have to worry.

251 konnte = could; konnte nicht = couldn't; durfte = was / were allowed to; durfte nicht = was / were not allowed to; mustn't = was not / were not allowed to; musste nicht, brauchte nicht = didn't have to / didn't need to

252

Setze die entsprechenden Vergangenheitsformen ein! Pass dabei auf, ob diesen Formen ein *to* folgt!

John ______________________ go home. (durfte)

He ______________________ stay in hospital. (musste nicht)

He ______________________ go to school. (brauchte nicht)

He ______________________ stay in bed for three days. (musste)

His friends ______________________ come to see him, … (konnten)

but they ______________________ stay more than half an hour. (durften nicht)

After 30 minutes, they ______________________ to leave. (mussten)

253

Stelle John die folgenden Fragen.

you / go home? ______________________ (durftest)

you / stay in hospital? ______________________ (musstest nicht)

you / go to school? ______________________ (brauchtest nicht)

you / stay in bed? ______________________ (musstest)

you / watch TV? ______________________ (durftest)

your friends / visit you? ______________________ (durften)

they / stay with you? ______________________ (durften)

they / talk with you? ______________________ (konnten)

When they / leave? ______________________ (mussten)

252 John was allowed to go home. He didn't have to stay in hospital. He didn't have to go to school. He had to stay in bed for three days. His friends could come to see him, but they were not allowed to stay more than half an hour. After 30 minutes they had to leave.

253 Were you allowed to go home? Didn't you have to stay in hospital? Didn't you have to go to school? Did you have to stay in bed? Were you allowed to watch TV? Were your friends allowed to visit you? Were they allowed to stay with you? Could they talk with you? When did they have to leave?

254

Gib Kurzantworten auf die Fragen, die seine Klassenkameraden ihm stellen.

Did you have to stay in hospital? No, ______

Did you have to stay in bed? Yes, ______

Did you have to take any medicine? Yes, ______

Were you allowed to watch TV? Yes, ______

Did you have to do any homework? No, ______

Were you allowed to call your friends? Yes, ______

Could you talk to them on the phone? Yes, ______

Were your friends allowed to visit you? Yes, ______

255

Stelle einem Freund von dir die Fragen. Gebrauche die Hilfsverben.

The last time you were ill …

______ go to hospital? (Musstest du)

______ stay in bed? (Wie lange musstest du)

______ see you? (Wie oft musste der Arzt)

______ get out of bed on your own*? (Konntest du)

______ do in hospital? (Was durftest du nicht)

______ do any homework? (Musstest du)

______ your friends ______ visit you? (Wie oft durften)

______ to go home? (Wann durftest)

* on your own = alleine, ohne Hilfe von anderen

254 No, I didn't.; Yes, I did.; Yes, I did.; Yes, I was.; No, I didn't.; Yes, I was.; Yes, I could.; Yes, they were.
255 Did you have to go to hospital? How long did you have to stay in bed? How often did the doctor have to see you? Could you get out of bed on your own? What weren't you allowed to do in hospital? Did you have to do any homework? How often were your friends allowed to visit you? When were you allowed to go home?

256

Kreuze die richtige Antwort an.

1. Nach *can*, *may*, *must*, *needn't*, *mustn't* steht in der Gegenwart immer ein Infinitiv.

   ja nein

2. Vor diesem Infinitiv steht nie ein *to*.

   ja nein

3. Diese Hilfsverben haben bis auf *can / can't* keine eigene Vergangenheitsform.

   ja nein

4. Für *must / needn't* mußt du in der Vergangenheit die entsprechenden Formen von *to have* to gebrauchen.

   ja nein

5. *to have to* ist ein Vollverb. Es wird im Unterschied zu *to be allowed to* mit *to do* gebraucht.

   ja nein

257

Setze die entsprechenden Hilfsverben ein.

The next time Mr Winterbottom went to the zoo on a class trip …

All of the pupils ____________________ sit in their seats.

Nobody ____________________ to stand up.

Nobody ____________________ to run around in the bus.

If anybody did, he or she ________________ do a lot of homework.

They ____________________ walk home.

They _________________ to go to zoo with him again.

256 1. ja; **2.** ja; **3.** ja; **4.** ja; **5.** ja

257 All of the pupils had to sit in their seats.; Nobody was allowed to stand up.; Nobody was allowed to run around on the bus.; If anybody did, he or she had to do a lot of homework.; They had to walk home.; They were not allowed to go to the zoo with him again.

258

Gebrauche das Vollverb *to have* für *have got*.

Mr Fletcher hasn't got anything. ____________________

He hasn't got a house. ____________________

He hasn't got a wife. ____________________

He hasn't got a family. ____________________

He hasn't got a job. ____________________

He hasn't got any money. ____________________

He hasn't got a car. ____________________

He hasn't got any friends. ____________________

He hasn't got anything. ____________________

259

Stelle dieselben Fragen mit *to have*.

Have your parents got a house? ____________________

Has Debbie got a hamster? ____________________

Have her parents got a cat? ____________________

Have you got a problem? ____________________

Has Mike got a bike? ____________________

Have these people got the tickets? ____________________

Has this girl got a friend? ____________________

Have you got a lot of courage? ____________________

258 Mr Fletcher doesn't have anything. He doesn't have a house. He doesn't have a wife. He doesn't have a family. He doesn't have a job. He doesn't have any money. He doesn't have a car. He doesn't have any friends. He doesn't have anything.
259 Do your parents have a house? Does Debbie have a hamster? Do her parents have a cat? Do you have a problem? Does Mike have a bike? Do these people have the tickets? Does this girl have a friend? Do you have a lot of courage?

260

Gib Kurzantworten. Achte dabei auf die Fragen.

a) Have you got a big family? No, ____________________

b) Have you got any pets? Yes, ____________________

c) Has your sister got a baby? No, ____________________

d) Does your grandma have a motorbike? Yes, ____________________

e) Do you have problems with your teachers? No, ____________________

f) Do you have problems at school? No, ____________________

g) Do your parents have problems with you? No, ____________________

h) Has Debbie got any letters from you? No, ____________________

i) Do you have a message for me? Yes, ____________________

j) Have you got any time for me? No, ____________________

k) Don't you have a little money for me? No, ____________________

l) Haven't you got anything else for me? No, ____________________

261

Schaue dir die folgenden Sätze genau an. Ergänze dann den Text.

She **has got** a house.

She **has** a house.

She's **having** a cup of tea.

She **has** a bath every evening.

1. *have got* und *to have* bedeuten „haben" im Sinne von ____________________.
2. *to have* kann ganz andere Bedeutungen haben, wie in der folgenden Wendung:

   to have a bath = ____________________. Hier ist *have got* nicht möglich.

260 a) No, I/we haven't. **b)** Yes, I/we have. **c)** No, she hasn't. **d)** Yes, she does. **e)** No, I/we don't. **f)** No, I/we don't. **g)** No, they don't. **h)** No, she hasn't. **i)** Yes, I/we do. **j)** No, I/we haven't. **k)** No, I/we don't. **l)** No, I/we haven't.
261 1. *have got* und *to have* bedeuten *haben* im Sinne von *besitzen*. **2.** *to have a bath* = ein Bad nehmen

262

Ordne die Ausdrücke mit *to have* den deutschen Bedeutungen zu.

to have an accident	ein Kind haben, ein Kind bekommen
to have fun	einen Tag frei haben
to have a bath	Spaß haben, sich amüsieren
to have breakfast	Mittag essen
to have a day off	plaudern, Schwätzen halten
to have lunch	eine Pause machen
to have a chat	einen Unfall haben
to have a break	ein Bad nehmen, baden
to have a baby	frühstücken
to have a shower	duschen
to have an argument	(sich) streiten

263

Dann setze die entsprechenden Wendungen sinngemäß ein.

a) It's twelve o'clock. Let's ____________________.

b) Oh dear, you smell bad! Go to the bathroom and ____________________.

c) My aunt is pregnant*. She will ____________________ a baby soon.

d) Be careful when you ride your bike! Don't ____________________.

e) You're going skiing this weekend? ____________________! Break a leg!

* pregnant = schwanger

262 to have an accident = einen Unfall haben; to have fun = Spaß haben, sich amüsieren; to have a bath = ein Bad nehmen, sich baden; to have breakfast = frühstücken; to have a day off = einen freien Tag haben; to have lunch = Mittag essen; to have a chat = plaudern, Schwätzchen halten; to have a break = eine Pause machen; to have a baby = ein Kind haben, ein Kind bekommen; to have a shower = sich duschen; to have an argument = streiten

263 a) Let's have lunch. **b)** … and have a bath / shower. **c)** … have a baby soon. **d)** … Don't have an accident. **e)** Have fun!

264

***Have got* oder *have*? Wo kannst du *have got* nicht einsetzen?**

It's early in the morning. The children are getting up for school. They always ________ an argument before they decide who can go to the bathroom first. The reason is that Alice always needs such a long time in the bathroom. First she ________ a shower, and then she washes her hair. After that she ________ a chat with her dolls. She keeps her dolls in the bathroom, and Alice ________ many of them. So when Alice goes to the bathroom first, the others ________ very little time to use it. They can't ________ a shower or a bath. They can only wash their faces, brush their teeth and then – maybe – they have time to ________ a very quick breakfast. Then they rush off to school on their bikes.

265

Welche Formen von *have/have got* musst du einsetzen?

Alice, can we come in now? No, you can't, I ________ a shower.

Come on, Alice, hurry up! We want to ________ a shower, too.

Just go and ________ your breakfast. You can ________ a shower after that.

Five minutes later they come back, but Alice is still in the bathroom. She ________ a chat with her dolls now. They ________ the day off, so they ________ a lot of time. So there is no need to ________ an argument today!

264 They always have an argument … First she has a shower … After that she has a chat with her dolls. … Alice has / has got many of them. So when Alice goes to the bathroom first, the others have / have got little time to use it. They can't have a shower or a bath. … they have time to have a very quick breakfast …
265 … No, you can't, I am having a shower. Come on, Alice, hurry up! We want to have a shower, too. Just go and have your breakfast. You can have a shower after that. … She is having a chat with her dolls now. They have the day off, so they have / have got a lot of time. So there is no need to have an argument today!

266

Schreibe auf, was kleine Kinder alles lernen müssen und nicht müssen.

Young kids / babies have to learn / don't have to learn

to walk	to go to the toilet	to eat by themselves
to shoot a gun	to watch TV	to change their own pampers
to do the cooking	to earn money	to get dressed
to help others	to play poker	to fly an airplane

____

____

____

267

Bilde Fragen und gib die entsprechenden Kurzantworten.

Beispiel: *Do you have to go to school? Yes, I do. No, I don't.*

a) ____________ you ____________ do your homework? ____________________

b) ________________________ make fun of others? ____________________

c) ________________________ find out what you like? ____________________

d) ________________________ like everybody? ____________________

e) ________________________ like all subjects? ____________________

f) ________________________ be like everybody? ____________________

g) ________________________ talk to everyone? ____________________

266 Young kids / babies have to learn: to walk, to go to the toilet, to eat by themselves, to get dressed, to help others. They don't have to learn: to shoot a gun, to watch TV, to change their own pampers, to do the cooking, to earn money, to play poker, to fly an airplane.

267 a) Do you have to do your homework? – Yes, I do. / No, I don't. **b)** Do you have to make fun of others? – Yes, I do. / No, I don't. **c)** Do you have to find out what you like? – Yes, I do. / No, I don't. **d)** Do you have to like everybody? – Yes, I do. / No, I don't. **e)** Do you have to like all subjects? – Yes, I do. / No, I don't. **f)** Do you have to be like everybody? – Yes, I do. / No, I don't. **g)** Do you have to talk to everyone? – Yes, I do. / No, I don't.

268

Bilde 4 Sätze mit den folgenden Angaben.

Beispiel: They had to clean their car though they didn't want to.

pay the bills ____.

clean the flat ____.

go to work ____.

listen to me ____.

269

a) Lies das Folgende bitte durch und finde die richtige Bedeutung der zwei folgenden Sätze.

Müssen kann im Englischen mit *to have to* und mit *must* übersetzt werden. Allerdings werden beide Ausdrücke unterschiedlich verwendet. Das Verb *to have to* drückt ein Müssen aus, das von außen / von jemand anderem kommt. (Beispiel: **I have to work.** Denn, wenn ich nicht arbeite, verdiene ich kein Geld zum Leben.) Bei *must* ist das Müssen dagegen oft ein innerer Zwang. (Beispiel: **I really must go now.** Denn ich möchte meine Freunde nicht warten lassen.)

1. *I must see you.* — a) My mother told me to see you.

2. *I have to see you.* — b) I really love you and can't live without you.

Im *simple past* gibt es diesen Unterschied allerdings nicht mehr. Hier heißt es immer "Ich had to" = „Ich musste".

I ______________ see you.

b) Setze *must* oder *have* to ein.

1. I really __________________ go now. My parents are waiting for me.

2. Where is Debbie? I ____________________ see her. I can't live without her.

3. I am afraid I can't come this afternoon. My mother told me I __________________ do my homework first.

4. I ______________________________ learn English. I need it for my job.

268 They had to (pay the bills / clean the flat / go to work / listen to me) though they didn't want to.
269 a) 1b), 2a); I had to see you.; **b) 1.** must, **2.** must, **3.** have to, **4.** have to

270

Setze *to* ein, wo es fehlt.

a) What do you want to do in your life?

I want
_______________ become a pilot.
_______________ see the world.
_______________ a lot of money.
_______________ spend it with you.
_______________ five children.
_______________ get a good job.

b) *to want* entspricht dem Deutschen _______________. Folgt ein Verb, dann musst du nach *to want* ein ________ einsetzen.

271

Setze *to* ein, wo es nötig ist.

Would you like
_______________ a cup of tea?
_______________ some orange juice?
_______________ have a drink?
_______________ some more meat?
_______________ go out with me?
_______________ be my friend?

Wo liegt der Unterschied zwischen **would like (to)** und **to want (to)**?

____

270 a) I want to become a pilot. I want to see the world. I want a lot of money. I want to spend it with you. I want five children. I want to get a good job. **b)** to want = wollen; *to want to* + Verb
271 a) Would you like a cup of tea? Would you like some orange juice? Would you like to have a drink? Would you like some more meat? Would you like to go out with me? Would you like to be my friend?
b) *I'd like to …* (*I would like to*) ist höflicher als *I want to …*; *Would like to …* bedeutet „ich möchte", *want to …* bedeutet „ich will".

272

Schaue dir die folgenden Sätze genau an und beantworte dann die Fragen.

Could you help me, please?

Could you come at three o'clock?

Could your sister come, too?

When we have finished, we could go for a walk.

Or we could have a drink somewhere.

a) Was bedeutet *could* in diesen Sätzen? Was kann *could* noch bedeuten?

____

b) Worum handelt es sich bei diesen Sätzen? Was drücken sie aus?

____

273

Übersetze bitte.

Möchtest du noch etwas Zucker?

____

Könntest du mir ein Stück Kuchen geben?

____

Willst du noch etwas Milch?

____

Ich will nicht nach Hause gehen.

____

272 a) *Could* bedeutet hier „ könnte(st)". *Could* kann auch noch „konnte" bedeuten. **b)** Mit *could* (könnte) kannst du höflich fragen oder ein Angebot oder eine Möglichkeit ausdrücken.
273 Would you like some more sugar? Could you give me a piece of cake? Do you want some more milk? I don't want to go home.

274

Mache Vorschläge mit *shall*.

buy a sandwich for you / do it for you / keep you company / carry it for you / find a place for you to sleep / explain it to you

"My schoolbag is so heavy." ______________________________

"I'm so tired." ______________________________

"I'm so hungry." ______________________________

"I can't do my homework." ______________________________

"This exercise is so difficult." ______________________________

"I am so lonely." ______________________________

275

Gib Ratschläge mit *should (= sollte)*. Welche Sätze passen zusammen?

a) "I'm so tired."	not eat so much
b) "My tests are so bad."	study* harder
c) "TV is boring."	ask her out on a date
d) "My jeans don't fit anymore."	look for them
e) "I'm getting so fat."	not stay up so late
f) "My skirt is so dirty."	go home now
g) "My room is a real mess."	wash it
h) "I've lost my keys."	tidy it up
i) "Alice likes me."	not watch so much TV
j) "My parents are waiting for me."	buy new ones

* to study = studieren, lernen/pauken

274 Shall I carry it for you? Shall I find a place for you to sleep? Shall I buy a sandwich for you? Shall I do it for you? Shall I explain it to you? Shall I keep you company?
275 a) You shouldn't stay up so late. **b)** You should study harder. **c)** You shouldn't watch so much TV. **d)** You should buy new ones. **e)** You shouldn't eat so much. **f)** You should wash it. **g)** You should tidy it up. **h)** You should look for them. **i)** You should ask her out on a date. **j)** You should go home now.

Das große Übungsbuch Englisch

Teil 2 (7. – 8. Klasse)

Inhalt

Inhalt

Inhalt

Inhalt

I do · *simple present* bei Gewohnheiten

1

Tom erzählt seinem Freund Mike in einer Mail von seinem Alltag. Schreibe seine Mail korrekt auf.
Tipp: Für regelmäßige Tätigkeiten wird *simple present* verwendet. Vergiss nicht, bei der 3. Person Singular auf das angehängte „s“ zu achten!

Dear Mike,

a go / from Monday to Friday / to school / I / always

____

b every afternoon / my homework / do / from 5 pm to 6:30 pm / I

____

c Maria / come over / usually / on Wednesday / and I / help her / with our maths homework

____

d visit / at the weekends / often / my grandmother / us

____

e play tennis / on Sunday / sometimes / I / with my friend Marc

____

f never / not like / I / go to the disco / loud music / so / I

____

2

In jedem der Sätze aus Kurztest 1 ist ein Signalwort versteckt, das darauf hinweist, dass in diesen Fällen das *simple present* verwendet werden muss. Findest du alle?

a I always go to school from Monday to Friday. **b** I do my homework every afternoon from 5 pm to 6:30 pm. **c** Maria usually comes over on Wednesday and I help her with our maths homework. **d** My grandmother often visits us at the weekends. **e** On Sunday I sometimes play tennis with my friend Marc. **f** I don't like loud music, so I never go to the disco.
2 always; every afternoon; usually; often; sometimes; never

3

Maria soll die junge Sportlerin Ashley interviewen und einen Bericht über deren Alltag schreiben. Sie hat schon Stichpunkte gesammelt, aber noch keine Fragen aufgeschrieben. Hilf ihr dabei.

Tipp: Im *simple present* braucht die Frage das Hilfsverb *do / does*, wenn keine Form von *to be* im Satz vorkommt.

a what / eat / every day? ____________________

b how long / be / the training? ____________________

c often / go out / with friends? ____________________

d your parents / be / proud? ____________________

e your parents / come / to every competition? ____________________

f you / go / to a normal school? ____________________

4

Maria sitzt Ashley gegenüber; aber sie ist so aufgeregt, dass sie sich völlig verhaspelt. Finde die Fehler und verbessere Marias Fragen. Schreibe sie neu auf.

a What do you in the afternoon? ____________________

b Where you train for the competitions? ____________________

c When your first competiton this year? ____________________

d You do an apprenticeship, too? ____________________

e What your favourite pop star? ____________________

f Have you time for relaxing with friends? ____________________

g What your hobbies? ____________________

h When you normally get up? ____________________

3 a What do you eat every day? **b** How long is the training? **c** Do you often go out with friends? **d** Are your parents proud? **e** Do your parents come to every competition? **f** Do you go to a normal school?

4 a What do you do in the afternoon? **b** Where do you train for the competitions? **c** When is your first competition this year? **d** Do you do … / Are you doing an apprenticeship, too? **e** Who is your favourite pop star? **f** Have you got time for relaxing with friends? / Do you have … **g** What are your hobbies? **h** When do you normally get up?

5

Tom hat Ferien und kann endlich mal was anderes tun als sonst immer! Er ruft Mike an und erzählt, was er während seiner Ferien macht. Kannst du seine Sätze vervollständigen?
Tipp: Für Handlungen oder Dinge, die gerade passieren, wird *present progressive* verwendet.

a Normally I have to study so hard for school, but guess what ______________________

__________ (I / do) right now. … Exactly – absolutely nothing!

b On school nights I always have to go to bed at 10 pm, so I can get up in time for school.
But ______________________________ (I / stay up) every night till midnight now!

c I usually have to read for school, but ______________________________ (I / play) video games all day now with my sister!

d Normally my sister really gets on my nerves, but ______________________________ (we / enjoy) our time together at the beach a lot – I mean, we're on holiday!

6

Maria und Tom liegen am Strand und beobachten, was um sie herum gerade passiert. Schreibe die Sätze im *present progressive*.

a Two little boys / play soccer

____

b The parents / talk to each other and they / not look after / the boys

____

c Now / one of the boys / jump / into the waves

____

d The other boy / shout / but his parents / not listen

____

5 a I am doing; **b** I am staying up; **c** I am playing; **d** we are enjoying
6 a Two little boys are playing soccer. **b** The parents are talking to each other and they aren't looking after the boys. **c** Now one of the boys is jumping into the waves. **d** The other boy is shouting but his parents are not listening.

7

Maria ist übers Wochenende bei ihrer Freundin Shawna. Doch dauernd ruft ihre Mutter auf dem Handy an und nervt sie mit allen möglichen Fragen! Schreibe die Fragen im *present progressive* auf.

Tipp: Im *present progressive* braucht die Frage das Hilfsverb *be*.

a ______________________ (you / eat) enough?

b ______________________ (you / help) with the housework?

c ______________________ (you / playing) with Shawna's little sister?

d ______________________ (you / sleep) long enough?

e ______________________ (you / watch) too much TV?

8

Shawnas Mutter ist eine alte Freundin von Marias Mutter. Deshalb stellt auch sie Maria unglaublich viele Fragen. Bringe die Wörter in die richtige Reihenfolge.

a mother / painting / beautiful / pictures / is / such / your / still

____ ?

b buying / she / clothes / is / every / still / new / month

____ ?

c delicious / cooking / still / she / those / is / vegetable dishes

____ ?

d sci-fi books / until / still / is / late / reading / at night / she

____ ?

e of / she / famous people / is / the autographs / still / collecting

____ ?

7 a Are you eating …? **b** Are you helping …? **c** Are you playing …? **d** Are you sleeping …? **e** Are you watching …?
8 a Is your mother still painting such beautiful pictures? **b** Is she still buying new clothes every month?
c Is she still cooking those delicious vegetable dishes? **d** Is she still reading sci-fi books until late at night?
e Is she still collecting the autographs of famous people?

9

Das *present progressive* kann nicht nur für Handlungen der Gegenwart benutzt werden, sondern auch für Verabredungen in der näheren Zukunft. Ergänze die Sätze dementsprechend in der Verlaufsform.

a This afternoon I can't come to help you. I ____________________ (visit) my aunt in hospital.

b Sorry, but tomorrow doesn't work for me. We ____________________ (paint) our living room.

c We ____________________ (fly) to France this year.

d I ____________________ (go) to a dance course this evening.

e She ____________________ (help) her neighbour with the children this afternoon.

f I won't do the shopping today. I ____________________ (go) to the cinema with my friends tonight and I don't want to be late again.

g What ____________________ (you / do) tonight? –

I ____________________ (go out) to dinner with my family.

10

Alles auf den nächsten Tag zu verschieben, ist typisch für Maria. Sie hat keine Lust, ihre Aufgaben heute zu erledigen, verspricht aber, dass sie es morgen tun wird. Ergänze ihre Sätze.

Tomorrow I …

a ____________________ the books back to the library. (zurückbringen)

b ____________________ the trousers from the tailor. (abholen)

c ____________________ my room, I swear! (aufräumen)

d ____________________ Grandma. (anrufen)

e ____________________ dinner for the whole family. (kochen)

f ____________________ all my clothes. (falten)

g ____________________ my bike. And Tom's, too! (reparieren)

9 a am visiting; **b** are painting; **c** are flying; **d** am going; **e** is helping; **f** am going; **g** are you doing; am going out
10 a am taking; **b** am picking up; **c** am tidying up; **d** am calling; **e** am cooking/preparing; **f** am folding; **g** am repairing

11

Marias Mutter ist wirklich ganz schön pessimistisch. Sie lehnt alles ab, was Maria vorschlägt, und meint, das ginge nicht. Maria widerspricht ihr jedes Mal! Was sagt sie zu ihrer Mutter?

Tipp: Im *simple present* braucht die Verneinung das Hilfsverb *don't / doesn't*, wenn keine Form von *to be* im Satz vorkommt.

Beispiel: "It is far too hot for shopping in London today, Maria."

Maria: "*It is not too hot for shopping in London!* It's only 25 degrees today!"

a "No, taking the car is really a bad idea because parking in London is very difficult."

Maria: "______________________________ because ______________________________! We can use one of the big car parks in the suburbs, Mum!"

b "You only have 20 pence left. How do you expect to buy anything with that?"

Maria: "______________________________!
I still have all my birthday money, that's about 100 pounds!"

12

Stevie und Kim tun so, als wären sie Agenten, und beobachten die nichtsahnende Nachbarin Mrs Otis. Sie haben beide ein Funkgerät und berichten einander, was gerade (nicht) passiert. Verwende das *present progressive*.

Tipp: Im *present progressive* braucht auch die Verneinung das Hilfsverb *be*.

a Kim: "Mrs Otis ______________________ (not park) the van in front of the house. She ______________________ (drive) it into the garage …"

b Stevie: "And her husband ______________________ (carry) a huge bag out of the house. But he ______________________ (not put) it into the dustbin … he ______________________ (drag = ziehen) it into the garage, too!"

c Kim: "That's strange … I hope he ______________________ (not drag) a dead body in this bag!"

11 a Taking the car is not a bad idea because parking in London isn't very difficult!
b I don't have only 20 pence left!
12 a is not parking; is driving; **b** is carrying; is not putting; is dragging; **c** is not dragging

13

Toms Klasse macht gerade einen Rundgang im Museum, aber ein paar von den Schülern haben keine Lust mehr auf die Ausstellung. Mit welchen Fragen fangen sie an zu quengeln? Stelle sie in der richtigen Form und achte auf die Satzstellung.

a when / go home / finally / we

____ ?

b have lunch / we / soon

____ ?

c we / go downtown / too

____ ?

14

Mütter sind von Natur aus neugierig. Toms Mutter besonders! Da sie übers Wochenende zu Besuch bei einer Freundin ist und wissen will, ob er auch „brav" ist, fragt sie ihn per Telefon aus. Bilde die Fragen zu Toms Antworten.

Tipp: Achte darauf, dass die Zeit der Frage mit der in der Antwort übereinstimmen muss!

Beispiel: *What are you doing right now?* — I'm doing my homework, Mum.

a ______________________ Yes, I always go to bed early, Mum.

b ______________________ I'm learning vocabulary, Mum.

c ______________________ No, I never eat fast food, Mum.

d ______________________ Yes, I always clean the kitchen.

e ______________________ I'm just watching the news on TV.

f ______________________ Yes, I'm helping Maria with maths.

13 a When are we finally going home? **b** Are we having lunch soon? **c** Are we going downtown, too?

14 a Do you go to bed early? **b** What are you learning? **c** Do you eat fast food? **d** Do you clean the kitchen? **e** What are you watching on TV? **f** Are you helping Maria with maths?

15

Wenn Schule ist, gelten strenge Regeln bei Tom. Am ersten Ferientag aber ist alles anders. Setze die Wörter in Klammern in der korrekten Zeit ein.
Tipp: Achte auf die Signalwörter!

a Tom normally ______________________ (get up) at 5:30 am. But today he ______________________ (sleep) until 9 am.

b Usually he ______________________ (have breakfast) at 6 am, but today he ______________________ (go out) for brunch with Maria.

c Every afternoon he ______________________ (study) for school. But today he ______________________ (go) for a walk with the neighbour's dog.

d He never ______________________ (go) to bed later than 9 pm, but today he ______________________ (read) a sci-fi book until 1 am.

16

Toms Mutter hat Geburtstag, und Tom und Maria bereiten etwas Besonderes für sie vor. Tom berichtet. Ergänze den Text in der jeweils richtigen Form.

It's Sunday afternoon, and on Sundays we usually a) ______________________ (chill) at home. But today Maria and I b) ______________________ (prepare) our mother's birthday present. It c) ______________________ (be) something very special: Home-made marmalade! Maria d) ______________________ (clean) the fruit, strawberries and apples. The recipe e) ______________________ (say): 'After cleaning, cut the fruit into little pieces and then cook it on medium heat.' … Oh no, Maria, what f) ______________________ (you / do)? The heat g) ______________________ (be) much too high! You h) ______________________ (burn) everything! I think Maria never i) ______________________ (cook) anything. She j) ______________________ (not know) how to cook!

15 a gets up / is sleeping; **b** has breakfast / is going out; **c** studies / is going; **d** goes / is reading
16 a) chill; b) are preparing; c) is; d) is cleaning; e) says; f) are you doing?; g) is; h) are burning; i) cooks; j) doesn't know

17

Tom schreibt seiner Mutter auch eine Geburtstagskarte. Streiche die falsche Verbform.

Dear Mum,

My best wishes for your birthday!!!

a I (promise / am promising) that I will help you as much as I can.

b You (do / are doing) so much for me. I just want to say: Thank you for everything you do for me!

c Because we (celebrate / are celebrating) your birthday today, I (do / am doing) the dishes for you on Saturday.

Happy birthday!

18

Tom erzählt seiner Oma vom Geschichtsunterricht. Doch die ist etwas schwerhörig und muss ständig nachfragen, weil sie etwas nicht verstanden hat. Frage nach den markierten Satzteilen.
Tipp: Denke an den Gebrauch der Hilfsverben und achte auf die Zeit des Aussagesatzes.

a We are going to a museum on Monday with our history teacher Mr Hollow.

____

b He thinks that it is very important to show us how people lived centuries ago.

____

c I really like going to museums and learning about the old times.

____

d But most of my classmates think it's very boring.

____

e They are not looking forward to it. What a shame!

____

17 falsch ist: **a** am promising; **b** are doing; **c** celebrate; do
18 a Where are you going on Monday? **b** What does he think is important to show you? **c** Who likes going to museums? **d** Who thinks it's very boring? **e** What are they doing?

19

Entscheide, ob es sich bei den Sätzen um eine gewohnheitsmäßige Handlung, um eine gerade stattfindende Tätigkeit oder um einen festen Plan für die Zukunft handelt. Trage die Buchstaben a, b etc. entsprechend in die Tabelle ein.

a She reads the newspaper every morning.

b Next week we are moving to Swindon.

c Right now she is cooking lunch.

d They are cleaning the car.

e Usually I take out the dog in the morning.

f You are leaving for Australia tomorrow, aren't you?

20

Welche Zeitform ist die richtige? Welche Handlung wird ausgedrückt? Markiere die korrekte Form und notiere, ob es sich um eine Gewohnheit, eine momentane Handlung, ein plötzlich eintretendes Ereignis oder einen Plan handelt.

a Every week I (am taking / take) judo lessons. = ____________________

b I (am learning / learn) judo because it's great fun! = ____________________

c Look at that woman over there! She (is attacked / is being attacked)!
We need to help her! = ____________________

d Tomorrow I (am taking / take) a test to be a yellow belt. = ____________________

19 Gewohnheit: a, e; momentane Handlung: c, d; Plan für die Zukunft: b, f
20 a take = Gewohnheit; **b** learn = Gewohnheit; **c** is being attacked = plötzliches Ereignis; **d** am taking = Plan

21

Am letzten Schultag erzählen Toms Mitschüler, was sie in den Ferien so tun. Setze das *simple present* bzw. *present progressive* ein.
Tipp: Achte auf die Signalwörter.

a In the holidays we usually ______________________ (go) to Cornwall

because my mother ______________________ (like) the climate there.

This afternoon, however, we ______________________ (fly) to France.

b Well, normally I ______________________ (go) swimming every day, but right

now I ______________________ (practise) inline skating

so I ______________________ (not have) enough time for swimming.

c This afternoon I ______________________ (make) cookies for my mother.

Every year on the first day of the holidays I ______________________ (do) something for her like cooking dinner, cleaning the kitchen or baking something nice.

22

Übersetze die Bruchstücke und bilde vollständige Sätze im *simple present* bzw. *present progressive*.

a im Sommer / regelmäßig / geht / joggen / Tom

____

b im Winter / für gewöhnlich / trainieren / Fitness-Studio / er

____

c Tom / diesen Sommer / Schwimmen und Rad fahren trainieren / für einen Triathlon

____

d er / mindestens / schwimmen und Rad fahren / zwei Stunden / jeden Tag

____

21 a go; likes; are flying; **b** go; am practising; don't have; **c** am making; do
22 a Tom goes jogging regularly in the summer. **b** In winter he usually trains at the gym. **c** This summer Tom is practising swimming and cycling for a triathlon. **d** He swims and cycles at least two hours every day.

23

Wann muss *since* und wann *for* benutzt werden? Kreuze an.

a since: ○ with specific points in time ○ with periods / spans of time

b for: ○ with specific points in time ○ with periods / spans of time

24

Trage in die Lücken ein, welche Übersetzung von *seit* jeweils richtig ist.

Beispiel: *for* 25 years

a ______________ yesterday

b ______________ 24 hours

c ______________ Friday morning

d ______________ two decades

e ______________ 45 minutes

f ______________ many days

g ______________ last Monday

h ______________ January 1st

i ______________ years

j ______________ Christmas

k ______________ 7 o'clock

l ______________ last weekend

25

Vervollständige die Sätze mit *since* oder *for*.

Beispiel: I've been living in Munich *for* ten years.

a Amy: How long has his dad been working here? Bill: ______________ a few weeks.

b Tom and I have only known each other ______________ last summer.

c I have had this shirt ______________ five years, and it still looks good!

d Amy's been waiting for us ______________ 7 o'clock this morning.

e She hasn't heard from her parents ______________ yesterday.

f We've been sitting here ______________ 45 minutes! Is the film ever going to start?

23 a with specific points in time; **b** with periods/spans of time
24 a since; **b** for; **c** since; **d** for; **e** for; **f** for; **g** since; **h** since; **i** for; **j** since; **k** since; **l** since
25 a for; **b** since; **c** for; **d** since; **e** since; **f** for

26

Im Deutschen ist es einfach: Man kann immer *seit* nehmen. Aber wenn man im Englischen *since* gegen *for* austauschen will, muss man alles umformulieren. Findest du für die untenstehenden Begriffe eine Umschreibung mit dem jeweils anderen Wort?

Beispiel: for 24 hours = *since* yesterday

a since the day before yesterday = ______________________________

b for 48 hours = ______________________________

c since 7 am this morning = ______________________________

d since January = ______________________________

e for five days = ______________________________

f since last Thursday = ______________________________

g for the last three hours = ______________________________

27

Vervollständige die Sätze mit *since* oder *for*.

a He needs to go to bed. He's been yawning (= gähnen) __________ hours.

b She hasn't heard from her boyfriend __________ he went on holiday.

c Sarah has wanted to meet you __________ a very long time. She's so excited!

d Bobby hasn't called me __________ several days. I think he's still angry.

e They need to go home. Their dad has been calling __________ they got here!

f Have you been here __________ the beginning? I didn't see you come in.

g We've been waiting for him to visit us __________ more than two years.

26 For example: **a** for 48 hours; **b** since the day before yesterday; **c** for eight hours; **d** for five months; **e** since Monday; **f** for two days; **g** since 10 am

27 **a** for; **b** since; **c** for; **d** for; **e** since; **f** since; **g** for

28

Vervollständige die folgenden Sätze. Bilde aus den Verben in Klammern das *present perfect* mit dem Hilfsverb *have / has* und dem Partizip Perfekt.
Tipp: Achte darauf, dass du das Substantiv aus den Klammern an die richtige Position stellst.

a How long ______________________________ on holiday? (Sarah / be)

b How long ______________________________ each other? (you / know)

c How long ______________________________ in New York? (she / live)

d How long ______________________________ that new car? (they / have)

e How long ______________________________ married? (Tim + Ann / be)

f How long ______________________________ this headache? (he / have)

29

Übersetze:

a Er wohnt schon seit 1984 in London.

____

b Sie kennen sich schon lange.

____

c Er wohnt seit vielen Jahren in München.

____

d Sie kennen sich seit ihrer Kindheit.

____

e Wie lange habe ich das jetzt schon satt?

____

28 a has Sarah been; **b** have you known; **c** has she lived; **d** have they had; **e** have Tim and Ann been; **f** has he had
29 a He has lived in London since 1984. **b** They have known each other for a long time. **c** He has lived in Munich for many years. **d** They have known each other since childhood. **e** How long have I been fed up with this?

30

Vervollständige die folgenden Sätze. Bilde aus den Verben in Klammern das *present perfect progressive* mit *have/has* + *been* + *-ing*-Form.

a Where have you been? We __________________________ for you since 8 o'clock this morning! (wait)

b You __________________________ for hours! (cook) We are so hungry!

c Those shoes __________________________ around all day. (lie) Who do you think is going to pick them up?

d He __________________________ with his grandparents since his parents moved to New York. (live)

e The weather in London is terrible! It __________________________ for four days now! (rain)

f They __________________________ TV all day. (watch) Can you believe that? And they haven't done any of their homework yet!

31

Welche Verben sollten hier im *present perfect progressive* stehen? Wenn du sie gefunden hast, schreibe sie in der richtigen Form auf.
Tipp: Achte auf die Signalwörter!

a My mother is in the kitchen, making hamburgers. She is cooking for almost one hour.

____

b My father works at the factory. He is working there for 12 years. He likes his job a lot.

____

c John is not doing his homework. He has surfed on the Internet since we had dinner.

____

d My parents and I are waiting to see my teacher. We were waiting for 30 minutes.

____

30 a have been waiting; **b** have been cooking; **c** have been lying; **d** has been living; **e** has been raining; **f** have been watching

31 a is cooking > has been cooking; **b** is working > has been working; **c** has surfed > has been surfing; **d** were waiting > have been waiting

32

Entscheide, welche Verbform für die folgenden Sätze richtig ist. Kreuze an.

a I have ____________ Mr Jones since I was a child.
- known
- been knowing

b He says that he has never ____________ in God. He's always been an atheist.
- believed
- been believing

c She has always ____________ London. I think she's been there a hundred times!
- liked
- been liking

d Puerto Rico has ____________ to the USA since the 19th century.
- belonged
- been belonging

e I know what she likes, and she has always ____________ chocolate.
- hated
- been hating

f What is special about the verbs above? ______________________________________

33

Entscheide, welche Verbform für die folgenden Sätze richtig ist. Kreuze an.

a All my Cokes in the fridge are gone! Someone ____________ them all.
- has drunk
- has been drinking

b Mr Smith has always been a Biology teacher. He ____________ Biology since my mother was in school.
- has taught
- has been teaching

c John is the author of many books. I think he ____________ nine, in total.
- has written
- has been writing

d Why is my bike so dirty? What ____________ with it?
- have you done
- have you been doing

e Why is my bike missing? What ____________ with it?
- have you done
- have you been doing

32 a known; **b** believed; **c** liked; **d** belonged; **e** hated; **f** They are normally never used in the progressive tense.
33 a has drunk; **b** has been teaching; **c** has written; **d** have you been doing; **e** have you done

34

Die folgenden Sätze sind richtig. Aber warum? Zwei mögliche Gründe stehen darunter. Kreuze die richtige Alternative an.

Tipp: Beginne die Begründungen mit *This sentence tells us* ...

a Mr and Mrs Smith have been living in the same house for twenty years.

- how many houses they've lived in
- the length of time they've been living there

b Stephen Spielberg has made 15 films since he became a director in the 70s.

- the number of film he's completed
- how long he's been directing films

c He has read four books over the past summer.

- the four books he's finished
- how long he's been reading

d He has been reading science fiction since he was a little boy.

- what he's been reading
- how long he's been reading

35

Schreibe zwei Sätze für jede Situation mit den jeweiligen Wörtern in Klammern.

Tim arrived in Germany two weeks ago. He's visiting friends in many parts of Germany.

a (Tim / travel round Germany / for two weeks) ____________________

____

b (Tim / visit many friends / since he arrived in Germany) ____________________

____

Rob and Lisa are playing in a tennis tournament. There are six matches in total, and five matches are already over. They came to the tournament 8 hours ago.

c (Rob and Lisa / play / five games) ____________________

____

d (Rob and Lisa / play / for eight hours) ____________________

____

34 a the length of time they've been living there; **b** the number of films he's completed; **c** the four books he's finished; **d** how long he's been reading

35 a Tim has been travelling round Germany for two weeks. **b** Tim has visited many friends since he arrived in Germany. **c** Rob and Lisa have played five games. **d** Rob and Lisa have been playing for eight hours.

36

Entscheide, welche Verbzeit man bei den folgenden Signalwörtern benutzen muss: *simple past* (SP) oder *present perfect* (PP)?

a ______ the day before yesterday

b ______ 45 minutes ago

c ______ since 3 o'clock

d ______ ever

e ______ last Christmas

f ______ already

g ______ this morning

h ______ not yet

i ______ in 1999

j ______ since last Christmas

k ______ three hours ago

l ______ last weekend

37

Vervollständige die folgenden Sätze mit der korrekten Verbform.
Tipp: Achte auf die Signalwörter.

a I (buy) ______________________ this book last weekend. Would you like to borrow it?

b I (read / never) ______________________ a Harry Potter book before.

c Oh, you'll like it! I (read) ______________________ all of them.

d (you / see / ever) ______________________ a Harry Potter movie?

e I (watch / only) ______________________ one of them. And you?

f I (see) ______________________ the first one when it first came out.

g Wow! That (be) ______________________ a long time ago!

h There (be) ______________________ many more Harry Potter movies since then. Should we rent the DVDs sometime and watch them at my place?

36 a SP; **b** SP; **c** PP; **d** PP; **e** SP; **f** PP; **g** SP; **h** PP; **i** SP; **j** PP; **k** SP; **l** SP
37 a bought; **b** have never read; **c** have read; **d** Have you ever seen; **e** have only watched; **f** saw; **g** was; **h** have been

38

Beantworte die Fragen und verwende dabei *simple past* oder *present perfect*. Achte auch auf die richtige Satzstellung.

a Have you seen John this evening? (No / I / see him / not / since last week)

---

b Have you done your homework? (No / I / do it / not yet)

---

c Have you ever been to the United States? (Yes / I / go to New York / in 1999)

---

d Have you ever met Mr Johnson's wife? (Yes / I / meet her / last year)

39

Übersetze und achte auf die richtige Zeitform.

a Tim hat fünf Jahre lang in London gewohnt.

---

b Joanne wohnt seit fünf Jahren in London.

---

c Steve hat sich gestern eine neue Jeans gekauft.

---

d Wir haben uns vor fünf Jahren kennengelernt.

---

e Wir kennen uns jetzt seit über fünf Jahren.

---

38 a No, I have not seen him since last week. **b** No, I have not done it yet. **c** Yes, I went to New York in 1999. **d** Yes, I met her last year.
39 a Tim lived in London for five years. **b** Joanne has lived in London for five years. **c** Steve bought a new pair of jeans yesterday. **d** We met five years ago./We got to know each other ...; **e** We have known each other for more than five years now.

40

Übersetze die folgenden Fragen.

a Seit wann wohnst du hier? How long ______

b Wann bist du hierher gezogen? When ______

c Seit wann kennst du ihn? ______

d Wann hast du ihn kennengelernt? ______

e Seit wann ist er tot? ______

f Wann ist er gestorben? ______

41

Entscheide, ob die hervorgehobenen Verben in der richtigen oder der falschen Zeit stehen. Falls eins falsch ist, schreibe die richtige Variante daneben.

a Shakespeare **has written** many plays. ______

b My father **has been born** in England. ______

c Our mother **grew up** in Ireland. ______

d **Did** you **see** Tom recently? ______

e **Have** you **finished** your homework? ______

f When **have** you **finished** your homework? ______

g Elvis **has died** in 1977. ______

h I**'ve lost** my wallet, and I have no money. ______

i **Have** you ever **seen** a baseball game? ______

j Where **have** they **been** last night? ______

40 a How long have you lived here? **b** When did you move here? **c** How long have you known him? **d** When did you meet him? **e** How long has he been dead? **f** When did he die?
41 a Shakespeare wrote many plays. **b** My father was born in England. **c** richtig; **d** Have you seen Tom recently? **e** richtig; **f** When did you finish your homework? **g** Elvis died in 1977. **h** richtig; **i** richtig; **j** Where were they last night?

42

Formuliere die Sätze im *simple past*.
Tipp: Bei einigen Verben musst du besonders auf die Schreibweise achten.

a Do you ask your friend for advice?

____

b Our teacher admits that he always uses yellow chalk.

____

c Dr. Riley looks at Tom's throat, takes his temperature and sends him to bed at once.

____

d We travel from Montana to Florida.

____

43

Welche Zeitangaben oder Signalwörter bezeichnen einen festen Zeitpunkt oder abgeschlossenen Zeitraum in der Vergangenheit? Unterstreiche.

in 1988 on Tuesday ever yesterday ago

yet while still last week at 12 o'clock when as long as

44

Welche Sätze stehen korrekt im *simple past*? Kreuze an.

a ◯ Did you listen to the news at ten? – No, I wasn't home at that time.

b ◯ The camera looks expensive. How much did you pay for it?

c ◯ Maria played on the computer …

d ◯ … while her mother prepared dinner.

e ◯ While I chatted with Clara …

f ◯ … the computer broke down.

42 a Did you ask your friend for advice? **b** Our teacher admitted that he always used yellow chalk. **c** Dr. Riley looked at Tom's throat, took his temperature and sent him to bed at once. **d** We travelled from Montana to Florida.
43 Signalwörter für *simple past* sind: in, on, yesterday, ago, last, at
44 Korrekt sind a b, c und f

45

Setze die Verben ins *past progressive*.
Tipp: Achte dabei auf die richtige Verwendung von *was* bzw. *were*.

a Peter / work ______
b We / correct ______
c They / play ______
d Sam and Tim / go ______
e You / answer ______
f She / pack ______
g I / eat ______
h The girls / wait ______

46

Setze die Verben ins verneinende *past progressive*. Achte auch hier darauf, ob es Singular oder Plural sein muss. Setze dann *wasn't* bzw. *weren't* entsprechend ein.

a Susan / cook ______
b Tim and Ben / drink ______
c I / draw ______
d It / fly ______
e The English / speak ______
f You / clean ______
g Mr Jones / enjoy himself ______
h He / download ______
i Steve / open ______

45 a Peter was working. **b** We were correcting. **c** They were playing. **d** Sam and Tim were going. **e** You were answering. **f** She was packing. **g** I was eating. **h** The girls were waiting.
46 a Susan wasn't cooking. **b** Tim and Ben weren't drinking. **c** I wasn't drawing. **d** It wasn't flying. **e** The English weren't speaking. **f** You weren't cleaning. **g** Mr Jones wasn't enjoying himself. **h** He wasn't downloading. **i** Steve wasn't opening.

47

Setze die Verben ins *past progressive*. Achte genau darauf, ob die Substantive Singular- oder Pluralbedeutung haben.

a The trousers / hang ____________________

b A pair of trousers / hang ____________________

c The People / sell ____________________

d The police / follow ____________________

e The news / repeat ____________________

48

Bilde auch hier das *past progressive*. Aber Vorsicht: Bei diesen Verben lauert die ein oder andere Falle in der Schreibung der *-ing*-Form!

a The sun / shine ____________________

b We / swim ____________________

c The cook / stir ____________________

d They / plan ____________________

e The girl / lie ____________________

f The children / hit each other ____________________

g Mrs Smith / practise ____________________

h The men / die ____________________

i The teacher / refer to it ____________________

j He / jog ____________________

k It / sit ____________________

l The family / move ____________________

47 a The trousers were hanging. **b** A pair of trousers was hanging. **c** The people were selling. **d** The police were following. **e** The news was repeating.

48 a The sun was shining. **b** We were swimming. **c** The cook was stirring. **d** They were planning. **e** The girl was lying. **f** The children were hitting each other. **g** Mrs Smith was practising. **h** The men were dying. **i** The teacher was referring to it. **j** He was jogging. **k** It was sitting. **l** The family was moving.

49

In den folgenden Sätzen hat sich je ein Fehler eingeschlichen. Findest du ihn? Unterstreiche das falsche Wort und schreibe es richtig daneben.

Beispiel: Peter weren't reading the book. wasn't

a The girls were planing a nice trip. ______

b The police was chasing the thief. ______

c Martin wasn't lieing. ______

d The lights were shineing on the actor. ______

e Megan was refering to the book. ______

f The news were constantly being repeated. ______

50

Vervollständige den Text und setze die Verbformen ins *past progressive*.

Yesterday at 2 o'clock, Peter Smith a) ______ (work) in the garden. The sun b) ______ (shine) and Peter's grandfather Joe c) ______ (sit) on the old bench with Grandma Josephine. His grandparents d) ______ (pet) the dog that e) ______ (lie) next to them. People f) ______ (pass) by. It was a beautiful Sunday, but in the woods nearby the police g) ______ (try) to catch a dangerous lion that had escaped from the zoo and h) ______ (run) around town! The Smiths i) ______ (not watch) the news. So they spent a peaceful day in their garden. But as she j) ______ (read) the newspaper on the next day, Mrs Smith almost fainted: "Oh my god! I am so glad I k) ______ (not jog) yesterday! I might have run into the lion!"

49 a planning; **b** were; **c** lying; **d** shining; **e** referring; **f** was

50 a) was working; b) was shining; c) was sitting; d) were petting; e) was lying; f) were passing; g) were trying; h) was running; i) weren't watching; j) was reading; k) wasn't jogging

51

Markiere mit ~ die Handlung, die länger andauerte, und mit / die kurze Handlung, die dazwischen eintrat.

a Megan **was talking** to Brian ◯ when the thief **stole** the car. ◯

b The musician **dropped** the instrument ◯ while the band **was playing**. ◯

c When Henry **started** driving ◯ it **was snowing**. ◯

d While Sarah **was writing** her essay ◯ the teacher **ate** an apple. ◯

e Andrew **took** the hammer ◯ while Jo **was repairing** the car. ◯

f Paula **was knitting** a sweater ◯ when Tyler **came** in. ◯

g While the fire **was burning** ◯ the house **collapsed**. ◯

h When Sabrina **heard** the noise ◯ she **was cleaning** her teeth. ◯

i Frank **was reading** the newspaper ◯ when the cat **jumped** on his lap. ◯

52

Finde heraus, welche Handlung über einen längeren Zeitraum andauerte und setze diese ins *past progressive*. Dann setze entsprechend die kurze Handlung, die dazwischen eintrat, ins *simple past*.

Beispiel: **read** a book — phone **ring**

While I *was reading* a book, the phone *rang*.

a **get** in the car — **rain**

We ______________________ in the car while it ______________________.

b **draw** picture — **sneeze**

The children ______________________ a picture when Peter ______________________.

c **cook** — **break** a plate

Mum ______________________ when Sarah ______________________ a plate.

51 a was talking (~); stole (/); **b** dropped (/); was playing (~); **c** started (/); was snowing (~); **d** was writing (~); ate (/); **e** took (/); was repairing (~); **f** was knitting (~); came (/); **g** was burning (~); collapsed (/); **h** heard (/); was cleaning (~); **i** was reading (~); jumped (/)
52 a We got in the car while it was raining. **b** The children were drawing a picture when Peter sneezed. **c** Mum was cooking when Sarah broke a plate.

53

Ergänze die Sätze und formuliere die Verben im *past progressive* oder *simple past*.
Tipp: *While* bedeutet: etwas war im Verlauf – *when* sagt dir, dass plötzlich etwas eintrat.

a When Judy ______________ (come) in, Steve ______________ (write) a letter.

b While the Millers ______________ (drive), they ______________ (not see) the radar control.

c Maggy and Jim ______________ (not swim) when it ______________ (begin) to rain.

d When the thief ______________ (have) an accident, the police ______________ (follow) him.

54

Übersetze. Unterscheide dabei die unterschiedliche Dauer der Handlungen, indem du *simple past* und *past progressive* richtig verwendest.
Tipp: „Das *past progressive* war im Verlauf und das *simple past* trat plötzlich auf."

a Während Simon aß, gingen die Lichter aus.

____

b Als Chris ankam, halfen bereits viele Menschen.

____

c Tamara ließ das Buch fallen, während sie und Jack die Straße überquerten.

____

d Als Marc die Treppe herunterfiel, nahm Selina gerade ein Bad.

____

53 a came; was writing; **b** were driving; didn't see; **c** weren't swimming; began; **d** had; were following
54 a While Simon was eating, the lights went out. **b** When Chris arrived, a lot of people were (already) helping. **c** Tamara dropped the book while she and Jack were crossing the street. **d** When Marc fell down the stairs, Selina was (just) taking a bath.

55

Bilde das *past perfect* mit *had* und dem *past participle*.
Tipp: Achte auf unregelmäßige Partizipien!

a visit ____________________

b not break ____________________

c prepare ____________________

d drive ____________________

e not paint ____________________

f swim ____________________

g have ____________________

h not be ____________________

i do ____________________

56

Finde heraus, welche Handlung zuerst geschehen sein muss.
Unterstreiche dann die richtigen Zeitformen.
Tipp: Die Handlung, die zuerst geschehen sein muss, steht im *past perfect*.

Beispiel: After Sam knew / had known Sue for only two months,
he asked / had asked her to marry him.

a When Sissy got / had got home, she noticed that someone broke / had broken into her house.

b Cecil was / had been nervous because he didn't fly / hadn't flown in a jet before.

c After the girls walked / had walked to the chapel, it began / had begun to rain.

d Suzy went / had gone to bed when I came / had come home. It was very quiet.

e Tim was / had been surprised because Sabrina wasn't / hadn't been late before.

f Some students were / had been late because they missed / had missed the bus.

55 a had visited; **b** hadn't broken; **c** had prepared; **d** had driven; **e** hadn't painted; **f** had swum; **g** had had; **h** hadn't been; **i** had done

56 a got; had broken; **b** was; hadn't flown; **c** had walked; began; **d** had gone; came; **e** was; hadn't been; **f** were; had missed

57

Ergänze die Sätze im richtigen zeitlichen Ablauf. Verwende dabei *simple past* oder *past perfect*.

a After Simon had finally found the camera, they ____________________ (leave) the house.

b Roger's mother told him to clean up his room because he ____________________ (make) such a big mess.

c The Walkers ____________________ (decide) not to buy a new car after the old one had been damaged in the accident.

d Daniel wasn't allowed to go to the pool until he showed his mother that he ____________________ (put on) suntan lotion. She thinks the sun is very dangerous.

e Anna ____________________ (not see) the movie before I told her about it.

f After he noticed that thieves ____________________ (break into) the house, John inspected it quickly and called the police.

58

Setze die Verben in die richtige Zeitform: *past perfect* oder *simple past*.

I a) ____________________ (get up) at 6 am this morning because the kids b) ____________________ (wake) me up with their screaming. I c) ____________________ (already shower), before I d) ____________________ (sit down) at the breakfast table. I wanted to read the paper, but it had coffee all over it. I e) ____________________ (cannot read) it any more because my cat f) ____________________ (tip over) my coffee cup. Because of all the stress I g) ____________________ (had) that morning at home, I h) ____________________ (miss) the bus. What a horrible day!

57 a left; **b** had made; **c** decided; **d** had put on; **e** hadn't seen; **f** had broken into
58 a) got up; b) had woken; c) had already showered; d) sat down; e) couldn't read; f) had tipped over; g) had had; h) missed

59

Bilde das *past perfect progressive* mit *had been* und der *-ing*-Form.

a wait ______________________

b not dream ______________________

c pay ______________________

d make ______________________

e go ______________________

f not tell ______________________

g plan ______________________

60

Stelle dir vor, welche Handlung zuerst geschehen sein muss und welche folgte.
Unterstreiche dann die richtigen Zeitformen.

Tipp: Das *past perfect progressive* findet zur selben Zeit statt wie das „normale" *past perfect*.

Beispiel: Sam practised / had been practising the guitar for two years, before he gave / had been giving his first concert.

Before Silvia a) decided / had been deciding to write a book about American history, she b) researched already / had already been researching the facts for years.

When Sarah c) arrived / had been arriving at Mike's house, he d) was already / had already been cooking for several hours.

Sina e) ran / had been running for two hours, so she f) felt / had been feeling exhausted.

The Millers were very worried. They g) called / had been calling Alice's mobile all morning when she h) finally arrived / had finally been arriving at noon.

Because Angelina i) watched / had been watching TV for two days straight, her eyes j) began / had been beginning to hurt a lot.

59 a had been waiting; **b** hadn't been dreaming; **c** had been paying; **d** had been making; **e** had been going; **f** hadn't been telling; **g** had been planning

60 a) decided; b) had already been researching; c) arrived; d) had already been cooking; e) had been running; f) felt; g) had been calling; h) finally arrived; i) had been watching; j) began

61

Setze die Verben in die richtige Zeitform: *past perfect progressive* oder *simple past*.

Before I a) ______________________________ (feel) the pain I b) ______________________________ (walk) for two hours.

Henry c) ______________________________ (drive) for several hours when the motor d) ______________________________ (stop).

The girl e) ______________________________ (wear) that shirt since last Friday when her mum finally f) ______________________________ (wash) it yesterday.

62

Setze die Verben in die richtige Zeitform: *past perfect* oder *past perfect progressive* und *simple past*.

Tipp: Das *past perfect progressive* und das *past perfect* liegen beide länger zurück. Beim *progressive* hast du aber die Dauer der Handlung im Blick!

I a) ______________________________ (shake) the bottle for ten seconds when I b) ______________________________ (notice) that I c) ______________________________ (forget) to put on the lid.

The mechanic d) ______________________________ (repair) my car after it e) ______________________________ (make) loud noises for the last three weeks and f) ______________________________ (break down) on the motorway.

After Eric g) ______________________________ (bleed) for 10 minutes, the nurse finally h) ______________________________ (give) him a Band-Aid.

61 a) felt; b) had been walking; c) had been driving; d) stopped; e) had been wearing; f) washed

62 a) had been shaking; b) noticed; c) had forgotten; d) repaired; e) had been making; f) had broken down; g) had been bleeding; h) gave

63

Maria stellt Vermutungen darüber an, wie sich ihre Sommerferien gestalten werden. Alle Vermutungen werden im Englischen mit dem *will-future* ausgedrückt.
Tipp: Das *will-future* wird mit *will* + Infinitiv gebildet.

a Probably I ____________________ (visit) my friend in Austria for a week and we ____________________ (spend) some days in Vienna.

b Maybe we ____________________ (go) to the mountains and I ____________________ (make) some sketches of the landscape.

c I think we ____________________ (also go out), and we ____________________ (dance) the whole night.

d I'm sure that we ____________________ (have) a lot of fun together, but I promise that I ____________________ (also write) postcards to my friends.

e I hope that the weather ____________________ (be) nice, but I know that we ____________________ (have) the greatest time even if it rains all the time!

64

Wenn das *will-future* für Vermutungen verwendet wird, gibt es dafür meist Signalwörter. Die wichtigsten Signalwörter tauchen oben in Kurztest 63 auf. Findest du sie? Schreibe auf.

a ____________________

b ____________________

c ____________________

d ____________________ ____________________

e ____________________ ____________________

63 a will visit; will spend; **b** will go; will make; **c** will also go out; will dance; **d** will have; will also write; **e** will be; will have

64 a probably; **b** maybe; **c** I think; **d** I'm sure; I promise; **e** I hope; I know

65

Bilde Sätze im *will-future* mit den Dingen, die Tom tun wird bzw. nicht tun wird.
Tipp: Die Verneinung wird mit *will* + *not* gebildet. Die Kurzform lautet *won't*.

Beispiel: Tom / help other students — *Tom will help other students.*

a He / not drink alcohol ______

b Tom / not take drugs ______

c He / work for his license ______

d Tom / get a scholarship ______

e He / go to Spain for a year ______

f That / be / exciting! ______

66

Tom ist sehr aufgeregt: Er hat ein Stipendium für Spanien erhalten! Nun will er eine Menge dazu wissen. Bilde die Fragen im *will-future*.

a The school / be / in Madrid? ______

b I / live with a family? ______

c How / I / get to school? ______

d When / I / return to Britain? ______

e I / go with a group of students? ______

f I / be able to take a language course? ______

g I / have time for sightseeing? ______

h Which town / I / live in? ______

i I / have to write a report? ______

65 a He will not/won't drink alcohol. **b** Tom will not/won't take drugs. **c** He'll work for his license. **d** Tom will get a scholarship. **e** He'll go to Spain for a year. **f** That will be exciting!
66 a Will the school be in Madrid? **b** Will I live with a family? **c** How will I get to school? **d** When will I return to Britain? **e** Will I go with a group of students? **f** Will I be able to take a language course? **g** Will I have time for sightseeing? **h** Which town will I live in? **i** Will I have to write a report?

67

Die folgenden Ereignisse werden eintreten, ohne dass der Sprecher sie beeinflussen kann. Schreibe die Sätze im *will-future* auf.

Tipp: *Will* zieht wie alle Hilfsverben stets den Infinitiv nach sich.

Beispiel: In September / Susan's brother / go / to school / from Monday to Friday.

In September Susan's brother will go to school from Monday to Friday.

a The weather / be / cold / next week

---

b Maria / be / 15 / next month

---

c They / move / to France / in May / for a new job

---

d The company rented a house for us. We / live / in the countryside

---

e The music in the disco / be / loud

---

f My mother / celebrate / her 50th birthday / in June

---

g I / be / an old woman / in 2050

---

h Monday is a public holiday. The shops / be / closed.

---

67 a The weather will be cold next week. **b** Maria will be 15 next month. **c** In May they will move to France for a new job. **d** We will live in the countryside. **e** The music in the disco will be loud. **f** My mother will celebrate her 50th birthday in June. **g** I will be an old woman in 2050. **h** The shops will be closed.

68

Auch für spontane Entschlüsse wird im Englischen das *will-future* verwendet. Setze ein.

a I ______________________ (chill) all day today.

b They ______________________ (order) a pizza for lunch.

c He ______________________ (be) home by two.

d We ______________________ (clean) the car now.

e She ______________________ (make) an apple pie.

f You ______________________ (call) your friends.

g I ______________________ (come) with you.

h That ______________________ (not work).

i They ______________________ (not help) with the dinner. They can't cook.

69

Tom freut sich auf seine Ferien in den USA und stellt sich vor, was er alles erleben wird. Schreibe die Sätze vollständig im *will-future* auf. Ergänze die fehlenden Wörter.

a probably / a lot of fast food / eat

____

b maybe / an I-Max theatre / visit

____

c I'm sure / a lot of interesting people / meet

____

d I hope / have time / go to a musical

____

68 a will chill; **b** will order; **c** will be; **d** will clean; **e** will make; **f** will call; **g** will come; **h** won't work; **i** won't help
69 a I'll probably eat a lot of fast food. **b** Maybe I'll visit an I-Max theatre. **c** I'm sure (that) I'll meet a lot of interesting people. **d** I hope (that) I'll have time to go to a musical.

70

Das *will-future* wird auch für das Konditional verwendet.
Tipp: *If, when* und *as soon as* stehen nie mit *will* im gleichen Satzteil.

a If you are right about that, I ________________ (give) you a call.

b When they have cleaned the car, we ________________ (take) a ride along the beach.

c As soon as I get the letter, I ________________ (answer) it.

d If I get in touch with Tom, I ________________ (give) him your regards.

e When I write him again, I ________________ (send) your photos, too.

f As soon as he returns home, we ________________ (come over) to see you.

71

Maria möchte unbedingt einen Hip-Hop-Tanzkurs besuchen, aber ihre Mutter ist dagegen. Maria bettelt so lange, bis ihre Mutter nachgibt. Aber sie stellt Bedingungen. Schreibe die Wörter in der richtigen Reihenfolge auf.

a you go / to the course, / If / do / , ok? / some extra vocabulary training / you will

____

b quit / will have to / your marks / you / get worse / will / the course / at school, / immediately. / If

____

c go / on the way home / If / I / you will / pay for the course, / and do the shopping. / to the supermarket

____

d there / during the week, / you / a performance / won't / take part. / is / If

____

70 a will give; **b** will take; **c** will answer; **d** will give; **e** will send; **f** will come over

***71* a** If you go to the course, you will do some extra vocabulary training, ok? **b** If your marks get worse at school, you will have to quit the course immediately. **c** If I pay for the course, you will go to the supermarket on the way home and do the shopping. **d** If there is a performance during the week, you won't take part.

72

Ergänze die Tabelle mit den richtigen Formen. Vervollständige dann die Sätze.

I		going to	go
you, we, they		going to	do
he, she, it		going to	read

a They ______________________ (move) on Saturday.

b She ______________________ (play) Anita in West Side Story.

c We ______________________ (make) some cakes for the party.

d I ______________________ (go) to Iceland for one year.

73

Tom schmiedet Pläne, was er alles in Spanien tun wird. Da es sich jetzt um seine Pläne handelt, verwendet er *going to*. Ergänze seine Aussagen.
Tipp: Verwende die Formen aus der Tabelle in Kurztest 72.

"As soon as I arrive in Spain, I a) ______________________ (buy) a really good dictionary. Also, I b) ______________________ (take) a language course. And when I come back to Britain I c) ______________________ (give) Spanish lessons to other students. I d) ______________________ (visit) a lot of museums in Madrid, and I e) ______________________ (read) a lot of books about the history of Spain. Of course, I f) ______________________ (learn) how to do the Flamenco. I g) ______________________ (meet) a lot of Spanish teenagers, and together, we h) ______________________ (see) the country."

72 I am going to go; you, we, they are going to do; he, she, it is going to read; **a** are going to move; **b** is going to play; **c** are going to make; **d** am going to go
73 a) I am going to buy; b) I'm going to take; c) I'm going to give; d) I'm going to visit; e) I am going to read; f) I'm going to learn; g) I'm going to meet; h) I'm going to see

74

Maria möchte natürlich eine Menge über Toms Spanien-Pläne wissen und fragt ihn aus. Wie lauten ihre Fragen im *going-to-future*?

a you / stay in Madrid for a long time?

____

b you / spend a lot of time on the beach?

____

c you / go shopping in Sevilla?

____

d you / make a video report?

____

75

Vor dem Klassenausflug versprechen die Schüler dem Lehrer alles Mögliche, was sie nicht tun werden. Bilde die verneinten Sätze im *going-to-future*.

a we / not miss the bus

____

b Maria / not be giggling all the time

____

c I / not chew gum in the museum

____

d we / not listen to loud music on the bus

____

***74* a** Are you going to stay in Madrid for a long time? **b** Are you going to spend a lot of time on the beach? **c** Are you going to go shopping in Sevilla? **d** Are you going to make a video report?
***75* a** We are not going to miss the bus. **b** Maria is not going to be giggling all the time. **c** I'm not going to chew gum in the museum. **d** We are not going to listen to loud music on the bus.

76

Maria muss in den Ferien zu einem Mathe-Nachhilfekurs, aber sie will nicht. Ihre Freunde wollen ihr helfen. Setze im *will-future* ein.

a Jane ____________________ (help) you with maths. She's really good at it! That way you needn't go to that stupid course.

b Marco ____________________ (talk) to your Mom.

c Maybe she ____________________ (listen) to him and cancel the course!

d Probably your mom ____________________ (not be) very happy when we all try to get you out of the course …

e Well, I think it's better to leave it up to Maria. We ____________________ (wait) outside until Maria has talked to her mother.

77

Maria hat überhaupt keine Lust auf Mathe-Nachhilfe in den Ferien! Sie notiert ihre Gedanken dazu in ihrem Tagebuch. Entscheide jeweils, ob *will-* oder *going-to-future* die korrekte Form ist.

How stupid! Ok, I'm not the best student in maths, I know that. But why do I have to join that stupid extra-course during my vacation?? I'm not that bad!

a I'm sure there ____________________ (be) a lot of stupid kids there, and

I ____________________ (not like) any of them.

b And I think it ____________________ (start) very early in the morning, so I can't sleep long.

c I ____________________ (act) really bad so that they don't want me and send me home!

d If I go to that stupid course, I ____________________ (not be able to go shopping) with my friends at all.

e I ____________________ (talk) to Mum again!

f Maybe I ____________________ (convince) her that the course is a bad idea if

I promise that I ____________________ (learn) maths for an hour every day instead.

76 a will help; **b** will talk; **c** will listen; **d** will not be; **e** will wait
77 a will be; won't like; **b** will start; **c** am going to act; **d** won't be able to go shopping; **e** am going to talk;
f will convince; will learn

78

Auch wenn man etwas fest eingeplant hat, kann es Überraschungen geben. Bilde aus den Bruchstücken vollständige Sätze im *will-* bzw. *going-to-future*.

a on Friday / I / fly / to Italy on business

____

b the plane / probably / be late

____

c I / take part / in a very important meeting

____

d I think / the meeting / be successful

____

79

Tom besucht mit seiner Stipendiatengruppe das Picasso-Museum in Barcelona. Natürlich hat er noch einige Fragen. Stelle sie im *will-* bzw. *going-to-future*.

a I / be able to / take photos?

____

b we / visit / the special exhibition, too?

____

c we / see / the most famous works by Picasso?

____

d we / eat / tapas afterwards?

____

78 a On Friday, I'm going to fly to Italy on business. **b** The plane will probably be late. **c** I am going to take part in a very important meeting. **d** I think the meeting will be successful.
79 a Will I be able to take photos? **b** Are we going to visit the special exhibition, too? **c** Will we see the most famous works by Picasso? **d** Are we going to eat tapas afterwards?

80

Tom schreibt seiner Mutter eine Postkarte. Welches Futur ist jeweils richtig? Streiche die falsche Verbform.

Dear Mum,

I have arrived in Spain and I really like it here. The people are very friendly!

a Tomorrow I (will buy / am going to buy) a dictionary.

b I (will sign up / am going to sign up) for a language course, so I think I (will need / am going to need) the dictionary.

c I (will probably go / am probably going to go) to Barcelona with some other students at the weekend.

d I think the weather (will be / is going to be) nice at the weekend. Then we (will also go / are also going to go) to the beach!

I'll write more soon. Love, Tom

81

Toms Mutter spricht mit Oma über ihn. Aber die hört nicht mehr gut und fragt nach den markierten Satzteilen. Kannst du ihre Fragen formulieren?

a "I think Tom will go to the beach every weekend."

b "He is going to learn a lot about the Spanish history."

c "Maybe his hostfamily will show him Madrid."

d "He knows that he'll like his year in Spain!"

80 richtig ist: **a** am going to buy; **b** am going to sign up; will need; **c** will probably go; **d** will be; will also go
81 a Where will he go every weekend? **b** What is he going to learn? **c** Who will show him Madrid?
d What will he like?

82

Viele Adverbien werden mit der Endung *-ly* aus Adjektiven gebildet. Wandle folgende Adjektive in Adverbien um.

a beautiful ______________________

b nervous ______________________

c public ______________________

d shy ______________________

e regular ______________________

f careless ______________________

g surprising ______________________

h usual ______________________

83

Achtung: Hier musst du bei der Schreibung des Adverbs gut aufpassen!

a simple ______________________

b happy ______________________

c economic ______________________

d whole ______________________

e dull ______________________

f busy ______________________

g full ______________________

h true ______________________

i angry ______________________

j noisy ______________________

84

Die folgenden Adjektive fallen bei der Umwandlung zu Adverbien etwas aus dem Rahmen. Wie lautet das Adverb jeweils?

a good ______________________

b fast ______________________

c silly ______________________

d daily ______________________

e friendly ______________________

f early ______________________

g straight ______________________

h lovely ______________________

82 a beautifully; **b** nervously; **c** publicly; **d** shyly; **e** regularly; **f** carelessly; **g** surprisingly; **h** usually
83 a simply; **b** happily; **c** economically; **d** wholly; **e** dully; **f** busily; **g** fully; **h** truly; **i** angrily; **j** noisily
84 a well; **b** fast; **c** in a silly way; **d** daily; **e** in a friendly way; **f** early; **g** straight; **h** in a lovely way

85

Ordne die folgenden Wörter der richtigen Spalte zu.

new	ill	carefully
black	nervously	fair
healthy	happily	gladly
well	good	truly

Adjektiv **Adverb**

86

Worauf bezieht sich das markierte Wort? Schreibe auf und entscheide dann, ob es sich um ein Adjektiv oder ein Adverb handelt.

Beispiel: He was a careful driver. *driver -> Adjektiv*

	bezieht sich auf		Adjektiv/Adverb
a He drove carefully.		→	
b He cooks well.		→	
c He is a good cook.		→	
d My dog barks loudly.		→	
e That was a loud noise.		→	

85 Adjektive: new; black; healthy; ill; good; fair;
Adverbien: well; nervously; happily; carefully; gladly; truly
86 a drove; Adverb; **b** cooks; Adverb; **c** cook; Adjektiv; **d** barks; Adverb; **e** noise; Adjektiv

87

Muss das Adjektiv oder das Adverb verwendet werden? Kreise die richtige Form ein.

a The girl was happy / happily.

b Pete is smiling friendly / in a friendly way.

c Marc had a calm / calmly voice.

d Marco is a good / well driver.

e He told me a surprising / surprisingly story.

f She screamed loud / loudly.

g The children ate their food quick / quickly.

88

Entscheide, ob ein Adjektiv oder ein Adverb benutzt werden muss.

a Steven was a ____________________ (good) student.

b He always learned ____________________ (good).

c Paula and Tony have been ____________________ (happy) married for 15 years.

d Have a ____________________ (happy) Easter.

e Andrew speaks Chinese ____________________ (fluent).

f His Chinese is ____________________ (fluent).

g The postman ____________________ (usual) comes around 2 pm.

h This is his ____________________ (usual) routine.

i It was a ____________________ (simple) explanation.

87 a happy; **b** in a friendly way; **c** calm; **d** good; **e** surprising; **f** loudly; **g** quickly
88 a good; **b** well; **c** happily; **d** happy; **e** fluently; **f** fluent; **g** usually; **h** usual; **i** simple

89

Adverbien können sich nicht nur auf Verben beziehen, sondern auch auf andere Adjektive und andere Adverbien und diese näher beschreiben. Unterstreiche das Wort, auf das sich das hervorgehobene Adverb jeweils bezieht. Handelt es sich um ein Verb, ein anderes Adverb oder ein Adjektiv?

Beispiel: You have driven **very** <u>carefully</u>. *Adverb*

a You are **extremely** nervous. ________________

b Paula played **unusually** well. ________________

c The children are **seriously** ill. ________________

d Marc played **nicely**. ________________

e She is always **highly** practical. ________________

f The waiter walks **very** fast. ________________

g Mrs Smith examined the patient **carefully**. ________________

90

Folgt dem Adverb ein Adjektiv oder ein weiteres Adverb?
Trage jeweils die richtige Form in die Lücken ein.

a The boxer was unbelievably ________________ (violent).

b She was really ________________ (slow).

c The hairdresser cut my hair extremely ________________ (fast).

d She was smiling absolutely ________________ (happy).

e She attends the classes fairly ________________ (regular).

f Megan is extremely ________________ (nervous).

g Her coat is extremely ________________ (dirty).

h The speaker spoke astonishingly ________________ (long).

i The boy is amazingly ________________ (intelligent).

89 a nervous; Adjektiv; **b** well; Adverb; **c** ill; Adjektiv; **d** played; Verb; **e** practical; Adjektiv; **f** fast; Adverb; **g** examined; Verb

90 a violent; **b** slow; **c** fast; **d** happily; **e** regularly; **f** nervous; **g** dirty; **h** long; **i** intelligent

91

Adverbien können sich auch auf einen ganzen Satz beziehen.
Dann setzt man sie meistens an den Satzanfang. Setze das passende Adverb ein.

unfortunately – obviously – strangely – suddenly – fortunately – maybe

a ______________________, she brought her key. Otherwise we would have been locked out.

b ______________________, he must have had a bad accident. Look at his face!

c ______________________, he didn't win the lottery. He needed the money so badly.

d ______________________ there was a loud noise!

e ______________________ the Jets will win this time.

f ______________________ my wallet disappeared. Has someone stolen it?

92

Hier ist einiges durcheinandergeraten: Wo gehört was hin? Und vor allem das Adverb?
Bringe die Satzteile in die richtige Reihenfolge.
Tipp: Das Adverb kann vorne, in der Mitte oder am Ende des Satzes stehen, aber niemals zwischen Verb und direktem Objekt!

a happily / the girl / at her parents / smiled

____

b had to stay / unfortunately / he / in hospital / for a few days

____

c opened / quickly / my sister / the letter / from her boyfriend

____

d he wasn't / fortunately / ill / seriously

____

91 a Fortunately; **b** Obviously; **c** Unfortunately; **d** Suddenly; **e** Maybe; **f** Strangely
92 a The girl smiled happily at her parents. **b** Unfortunately, he had to stay in hospital for a few days. **c** My sister opened the letter from her boyfriend quickly. **d** Fortunately, he wasn't seriously ill.

93

Welche Verben drücken eine Sinneswahrnehmung aus, beschreiben aber keine Tätigkeit? Kreuze an.

- **a** to look pretty ○
- **b** to cheer ○
- **c** to turn around ○
- **d** to taste bad ○
- **e** to drive away ○
- **f** to listen to music ○
- **g** to sound terrible ○
- **h** to work hard ○
- **i** to feel cold ○
- **j** to eat much ○
- **k** to smell funny ○
- **l** to eat sweets ○

94

Setze bei Verben der Sinneswahrnehmung ein Adjektiv und bei Tätigkeitsverben ein Adverb.

a The cake tasted ______________________ (fantastic).

b She ate the cake ______________________ (quick).

c The cake smelt ______________________ (wonderful).

d The model looked ______________________ (beautiful).

e They sang ______________________ (loud) at the soccer match.

f The snowman was built ______________________ (fast).

g The snow felt ______________________ (cold).

h Judy ______________________ (quiet) listened to the choir.

i The choir sounded ______________________ (terrible).

j Harry played ______________________ (good).

93 a to look; **d** to taste; **f** to listen; **i** to feel; **k** to smell
94 a fantastic; **b** quickly; **c** wonderful; **d** beautiful; **e** loudly; **f** fast; **g** cold; **h** quietly; **i** terrible; **j** well

95

Welche Verben drücken einen Zustand aus, beschreiben aber keine Tätigkeit? Kreuze an.
Tipp: Ein Zustandsverb lässt sich mit „sein" ersetzen.

- **a** to be glad ○
- **b** to scream ○
- **c** to stay happy ○
- **d** to make ○
- **e** to walk by ○
- **f** to seem quiet ○
- **g** to lift up ○
- **h** to appear dead ○
- **i** to sleep long ○
- **j** to ride ○

96

Setze bei Verben des Zustands ein Adjektiv und bei Tätigkeitsverben ein Adverb.
Tipp: Ein Zustandsverb lässt sich mit „sein" ersetzen, dann wird ein Adjektiv verwendet.

- **a** She had been a ____________________ (great) listener.
- **b** The car didn't seem ____________________ (perfect).
- **c** She was ____________________ (amazing) in the play.
- **d** Gerald ____________________ (immediate) noticed the danger.
- **e** The gym teacher helped the students ____________________ (patient).
- **f** Martin seemed ____________________ (friendly) to me.
- **g** The elephant walked to the water ____________________ (slow).
- **h** Three mice grabbed the cheese ____________________ (quick).
- **i** Marcus stayed absolutely ____________________ (quiet), even though the others went crazy.
- **j** The hunter loaded his gun ____________________ (careful).

95 a to be; **c** to stay; **f** to seem; **h** to appear
96 a great; **b** perfect; **c** amazing; **d** immediately; **e** patiently; **f** friendly; **g** slowly; **h** quickly; **i** quiet; **j** carefully

97

Welche Verben drücken eine Zustandsveränderung aus, beschreiben aber keine Tätigkeit? Kreuze an.

Tipp: Eine Zustandsveränderung erkennst du daran, dass das Verb mit „werden" ersetzt werden kann.

a to play soccer ○

b to get rich ○

c to cook a meal ○

d to fly a plane ○

e to hide a present ○

f to become old ○

g to cycle alone ○

h to go crazy ○

98

Setze bei Verben der Zustandsveränderung ein Adjektiv und bei Tätigkeitsverben ein Adverb.

a Everyday my mother says that she's getting ____________________ (sick) of my loud music.

b The tennis player finished the match ____________________ (successful).

c This small soccer club has become ____________________ (famous) here.

d My grandfather thinks that he is going ____________________ (crazy) because he hears funny sounds.

e Rita forgot the numbers ____________________ (instant).

f Britney became very ____________________ (popular) in the 90s.

g The knights fought ____________________ (brave) in the last battle.

h The wind blew ____________________ (heavy) against my window.

i My uncle had become ____________________ (rich) before he met my aunt.

j The tiger got ____________________ (angry) when the man hit its cage.

97 b to get; **f** to become; **h** to go

98 a sick; **b** successfully; **c** famous; **d** crazy; **e** instantly; **f** popular; **g** bravely; **h** heavily; **i** rich; **j** angry

99

Handelt es sich um ein Verb des Zustands, der Zustandsveränderung oder der Sinneswahrnehmung? Oder um ein Tätigkeitsverb? Entscheide und füge dementsprechend ein Adjektiv oder ein Adverb ein.

a The music sounds ______________________________ (strange).

b Matthew always stays ______________________________ (quiet).

c My brother felt ______________________________ (weak).

d My parents are going ______________________________ (crazy).

e The spaghetti tasted ______________________________ (wonderful).

f The teacher was shouting very ______________________________ (loud).

g She accepted the money ______________________________ (glad).

h The bride looked ______________________________ (beautiful) yesterday.

i After two hours, he became ______________________________ (nervous).

j Natasha was reading ______________________________ (slow).

100

Bei diesen Verben musst du entscheiden, ob sie in diesem Zusammenhang eine Tätigkeit oder einen Zustand beschreiben. Setze dann entsprechend ein Adverb oder ein Adjektiv ein.

a The girl looked very ______________________________ (nice) in her yellow shirt.

b Look ______________________________ (careful) before you give the test back.

c The teacher looked ______________________________ (angry) at the girl.

d She smelled the chemical ______________________________ (careful). Her teacher said that it was a very strong chemical and could have hurt her.

e The fish smelled ______________________________ (interesting).

99 a strange; **b** quiet; **c** weak; **d** crazy; **e** wonderful; **f** loudly; **g** gladly; **h** beautiful; **i** nervous; **j** slowly
100 a nice; **b** carefully; **c** angrily; **d** carefully; **e** interesting

101

Ordne die Adjektive richtig zu. Vergiss den Artikel *the* nicht, denn es geht hier um eine Gruppe von Personen.

lonely – sick – disabled – famous – weak – poor – young

a This group of people is known all over the world: ______________________

b This group of people hardly has any money: ______________________

c This group of people is ill: ______________________

d This group of people isn't very strong: ______________________

e This group of people includes children and teenagers: ______________________

f This group of people doesn't have any friends: ______________________

g This group of people includes people who cannot walk: ______________________

102

Ergänze die folgenden Sätze. Achte darauf, ob es sich um eine Gruppe von Menschen handelt oder um eine Einzelperson.

Tipp: Bei Einzelpersonen musst du das Adjektiv durch ein passendes Nomen ergänzen (z. B. *man, woman, …*).

a Die Reichen können sich jedes Jahr ein Auto leisten.

______________________ can afford to buy a car every year.

b Der Arme hatte einen alten Mantel an.

______________________ was wearing an old coat.

c Die Behinderte wurde ständig diskriminiert.

______________________ was constantly discriminated against.

d Die Alten müssen lernen mit Computern zu arbeiten.

______________________ have to learn to work with computers.

e Das ist eine Party für die Berühmten.

This is a party for ______________________.

101 a the famous; **b** the poor; **c** the sick; **d** the weak; **e** the young; **f** the lonely; **g** the disabled

102 a The rich; **b** The poor man; **c** The disabled woman / The handicapped woman; **d** The old; **e** the famous

103

Partizipien können auch wie ein Adjektiv gebraucht werden. Das *present participle* (Endung *-ing*) drückt dabei aktive Bedeutung aus, das *past participle* hingegen hat passive Bedeutung. Setze die richtigen Partizipien in die Lücken ein.

bored – stolen – frightening – boring – frightened – entertaining – written

a The man had a ______________________________ voice. I was scared!

b That was a ______________________________ presentation.

c A lot of people were ______________________________ during the presentation.

d They finally found the ______________________________ pictures.

e Lissy is a very ______________________________ girl. She knows a lot of jokes!

f The police caught the ______________________________ man. He was hiding.

g The detectives found the ______________________________ note on the table.

104

Kreise das richtige Partizip ein.

a This movie was exciting / excited.

b The boy saw an unexpecting / unexpected show.

c The news was surprising / surprised.

d It was a well-knowing / well-known fact.

e This was a very interesting / interested book.

f A lot of people were very worrying / worried. You could see it in their faces.

g They loaded the packing / packed suitcases.

h They collected all the using / used plates.

103 a frightening; **b** boring; **c** bored; **d** stolen; **e** entertaining; **f** frightened; **g** written
104 a exciting; **b** unexpected; **c** surprising; **d** well-known; **e** interesting; **f** worried; **g** packed; **h** used

105

Es gibt zwei Möglichkeiten, Adjektive zu steigern: mit der Endung *-er/-est* oder mit *more/most*. Ordne die Möglichkeiten richtig zu.

106

Verteile die Adjektive in die richtigen Spalten.

Tipp: Laut lesen hilft bei der Bestimmung der Silbenzahl.

a horrible
b unexpected
c angry
d sad
e careful
f noisy
g nervous
h hot
i happy
j glad
k wonderful
l extreme

105 einsilbige: „-er/-est"; zweisilbige auf „y": „-ier/-iest"; zwei- oder mehrsilbige: „more/most"
106 einsilbig: **d** sad; **h** hot; **j** glad; zweisilbig auf „y": **c** angry; **f** noisy; **i** happy; zweisilbig nicht auf „y": **e** careful; **g** nervous; **l** extreme; mehrsilbig: **a** horrible; **b** unexpected; **k** wonderful

107

Steigere folgende Adjektive. Achte dabei auf Endung und Silbenzahl.

a fast		
b nervous		
c interesting		
d exciting		
e soon		
f careful		
g dark		
h beautiful		
i terrible		
j high		

108

Bei diesen Adjektiven musst du bei der Steigerung auf die Schreibweise achten.

a pure		
b hot		
c happy		
d angry		
e fat		

107 a faster, fastest; **b** more nervous, most nervous; **c** more interesting, most interesting; **d** more exciting, most exciting; **e** sooner, soonest; **f** more careful, most careful; **g** darker, darkest; **h** more beautiful, most beautiful; **i** more terrible, most terrible; **j** higher, highest
108 a purer, purest; **b** hotter, hottest; **c** happier, happiest; **d** angrier, angriest; **e** fatter, fattest

109

Verwende die Steigerungsformen der Adjektive und bilde Sätze.

Beispiel: David • / Pat •• / Simon ••• (fast)

David is fast, but Pat is faster. Simon is the fastest of all.

a Carina • / Tina •• / Selina ••• (nice)

____

b Fred • / Steven •• / Thomas ••• (helpful)

____

c The rat • / the tiger •• / the elephant ••• (big)

____

d soccer • / rock climbing •• / skydiving ••• (dangerous)

____

110

Die Steigerungsformen dieser Adjektive haben nicht viel mit der Grundform gemeinsam. Kannst du sie trotzdem nennen?

a good		
b far		
c much		
d a little		
e bad		
f many		

109 a Carina is nice, but Tina is nicer. Selina is the nicest of all. **b** Fred is helpful, but Steven is more helpful. Thomas is the most helpful of all. **c** The rat is big, but the tiger is bigger. The elephant is the biggest of all. **d** Soccer is dangerous, but rock climbing is more dangerous. Skydiving is the most dangerous of all.

110 a better, best; **b** farther/further, farthest/furthest; **c** more, most; **d** less, least; **e** worse, worst; **f** more, most

111

Prüfe, ob die genannten Dinge die gleiche Punktzahl haben oder nicht.
Bilde dann Sätze mit dem Adjektiv in Klammern.
Tipp: Ist etwas ungleich, verwende *than* oder *not as . . . as*.
Ist etwas gleich, nimm *as . . . as*.

a The green sweater •• / the blue sweater • (nice).

The green ______________________________

b The book •• / the CD • (heavy)

The book ______________________________

c The mouse • / the elephant •• (intelligent)

The mouse ______________________________

d The girl • / the woman • (nervous)

The girl ______________________________

e The cake • / the pudding •• (good)

The cake ______________________________

112

Findest du heraus, was gemeint ist? Ergänze die Sätze in der richtigen Steigerungsform.

a Oh, look at that shirt. It is much nicer ______________ my red one!

b I know ______________ (cool) shop ever!

c This is not as ______________ (expensive) the green shirt.

d Mmmmh. These potatoes taste ______________ (good) the noodles. They were terrible.

e I think this bag is as ______________ (practical) the suitcase.

f The striped skirt makes me look ______________ (big) than I am.

g This is the ______________ (interesting) film I have seen. Just look at its title!

111 a The green sweater is nicer than the blue sweater. **b** The book is heavier than the CD. **c** The mouse isn't as intelligent as the elephant. **d** The girl is as nervous as the woman. **e** The cake is not as good as the pudding.
112 a than; **b** the coolest; **c** expensive as; **d** better than; **e** practical as; **f** bigger; **g** most interesting

113

Es gibt auch bei den Adverbien zwei Möglichkeiten der Steigerung: mit der Endung *-er/-est* oder mit *more/most*. Ordne die Möglichkeiten den richtigen Adverbien zu.

114

Verteile die Adverbien in die richtigen Spalten.
Tipp: Laut lesen hilft bei der Bestimmung der Silbenzahl.

a high
b intelligently
c simply
d pleasantly
e gladly
f soon
g shyly
h fast
i fairly
j happily
k early
l nicely

113 einsilbige Adverbien und „early": -er/-est; zweisilbige: more/most; mehrsilbige: more/most
114 wie einsilbige behandelt: **a** high; **f** soon; **h** fast; **k** early; zweisilbige: **c** simply; **e** gladly; **g** shyly; **i** fairly; **l** nicely; mehrsilbige: **b** intelligently; **d** pleasantly; **j** happily

115

Steigere folgende Adverbien. Achte dabei auf Endung und Silbenzahl.

a angrily		
b soon		
c strategically		
d high		
e tidily		
f fast		
g excitingly		
h truly		
i carefully		
j simply		

116

Bei diesen Adverbien gibt es beide Möglichkeiten der Steigerung. Wie lauten sie?
Tipp: Achte auf die Schreibweise.

a loudly		
b quickly		
c slowly		

115 a more angrily; most angrily; **b** sooner; soonest; **c** more strategically; most strategically; **d** higher; highest; **e** more tidily; most tidily; **f** faster; fastest; **g** more excitingly; most excitingly; **h** more truly; most truly; **i** more carefully; most carefully; **j** more simply; most simply
116 a louder/more loudly; loudest/most loudly; **b** quicker/more quickly; quickest/most quickly; **c** slower/more slowly; slowest/most slowly

117

Verwende die Steigerungsformen der Adverbien und bilde Sätze.

Beispiel: Selina drives carefully. (Peter •• / Tim •••)

Peter drives more carefully, and Tim drives the most carefully of all.

a Sven jumps high. (Hector •• / Justin •••)

____

b Randy reads fast. (Zack •• / Jill •••)

____

c The boy screams loudly. (the girl •• / the woman •••)

____

d Sabrina is speaking nervously. (Roger •• / Andrew •••)

____

118

Die Steigerungsformen dieser Adverbien haben nicht viel mit der Grundform gemeinsam. Kannst du sie trotzdem nennen?
Tipp: Sie sind identisch mit den Sonderformen der Adjektive!

a badly		
b well		
c far		
d much		
e a little		
f a lot		

117 a Hector jumps higher, and Justin jumps the highest of all. **b** Zack reads faster, and Jill reads the fastest of all. **c** The girl screams louder/more loudly, and the woman screams the loudest/most loudly of all. **d** Roger is speaking more nervously, and Andrew is speaking the most nervously of all.
118 a worse, worst; **b** better, best; **c** farther/further, farthest/furthest; **d** more, most; **e** less, least; **f** more, most

119

Prüfe, ob die genannten Dinge die gleiche Punktzahl haben oder nicht.
Bilde dann Sätze mit dem Adverb in Klammern.
Tipp: Ist etwas ungleich, verwende *than* oder *not as ... as.*
Ist etwas gleich, nimm *as ... as.*

a The boy •• / the man •• (hard)

The boy worked ______________________________

b Mr Hanks •• / Mr Brown • (powerfully)

Mr Hanks sings ______________________________

c Megan •• / Mary • (easily)

Megan understands maths ______________________________

d Mr Brooks •• / Mr Temper • (soon)

Mr Brooks arrived ______________________________

e The girl •• / the boy • (well)

The girl cooks ______________________________

120

Findest du heraus, was Jim alles besser kann? Ergänze die Sätze.

a Jim reads better ______________ Jeff!

b And Jeff doesn't understand maths as ______________ (quickly) Jim!

c Jim always tells stories ______________ (entertainingly) of all!

d Jennifer cooks much ______________ (badly) Jim.

e Jim knows a lot ______________ (much) Elizabeth.

f Jim speaks Chinese ______________ (fluently) of all pupils.

g He can dance ______________ (beautifully) than Gill.

119 a as hard as the man. **b** more powerfully than Mr Brown. **c** easier /more easily than Mary. **d** sooner than Mr Temper. **e** better than the boy.
120 a than; **b** quickly as; **c** the most entertainingly; **d** worse than; **e** more than; **f** the most fluently; **g** more beautifully

121

Stelle fest, ob es sich um ein Adjektiv oder Adverb handeln muss, und kreise die richtige Steigerungsform ein.

a Trish prepared her food more careful / more carefully than Sarah.

b Henry was more careful / more carefully than Gerd.

c Fred's dog barked the noisiest / most noisily of all the dogs in the neighbourhood.

d Jack became happier / more happily when he heard the good news.

e Emily sang the most interesting / most interestingly of all the girls in the contest.

f Tyler attended classes more regular / more regularly than Andrew.

g Marina is the most beautiful / most beautifully girl at school.

h Dan is more careless / more carelessly than Steve.

122

**Muss hier ein Adjektiv oder ein Adverb eingesetzt werden?
Wähle dann die richtige Steigerungsform. In der Klammer steht das Adjektiv.**

a Megan seems ______ (nice) than she really is.

b Leon rides the bike ______ (elegant) than Mark.

c Jen writes essays ______ (interesting) than Phil.

d My mom prepares food ______ (fast) than anybody else.

e My uncle drives the ______ (careless) of all our relatives.

f This feels ______ (soft) than a pillow.

g My daughter is ______ (happy) in school now.

h She comes home ______ (quickly) than before.

i The manager looks ______ (busy) than the assistant.

121 a more carefully; **b** more careful; **c** most noisily; **d** happier; **e** most interestingly; **f** more regularly; **g** most beautiful; **h** more careless

122 a nicer; **b** more elegantly; **c** more interestingly; **d** faster; **e** most carelessly; **f** softer; **g** happier; **h** more quickly; **i** busier

123

In den folgenden Sätzen wurden die Relativpronomen ausgelassen. Setze *who* oder *which* richtig ein.
Tipp: Bei den notwendigen Relativsätzen ist das Relativpronomen Subjekt des Satzes, daher sind die Pronomen unerlässlich!

a The man ____________________ stole the car was caught by the police.

b The girl ____________________ shouted at me was Megan.

c Please take the book ____________________ I left on the shelf.

d This is the list of tourists ____________________ want to stay in this hotel.

e This is the dog ____________________ is always barking.

f This is the family ____________________ likes to go to Spain in summer.

g Peter is the boy ____________________ eats a lot of fish.

h I like the mobile ____________________ comes in black. I don't like the silver one.

124

Entscheide in den folgenden Sätzen, welches Relativpronomen eingesetzt werden muss: *who*, *which* oder *whose*.
Tipp: Das Relativpronomen *whose* setzt man dann ein, wenn man im Deutschen „dessen" oder „deren" benutzt.

a This is the man _______________ wife is from Greece.

b This is the man _______________ came from Greece.

c Mark found the pen _______________ I had lost.

d Mark found the pen _______________ cap I had lost.

e These were the houses _______________ roofs got blown off in the last storm.

f These were the houses _______________ got blown away in the last storm.

g This is the famous soccer player _______________ manager died last year.

h This is the famous soccer player _______________ made a lot of money last year.

Anmerkung: *that* ist bei notwendigen Relativsätzen sowohl für *who* als auch für *which* einsetzbar.
123 a who; **b** who; **c** which; **d** who; **e** which; **f** who/which; **g** who; **h** which
124 a whose; **b** who; **c** which; **d** whose; **e** whose; **f** which; **g** whose; **h** who

125

Fasse die beiden Sätze zusammen und benutze das Relativpronomen *whose*.

Beispiel: Steven is a student at Harvard. / Steven's mother is my mother's best friend.

Steven, whose mother is my mother's best friend, is a student at Harvard.

a I sold my car to the guy. / The guy's old car was destroyed in an accident.

____

b The students don't like Mr Smith. / Mr Smith's wife is a teacher at another school.

____

c That man is the one. / That man's father is a Member of Parliament.

____

d That's the family. / That family's gifts were stolen the day before Christmas.

____

126

Setze aus den Satzteilen eine Definition für das markierte Wort zusammen.
Verwende dabei die Relativpronomen *who*, *which* oder *whose*.

a headlines / the large words / start an article / are

____

b a burglar / person / break into houses and steal things / is

____

c a cousin / girl or a boy / is / parents are the brother or sister of your mother or father

____

d a microwave / electronic device / heat up food fast / is (device = Gerät)

____

125 a I sold my car to the guy whose old car was destroyed in an accident. **b** The students don't like Mr Smith, whose wife is a teacher at another school. **c** That man is the one whose father is a Member of Parliament. **d** That's the family whose gifts were stolen the day before Christmas.

126 a Headlines are the large words which start an article. **b** A burglar is a person who breaks into houses and steals things. **c** A cousin is a girl or a boy whose parents are the brother or sister of your mother or father. **d** A microwave is an electronic device which heats up food fast.

127

Die folgenden Sätze benötigen eigentlich kein Relativpronomen, denn es ist „nur“ Objekt des Satzes. Deshalb werden sie auch Kontaktsätze genannt. Zeige, was man jedoch einsetzen könnte: *who* oder *which*.

a The man (________________) I met is called Mr Heinz.

b I lost the pencil (________________) I bought yesterday.

c There are a lot of things (________________) she needs to take care of.

d A lot of people like the movies (________________) Steven Spielberg made.

e Brad Pitt is a man (________________) many people know.

f Susan is the doctor (________________) my sister called when she was sick.

g Mrs Miller is the old lady (________________) I called last night.

h Jennifer is the waitress (________________) Mike likes a lot.

i The "Wedding Singer" is the only movie (________________) I've watched nine times.

128

Bilde aus den folgenden Satzteilen einen Satz. Schreibe in Klammern das Relativpronomen, das man auch weglassen könnte, da es Objekt des Satzes ist.

Beispiel: a picture – I like a lot

This is the picture (which) I like a lot.

a the car – Mr Robinson bought

____

b the woman – Henry talked to last night

____

c the list of people – I want to invite

____

127 a who; **b** which; **c** which; **d** which; **e** who; **f** who; **g** who; **h** who; **i** which

128 a This is the car (which) Mr Robinson bought. **b** This is the woman (who) Henry talked to last night. **c** This is the list of people (who) I want to invite.

129

Bei den folgenden Relativsätzen können manche Relativpronomen weggelassen werden. Klammere diese Relativpronomen ein.
Tipp: Wenn nach *who, which* oder *that* ein Verb folgt, dann ist das Relativpronomen Subjekt des Satzes und kann nicht weggelassen werden. *Whose* darf man nie weglassen!

a Salma Hajek is the actress who I saw yesterday.

b DSDS is the show that is on every Friday evening.

c This is the football club whose players went on strike.

d They arrested the thief who stole the jewels.

e The teacher took the book which I had on my desk.

f Harry is the salesman whose car got stolen on his last trip.

g They invented a machine which can help you translate texts.

h I think we can rely on the boy who I was talking to. (rely on = sich verlassen auf)

130

Nicht überall sind die Relativpronomen notwendig. Füge nur die Relativpronomen ein, die eingesetzt werden müssen. Verwende *who, which* oder *whose*.

a They recognized the player ________________ knee got hurt.

b Martina is the woman ________________ Eric saw on the new TV show yesterday.

c Danny likes the potatoes ________________ are almost burnt.

d My aunt always helps people ________________ relatives live far away.

e Diana is the princess ________________ died in a car crash.

f This is the new TV set ________________ my husband bought last week.

g Egypt is a country ________________ offers a lot of interesting sights to see.

h Henry always takes the pills ________________ my aunt gave him.

i Sandra likes to take in animals ________________ owners don't want them anymore.

129 eingeklammert werden müssen: **a** (who); **e** (which); **h** (who)
130 a whose; **c** which; **d** whose; **e** who; **g** which; **i** whose

131

Hier hat jemand seine ganz persönliche Sicht zu verschiedenen Dingen. Bilde Sätze aus den Bruchstücken und verwende dabei ein Relativpronomen. Klammere das Relativpronomen ein, wenn du es auch weglassen kannst.

Beispiel: an SUV / car / most people don't really need

An SUV is a car (which) most people don't really need.

a a celebrity / person / enjoy being admired by other people

____

b an actress / woman / get paid too much

____

c a vegetarian / person / I cannot understand

____

d gold / metal / all people like around their fingers

____

132

Bilde einen Satz und achte dabei auf die Stellung der Präposition. Schreibe das passende Relativpronomen in Klammern, da man es hier auch weglassen kann.

Beispiel: the house – A burglar broke in this house.

This is the house (which) a burglar broke in.

a the magazine – My English teacher took away my magazine.

____

b the dogs – Our neighbours take care of the dogs.

____

c my friends – I play tennis with my friends.

____

131 a A celebrity is a person who enjoys being admired by other people. **b** An actress is a woman who gets paid too much. **c** A vegetarian is a person (who) I cannot understand. **d** Gold is a metal (which) all people like around their fingers.

132 a This is the magazine (which) my English teacher took away. **b** These are the dogs (which) our neighbours take care of. **c** These are my friends (who) I play tennis with.

133

Die folgenden Sätze tauchen in sehr förmlichem Englisch auf. Sie klingen aber auch etwas altmodisch. Weißt du, wie modernes Englisch klingt? Wandle die Sätze aus der förmlichen Schreibweise um.
Tipp: Achte auf die Satzstellung!

Beispiel: This is the man with whom I played tennis.

This is the man who I played tennis with.

a This is the girl with whom Maria drove home.

b These are the stories about which I like to read.

c Mike is the man to whom I like to talk for hours.

d This is the guestbook in which Kandra wrote.

134

In jeden der folgenden Sätze hat sich ein Fehler eingeschlichen. Findest du sie? Schreibe den Satz richtig darunter.

a The kitchen is the room who I like the best.

b These are the players that coach is always very nervous during a match.

c Mr Gulliver is the man which works in the restaurant across the street.

d Mrs Berger is a woman whom always has good advice.

133 a This is the girl who Maria drove home with. **b** These are the stories which I like to read about.
c Mike is the man who I like to talk to for hours. **d** This is the guestbook which Kandra wrote in.
134 a The kitchen is the room (which/that) I … **b** These are the players whose coach …
c Mr Gulliver is the man who/that works … **d** Mrs Berger is a woman who/that always …

135

In den folgenden Sätzen fehlen die Relativpronomen. Setze *who, which* oder *whose* richtig ein.

a Andrew, ________________ usually talks a lot, won't be at the party tonight.

b Madonna, ________________ is a famous singer, gave a concert in Munich last week.

c Berlin, ________________ is the capital of Germany, has a lot of sights to see.

d Sandra, ________________ parents got divorced last month, lives in New York now.

e English grammar, ________________ a lot of students don't like, is not so bad.

f Drinking, ________________ is a bad habit, has a very bad effect on your body.

g My Aunt Carol, ________________ husband works in a big company, came for a visit.

h Debbie, ________________ became a dentist, flew to Hawaii last summer.

136

Trenne mithilfe von Kommas die zusätzlichen Informationen ab.

a Peter who is the director of the show did a great job.

b Coca-Cola which was invented in 1892 became a popular soft drink.

c Prince Charles whose real name is Charles Philip Arthur George was born in 1948.

d The Guinness Book which is a book with amazing records first came out in 1955.

e Richard whose songs were never successful became a baker.

f Mr Stevenson who was my English professor retired two years ago.

g "Letters from the Inside" which is the title of the book I got from you was great.

h Herbert and Maria who are my aunt's children fight a lot.

i The members of The Rolling Stones whose careers started in 1962 formed a unique band.

135 a who; **b** who; **c** which; **d** whose; **e** which; **f** which; **g** whose; **h** who

136 a …, who is the director of the show, …; **b** …, which was invented in 1892, …; **c** …, whose real name is Charles Philip Arthur George, …; **d** …, which is a book with amazing records, …; **e** …, whose songs never were successful, …; **f** …, who was my English professor, …; **g** …, which is the title of the book I got from you, …; **h** …, who are my aunt's children, …; **i** …, whose careers started in 1962, …

137

Mache aus zwei Sätzen einen: Füge die im zweiten Satz gegebene Zusatzinformation als nicht notwendigen Relativsatz ein.

Beispiel: Frederick is my uncle. He is 57 years old.

Frederick, who is 57 years old, is my uncle.

a Selina likes shopping. She is my niece.

____

b Mr Gruber is my neighbour. His cat ate my bird.

____

c My brother didn't win his last tennis match. He was sick.

____

d Hamburg has got a big harbour. It is a city in Germany.

____

138

Entscheide in den folgenden Sätzen, ob es sich um einen notwendigen oder einen nicht notwendigen Relativsatz handelt. Setze ein Relativpronomen und Kommas nur da, wo sie nötig sind.

a Eton ______________ has a famous college is a very old town.

b There are a lot of things ______________ Tina needs to do by tomorrow.

c My PE teacher ______________ name I cannot pronounce is really nice.

d The Queen ______________ was crowned in 1953 is the oldest reigning monarch in UK history.

e The runner ______________ came in first was George Benton.

137 a Selina, who is my niece, likes shopping. **b** Mr Gruber, whose cat ate my bird, is my neighbour. **c** My brother, who was sick, didn't win his last tennis match. **d** Hamburg, which is a city in Germany, has got a big harbour.
138 a Eton, which … college, is a very old town. **b** —; **c** My PE teacher, whose … pronounce, is really nice. **d** The Queen, who … in 1953, is the oldest…. **e** The runner who came in first was George Benton.

139

Ordne den Modalverben die passende Bedeutung zu:

Erlaubnis Pflicht Fähigkeit Vorschlag/Wunsch

Verbot etwas Unnötiges

		Maria can sing well.
		She must do her homework.
		She may go out until 10 p.m..
		Shall I help you?
		You mustn't smoke at the age of 13.
		You needn't help in the garden.

140

Tom und Maria müssen eilig ihre Sachen zusammenpacken. Maria schafft es nicht allein. Tom überlegt, wie er ihr helfen kann. Schreibe seine Vorschläge auf.

Tipp: Das Modalverb *shall* leitet die Frage ein.

Beispiel: Maria: "I don't have any more pencils. And I don't have time to buy new ones."

Tom: "*Shall I buy them for you?*" (buy / them for you)

a Maria: "Where is my drawing block? I can't find it now."

Tom: "______________________________" (give / you one of mine)

b Maria: "We need an old shirt for the painting lessons. But all my clothes are new!"

Tom: "______________________________" (get one / from my sister)

c Maria: "I lost my rubber somewhere! But I need one for the drawing lesson …"

Tom: "______________________________" (bring / an extra one)

139 can: Fähigkeit; must: Pflicht; may: Erlaubnis; shall: Vorschlag/Wunsch; mustn't: Verbot; needn't: etwas Unnötiges

140 a „Shall I give you one of mine?" **b** „Shall I get one from my sister?" **c** „Shall I bring an extra one?"

141

Maria und Tom wollen an dem Schülerworkshop *Young Artists* teilnehmen.
Sie lesen gemeinsam die Infobroschüre. Setze ein: *can/can't, must, mustn't, needn't.*
Tipp: *must* = müssen und *mustn't* = nicht dürfen!

a For *Young Artists* you __________ have an audition (=Vorsprechen). This is obligatory.

b But you __________ practise for it. It's rather easy.

c YA offers courses for painting, sculpture and drawing. But you __________ attend all three courses, only one.

d Most students __________ come during the week. Therefore, YA lessons are on Saturdays.

e There is no uniform for the YA students, but you __________ buy one if you want to.

142

Mrs Gable organisiert nach dem Workshop eine Ausstellung mit ihren Schülern.
Welches Modalverb passt? Unterstreiche es.

Beispiel: You (can / needn't / must) finish your pictures by next Saturday!

a The visitors (can't / shall / needn't) pay anything at the entrance. It's free.

b You (mustn't / needn't / can't) show pictures that are not from our workshop. It's against the rules.

c You (may / can't / shall) prepare invitations for our exhibition and hand them out to everybody, remember.

d You (mustn't / needn't / shall) write anything about your pictures. But of course you (may / must / shall) explain your works with a short note next to them.

e If you (must / can / mustn't) help me with the arrangements (=Vorbereitungen), please tell me. I would very much appreciate the help. Thank you.

141 a must; **b** needn't; **c** mustn't; **d** can't; **e** can
142 a needn't; **b** mustn't; **c** shall; **d** needn't/may; **e** can

143

Weil nicht alle Modalverben in andere Zeiten umgeformt werden können, gibt es sogenannte Ersatzformen. Verbinde die passenden Bedeutungen.
Tipp: *Can* kann mit *be able to* ersetzt werden (dann ist eine Fähigkeit gemeint) oder mit *be allowed to* (Bitte oder Erlaubnis, wie bei *may*).

a Maria must go to *Young Artists* by bus.	**f** She is allowed to go by train, too.
b She needn't pay extra for the bus.	**g** She isn't able to walk all the way.
c She can't walk all the way.	**h** She isn't allowed to hitchhike.
d She mustn't hitchhike.	**i** She doesn't have to pay extra for the bus.
e She may go by train, too.	**j** Maria has to go to Young Artists by bus.

144

Setze in die Tabelle ein:

be able to · have to · not be allowed to (2x)

not be able to · be allowed to (2x) · not have to

can	
can't	
must	
mustn't	
may	
needn't	

143 a+j; b+i; c+g; d+h; e+f
144 can: be able to/be allowed to; can't: not be able to/not be allowed to; must: have to; mustn't: not be allowed to; may: be allowed to; needn't: not have to

145

Bei den folgenden Sätzen wurden die Ersatzformen verwendet. Formuliere um, indem du die ursprünglichen *modals* wieder einsetzt. Manchmal wird in der Umgangssprache auch im *simple present* üblicherweise eher die Ersatzform als das *modal* verwendet. Weißt du, wann?

Beispiel: Tom *can* (is able to) paint beautifully.

a But he ____________________ (has to) practise sports.

b His mother says: "You ____________________ (don't have to) practise painting but you ____________________ (have to) work hard to improve at sports!"

c Because Tom ____________________ (isn't able to) say no, he agrees to join a soccer club.

d He is a very bad soccer player, so he ____________________ (has to) work really hard to get better.

e He ____________________ (is able to) play three times a week.

146

Setze die Modalverben passend in die Lücken ein:

must (2x) **can't** **may** **mustn't** **needn't** **can (2x)**

a After playing soccer, Tom ____________________ go to the cinema with his friends. If he doesn't play soccer, his mother won't allow him to go out with his friends.

b He ____________________ help with the housework, and he is very happy about that.

But he ____________________ study two hours every day. Otherwise, his marks will be bad.

c Tom ____________________ watch too much TV. This way he will get better marks.

d Tom ____________________ cook very well. His mother is proud of him.

e She also says: "If you ____________________ paint and draw nicely, other people will admire you."

f But Tom ____________________ go to YA and learn how to paint. He ____________________ play soccer all the time.

145 a must; **b** needn't / must; **c** can't; **d** must; **e** can
146 a may; **b** needn't / must; **c** mustn't; **d** can; **e** can; **f** can't / must

147

Maria lernt die anderen Schüler in ihrem Kurs kennen. Sie erzählen über sich. Setze die Ersatzform im *simple present* in die Lücken ein.

Beispiel: Maria: "I have to (must) help my mother at home."

a Susan: "I ______________________ (may) go out to the disco every evening."

b Andrew: "I ______________________ (mustn't) meet with friends before I have finished my homework."

c Sam: "I ______________________ (can) speak four languages fluently."

d Betty: "I ______________________ (needn't) look after my little sisters."

e Mariah: "I ______________________ (can't) eat meat when I think of the animals. So I'm a vegetarian."

f Charly: "I ______________________ (must) practise the piano every day for the competition next month."

148

Mrs Gable, die Zeichenlehrerin, informiert die Schüler über ihren Workshop bei *Young Artists*. Welches *modal* muss sie jeweils verwenden? Unterstreiche die richtige Lösung.

a You (may / must / can) be in the classroom on time. The lesson starts at 10 am every Saturday.

b If you (needn't / must / can't) come, please call the secretary Mrs Glenford.

c You (must / can't / may) come to an information evening tonight – if you have time.

d But you (need / needn't / can't) come, if you don't have any more questions.

e Pencils and rubber are the most important tools for our workshop. You (can / needn't / mustn't) forget them next Saturday!

f If the weather is nice, we (needn't / must / can) go out and collect objects for drawing.

g You (can't / mustn't / may) also bring photos of flowers and draw them.

147 **a** am allowed to; **b** am not allowed to; **c** am able to; **d** don't have to; **e** am not able to; **f** have to
148 **a** must; **b** can't; **c** may; **d** needn't; **e** mustn't; **f** can; **g** may

149

Setze in die Tabelle ein.
Tipp: *Was* bzw. *wasn't* wird bei *he / she / it* verwendet.

did not have to | was / were able to | had to | wasn't / weren't allowed to (2x) | wasn't / weren't able to | was / were allowed to (2x)

can	
can't	
must	
mustn't	
may	
needn't	

150

Zu Hause erzählt Tom seiner Mutter von der ersten Stunde. Setze hier die Ersatzform im *simple past* in die Lücken ein.

Beispiel: First we *had to* (must) introduce ourselves to the class.

a Everybody ______________ (must) talk about his favourite artists.
We ______________ (may) talk about our family and hobbies, too.

b I ______________ (needn't) explain anything about rock climbing.
Everybody there already knew about it. Sam ______________ (can even) try rock climbing during his last holidays!

c A lot of students ______________ (can't) stay silent for more than an hour. They didn't listen to the teacher anymore.

d Andrew ______________ (mustn't) chew his gum during the lesson. He ______________ (must) to spit it out.

149 can: was / were able to oder was / were allowed to; can't: wasn't / weren't able to oder wasn't / weren't allowed to; must: had to; mustn't: wasn't / weren't allowed to; may: was / were allowed to; needn't: did not have to
150 a had to / were allowed to; **b** didn't have to / was even able to; **c** weren't able to; **d** wasn't allowed to / had to

151

Vor lauter Aufregung benutzt Tom die falsche Zeit. Setze die Ersatzformen seiner Erzählung ins *simple past*.

a But Andrew is a real bully (= Rüpel) anyway. He __________ (isn't) able to listen to anybody and he __________ (isn't) able to stay in his chair.

b He __________ (isn't) allowed to walk around the classroom, but he did it anyway.

c He __________ (is) allowed to go to the bathroom, but he didn't come back.

d Sam __________ (has) to go get him after twenty minutes. He found Andrew in the cafeteria. None of us could believe it!

e Then we __________ (are) allowed to go out and look for flowers to draw.

f But Sam didn't look for flowers, and he lied to Mrs Gable when we got back to the classroom: "Sorry, but I __________ (am) not able to find any flowers."

152

Übersetze die Wörter in Klammern. **Tipp: Bei *can* hast du zwei Möglichkeiten!**

Hi Marc,

I went to *Young Artists* last Saturday. You know, my mother wants me to improve my drawing skills. First, we a) __________ (mussten) play some games to warm up with the others. I don't like games, and I b) ______________ (konnte) play enough at home. Well, anyway, then I c) ______________ (durfte) compare my pictures with the others. But I d) ______________ (brauchte nicht) feel bad about my pictures. There were a lot of students whose pictures were worse. Unfortunately we e) ____________________ (durften nicht) take them home. My mother would have loved to see them!

See you soon, Tom

151 a wasn't / wasn't; **b** wasn't; **c** was; **d** had; **e** were; **f** was

152 a) had to; b) was able to oder could; c) was allowed to; d) didn't have to; e) weren't allowed to

153

Setze den Text in die Vergangenheit.

Beispiel: The visitors *were able to* (can) talk to the students about their pictures.

a The students __________ (needn't) write any explanations about their works but of course they __________ (may).

b Unfortunately Tom __________ (can't) come because he was ill.

c Maria said that she __________ (must) work hard to finish the picture in time for the show.

d Mrs Brown __________ (can) come and help with the coffee bar.

e The students __________ (mustn't) show any pictures other than their YA works.

154

Übersetze und achte auf die korrekte Zeit: *simple present* oder *simple past*?
Tipp: Im *simple present* gibt es immer zwei mögliche Übersetzungen!

a We __________ (mussten) work really hard for the exhibition.

b We __________ (durften nicht) show pictures that we had painted at home. Mrs Gable says that's against the rules because someone else might have painted them.

c But we __________ (durften) to bring leaflets and photographs of our other pictures and hand them out to the visitors.

d I asked her: "__________ (dürfen) we sell some of our pictures?"

e She laughed and said: "Well, if someone wants to buy them, you __________ (dürft) sell them. I don't mind."

f Luckily we __________ (müssen nicht) give interviews.

g Some students want to, but I have the flu. I __________ (nicht dürfen) talk too much.

153 a didn't have to / were allowed to; **b** wasn't able to; **c** had to; **d** was able to; **e** weren't allowed to
154 a had to; **b** weren't allowed to; **c** were allowed to; **d** May / Can; **e** may / can; **f** needn't / don't have to; **g** mustn't / am not allowed to

155

Mrs Brown und Mrs Miller überlegen, was in der ersten Stunde alles passiert sein muss.
Tipp: Lasse alle Sätze mit *must have* beginnen und verwende das *past participle* der Wörter in Klammern.

Beispiel: Maria *must have found* (find) a new friend. She talks about Tracy all the time.

a Tom was really angry with Andrew. He ______________________ (act) terribly.

b Maria ______________________ (be) impressed by Tracy.

c They ______________________ (help) Mrs Gable clean the room; they got home very late.

d No, I think they ______________________ (take) a break at McDonald's on the way back.

156

Mrs Brown und Mrs Miller jammern sich gegenseitig vor, wozu sie ihre Kinder ständig ermahnen müssen. Dabei wird *can* zu *could, may* zu *might* und *shall* zu *should.*
Tipp: Achte auf die Pronomen, sie ändern sich von der 1. zur 3. Person Singular!

Beispiel: "Maria, you are always late. You shall pack earlier this time!"

I told her that she should pack earlier.

a "Tom, you know that soccer on Saturdays can be a problem!"

____

b "Tom, you can't go to the Young Artists with your soccer gear on."

____

c "Maria, you shall always clean up your room before you leave!"

____

d "Maria, I may be strict, but you shall clean up your room yourself!"

____

155 a must have acted; **b** must have been; **c** must have helped; **d** must have taken
156 a I told him that soccer on Saturdays could be a problem. **b** I told him that he couldn't go to the YA with his soccer gear on. **c** I told Maria that she should always clean up her room before she leaves. **d** I told her that I might be strict, but she shoud clean up her room herself.

157

Vervollständige die Sätze mit der richtigen Form der Wörter in Klammern.
Tipp: *If* und *will* können niemals im gleichen Satzteil stehen!

Beispiel: Tom will buy the DVD if ____________________ (he / like the movie).

Tom will buy the DVD *if he likes the movie.*

a Tom will go rock climbing this weekend if ____________________ (Marc / come with him).

b Marc will come with Tom if ____________________ (his parents / say yes).

c His parents ____________________ (say yes) if Marc promises to be careful.

d Tom and Marc ____________________ (have fun) at the weekend if the weather is nice.

158

Kannst du die Sätze richtig vervollständigen?

Beispiel: If I __________ (come) home early, I __________ (make) a cake.

If I *come* home early I *will make* a cake.

a If I __________ (lose) my mobile, I __________ (go) to the police.

b If I __________ (get up) too late, I __________ (call) the school and tell them that I __________ (be) late this morning.

c If I __________ (miss) the bus to school, I __________ (ride) my bike.

d If I __________ (forget) my friend's birthday, I __________ (tell) her that I'm sorry.

e If I __________ (finish) the homework early, I __________ (go shopping) with my friends.

157 a Marc comes with him; **b** his parents say yes; **c** will say yes; **d** will have fun
158 a lose / will go; **b** get up / will call / will be; **c** miss / will ride; **d** forget / will tell; **e** finish / will go shopping

159

Was gehört zusammen? Verbinde die passenden Satzteile. Schreibe dann noch einmal den vollständigen Satz auf.

a If / my grandmother / visit us — d) I / go for a walk with her dog.

b If / my friend Susan / be ill — e) we / invite him to the party tonight.

c If / we / see Tom — f) my mother / make a delicious cake.

160

Kreuze zuerst den Satzteil an, in dem das *if* stehen muss. Schreibe dann die Sätze noch einmal vollständig in der richtigen Form auf.

Beispiel: Maria / practise more X — she / win the dancing competition.

If Maria practises more, she will win the dancing competition.

a we / buy the jeans — they / not be too expensive.

b you / like the food — you / get more.

c I / wear my jacket — I / be cold.

d they / get stuck in rush hour — they / leave after 4 o'clock.

159 a + f): If my grandmother visits us, my mother will make a delicious cake.
b + d): If my friend Susan is ill, I will go for a walk with her dog.
c + e): If we see Tom, we'll invite him to the party tonight.
160 a We will buy the jeans if they aren't too expensive. **b** If you like the food, you will get more.
c I will wear my jacket if I'm cold. **d** They will get stuck in rush hour if they leave after 4 o'clock.

161

Wie lauten die Verbformen, wenn man etwas verneinen will?
Formuliere die Sätze ins Negativ um.
Tipp: In der Gegenwart *(simple present)* muss in der Verneinung oft *do / does* verwendet werden.

Beispiel: If Maria helps her mother, she will give her some extra pocket money.

If Maria doesn't help her mother, she will not give her some extra pocket money.

a If Tom gets his luggage ready in time, he will catch the bus easily.

____

b If Mrs Brown is at home, she can take Tom to his soccer training.

____

c Mrs Miller will pick up Maria at the station if the car is ok again.

____

d Maria can visit her friend if she finishes her homework before 4 o'clock.

____

162

Fülle die Lücken mit der jeweils richtigen Form.

a We ______________ (not buy) the pullover if it ______________ (not be) on sale.

b The shop ______________ (not sell) anything if they ______________ (not open) in the afternoon, too.

c She ______________ (not win) the race if she ______________ ______________ (not practise) more.

d If you ______________ (not help) me, I ______________ (not finish) the housework in time.

161 a If Tom doesn't get his luggage ready in time, he will not/won't catch the bus easily. **b** If Mrs Brown isn't at home, she can't take Tom to his soccer training. **c** Mrs Miller will not/won't pick up Maria at the station if the car isn't ok again. **d** Maria can't visit her friend if she doesn't finish her homework before 4 o'clock.

162 a won't buy / isn't; **b** won't sell / don't open; **c** won't win / doesn't practise; **d** don't help / won't finish

163

Maria würde am Wochenende gerne nach London fahren, wenn …
Vervollständige die Sätze mit dem *simple past* bzw. *would* + Infinitiv.
Tipp: *If* und *would* können nicht im selben Satzteil stehen!

Beispiel: Maria would go to London if her parents *paid* (pay) the train ticket.

a Maria's mother __________ (take) her to London by car if she had time on Saturday.

b Maria would hitchhike to London if her parents __________ (agree). But her parents don't allow her to hitchhike.

c Maria's friend Stella would come with her if she still __________ (live) nearby. But Stella has moved to Greece.

d Maria __________ (go) to London with the neighbours if they went to London. They go to London every weekend but right now they are on holiday in Spain.

164

Maria ärgert sich, dass es mit ihrem Ausflug nach London nicht klappt. Sie sitzt zu Hause auf dem Sofa und stellt sich vor, was sie dort alles unternehmen könnte. Vervollständige die Sätze mit der korrekten Form.
Tipp: *If* und *would* können nicht im gleichen Satzteil stehen!

Beispiel: If I __________ (win) in the lottery, I __________ (hire) a chauffeur.

If I *won* in the lottery, I *would hire* a chauffeur.

a If I __________ (have) money, I __________ (buy) a lot of nice clothes in London.

b If I __________ (get) a ticket, I __________ (visit) Madame Tussaud's.

c If I __________ (like), I __________ (see) the Tower, too.

d If I __________ (find) a nice park, I __________ (have) a picnic.

e If I __________ (be) in London, I __________ (do) so many things!

163 a would take; **b** agreed; **c** lived; **d** would go
164 a had / would buy; **b** got / would visit; **c** liked / would see; **d** found / would have; **e** was / would do

165

Verbinde richtig und schreibe dann noch einmal den ganzen Satz.

a If / our teacher / help us

b If / I / go shopping

c If / Sam / like dogs

d) he / go for a walk with Bonzo.

e) we / understand the exercise.

f) I / pick up the groceries for you.

166

Kreuze den Satzteil an, in dem das *if* stehen muss. Schreibe dann die Sätze in der richtigen Form auf.

Beispiel: Tom / take part in the competition ☐ he / have more practice ☒

Tom would take part in the competition if he had more practice.

a Maria / improve in Maths ☐ she / do the homework with Tom ☐

b Tom / help her with the homework ☐ his friends / make fun of him ☐

c Maria's mother / give her more pocket money ☐ Maria / get better marks at school ☐

d Maria / get more pocket money ☐ she / take dancing lessons ☐

165 a + e): If our teacher helped us, we would understand the exercise. **b + f)**: If I went shopping, I would pick up the groceries (= Lebensmittel) for you. **c + d)**: If Sam liked dogs, he would go for a walk with Bonzo.
166 a Maria would improve in Maths if she did the homework with Tom. **b** If Tom helped her with the homework, his friends would make fun of him. **c** Maria's mother would give her more pocket money if Maria got better marks at school. **d** If Maria got more pocket money, she would take dancing lessons.

167

Wie lauten die Verbformen, wenn die Sätze in der Vergangenheit verneinend formuliert werden sollen?
Tipp: In der Vergangenheit (*simple past*) muss in der Verneinung oft *did* verwendet werden.

Beispiel: If we had time this weekend, we would help you with your gardening.

If we *didn't* have time this weekend, we *wouldn't* help you with your gardening.

a If we went shopping, we would have enough food for the weekend.

___

b If Mrs Miller earned a lot of money, she would buy the new Porsche.

___

c If Maria got up too late, she would miss the school bus.

___

d Tom would go to the soccer training twice a week if Mrs Brown took him there by car.

___

168

Fülle die Lücken mit der jeweils richtigen Form.

a We ___ (not fly) to Australia if we ___ (not have) the money.

b Tom ___ (not help) Maria with the homework if his mother ___ (not tell) him to.

c If Marc ___ (not stay) with his grandparents this weekend, he ___ (not miss) the soccer game at his school.

d If they ___ (not watch) TV all the time, they ___ (not get in trouble) with their parents every day.

167 a If we didn't go shopping, we wouldn't have enough food for the weekend. **b** If Mrs Miller didn't earn a lot of money, she wouldn't buy the new Porsche. **c** If Maria didn't get up too late, she wouldn't miss the school bus. **d** Tom wouldn't go to the soccer training twice a week if Mrs Brown didn't take him there by car.
168 a wouldn't fly / didn't have; **b** wouldn't help / didn't tell; **c** didn't stay / wouldn't miss; **d** didn't watch / wouldn't get in trouble

169

Maria hatte in Schwierigkeiten gesteckt. Was hättest du an ihrer Stelle getan? Finde die richtige Form der Wörter in Klammern und vervollständige die Sätze.
Tipp: *If* und *would have* können niemals im gleichen Satzteil stehen!

Beispiel: If I *had missed* (miss) the last bus, I *would have called* (call) a taxi.

a If I ______ (forget) my homework, I ______ (tell) my teacher right away.

b If I ______ (break) the window, I ______ (pay) a new one.

c If I ______ (ruin) the food, I ______ (order) a pizza.

d If I ______ (lose) my purse, I ______ (call) the bank to cancel my credit card.

170

Marias Wochenende war wieder mal nicht sehr erfolgreich. Kannst du die Sätze richtig vervollständigen?
Tipp: Typ III wird mit *would have* + Infinitiv und *past perfect* gebildet.

Beispiel: Maria would have bought the present for her mother if *she had had* (she / have) enough money.

a She would have cleaned her room if ______ (she / think of) it.

b Maria ______ (write) her friend an e-mail if her computer had been working.

c She ______ (clean) her bicycle if the weather had been better.

d Maria would have gone to the cinema with her friends if they ______ (have) time to watch the film.

169 a had forgotten / would have told; **b** had broken / would have paid; **c** had ruined / would have ordered; **d** had lost / would have called
170 a she had thought of; **b** would have written; **c** would have cleaned; **d** had had

171

Verbinde zuerst die zusammengehörenden Satzteile und schreibe dann den vollständigen Satz auf.

a If / you / called Maria

b If / the bus / arrive on time

c If / Tom / bring his climbing equipment

d) she / come to the cinema with you.

e) he / go / rock climbing with Marc.

f) we / catch the plane.

172

Kreuze zuerst den Satzteil an, in dem das *if* stehen muss.
Schreibe dann die Sätze vollständig in der richtigen Form auf.

Beispiel: Maria / make a cake ☒ she / bring it to Tom's party. ○

If Maria had made a cake, she would have brought it to Tom's party.

a We / buy a new car ○ we / not go on holiday this year. ○

b They / visit us ○ they / find a dogsitter for Bonzo. ○

c Mrs Brown / meet Mrs Miller ○ the women / talk about their children. ○

d Maria / write a good essay ○ she / read the book. ○

171 a + d: If you had called Maria, she would have come to the cinema with you. b + f: If the bus had arrived on time, we would have caught the plane. c + e: If Tom had brought his climbing equipment, he would have gone rock climbing with Marc.
172 a If we had bought a new car, we would not have gone on holiday this year. **b** They would have visited us if they had found a dogsitter for Bonzo. **c** If Mrs Brown had met Mrs Miller, the women would have talked about their children. **d** Maria would have written a good essay if she had read the book.

173

Formuliere die Sätze zu einer negativen Aussage um.

Beispiel: If I had forgotten my keys, I would have stayed at my friend's house for the night.

If I *hadn't forgotten* my keys, I *wouldn't have stayed* at my friend's house for the night.

a If I had stayed at my friend's house, we would have watched a nice film.

____

b If we had watched a nice film, we would have had crisps and popcorn.

____

c I would have gained weight (= zunehmen) if we had had crisps and popcorn.

____

d I would have gone to the fitness club if I had gained weight.

____

174

Fülle die Lücken mit der jeweils richtigen Form.

a We ____________________ (not buy) the car if our old car ____________________ (not break down).

b Maria ____________________ (not get) a good mark if she ____________________ (not study) very hard before.

c If they ____________________ (not move) to Greece, we ____________________ (not have) the possibility to go there this year.

d If he ____________________ (not help) her with the housework, she ____________________ (not have) time to go out at night.

173 a If I hadn't stayed at my friend's house, we wouldn't have watched a nice film. **b** If we hadn't watched a nice film, we wouldn't have had crisps and popcorn. **c** I wouldn't have gained weight if we hadn't had crisps and popcorn. **d** I wouldn't have gone to the fitness club if I hadn't gained weight.
174 a wouldn't have bought / hadn't broken down; **b** wouldn't have got / hadn't studied; **c** hadn't moved / wouldn't have had; **d** hadn't helped / wouldn't have had

175

Die Mütter von Tom und Maria unterhalten sich miteinander. Was wird gesagt? Verbinde die zusammengehörenden Satzteile.

a If Tom helped her with the homework,	e) it would have looked much nicer.
b If Maria works harder,	f) we'll take a trip to Dublin.
c If we have time,	g) she wouldn't learn anything.
d If you had cleaned your room,	h) she will get better marks at school.

176

simple past   will-future   conditional II   simple present   past perfect   conditional I

177

	a If I like the movie,	I will get it on DVD.
	b If I had had enough money,	I would have bought the game.
	c If I understood maths,	I would like the subject.

175 **a** + g); **b** + h); **c** + f); **d** + e)
176 Typ I: simple present – will-future; Typ II: simple past – conditional I; Typ III: past perfect – conditional II
177 **a** Typ I; **b** Typ III; **c** Typ II

178

Ergänze die Unterhaltung der beiden Mütter mit den Sätzen aus Kurztest 175.

Mrs Miller: "Maria only gets bad marks at school. I think she doesn't want to learn. But I'm sure ____

______________________________. I think she is just lazy."
Mrs Brown: "Maybe it is really difficult for her. Tom is very intelligent and he always gets very good marks. I'm very proud of him. I will ask him, I think he can help Maria with the homework."

Mrs Miller: "____

______________________________. She has to work more. But the only thing that she likes is going shopping with her friends. And her room! It is so dirty! She never cleans."

Mrs Brown: "Yes, right. That's the same with Tom. I always tell him: ____________________

______________________________. But Tom likes it like that!"

Mrs Miller: "Well, it's always the same with the children. What will you do at the weekend?"

Mrs Brown: "____.
We have always wanted to go there for a weekend trip."

179

Ergänze die Lücken. Prüfe zuerst, ob es ein *if*-Satz vom Typ I, II oder Typ III ist.

"If my mother hadn't told me to clean all the time, I ____________________ (like to tidy up). I won't tell her anything about school anymore if she ____________________ (go on) telling everybody. If Mom didn't meet Mrs Miller every Friday and didn't tell her everything, Maria ____________________ (not make fun) of me every Monday. And if Maria ____________________ (not make fun) of me all the time, the others wouldn't laugh about me all the time."

178 If Maria works more, she will get better marks at school. / If Tom helped her with the homework, she wouldn't learn anything. / If you cleaned your room, it would look much nicer. / If we have time, we'll take a trip to Dublin.
179 would like to tidy up. / goes on / wouldn't make fun / didn't make fun

180

Übersetze die hervorgehobenen Personalpronomen und trage sie in die Lücken ein.

a Ich mag **ihn** sehr. = I like ____________ very much.

b Er mag **mich** noch mehr. = He likes ____________ even more.

c Die Schüler mögen **uns**. = The pupils like ____________.

d Wir Lehrer mögen **sie**. = We teachers like ____________ (die Schüler).

e Ihr mögt **sie** nicht? = You don't like ____________ (die Schülerin)?

f Sie mag **euch** auch nicht. = She doesn't like ____________ either.

g Kennt sie **dich**? = Does she know ____________?

h Kennst du **sie**? = Do you know ____________ (die Engländerin)?

i Er versteht **mich** gut. = He understands ____________ well.

j Ich verstehe **ihn** nicht. = I don't understand ____________.

181

Übersetze die folgenden Sätze und beachte bei der Wahl des Reflexivpronomens, ob es sich um Singular oder Plural handelt.

a Sie redet mit sich selbst. = ____

b Sie reden mit sich selbst. = ____

c Bedien' dich! = ____

d Bedient euch! = ____

e Amüsierst du dich? = ____

f Amüsiert ihr euch? = ____

g Ich habe mich verletzt. = ____

h Wir haben uns verletzt = ____

180 a him; **b** me; **c** us; **d** them; **e** her; **f** you; **g** you; **h** her; **i** me; **j** him
181 a She is talking to herself. **b** They are talking to themselves. **c** Help yourself! **d** Help yourselves! **e** Are you enjoying yourself? **f** Are you enjoying yourselves? **g** I hurt myself. **h** We hurt ourselves.

182

Welches Pronomen vervollständigt jeweils am besten die folgenden Sätze? Kreuze an.
Tipp: Wenn nichts im Satz fehlt, wähle „nichts".

a Tony broke up (= Schluss machen) with Amy. Tony hurt ____________________.

○ nichts ○ herself ○ her

b Tom dropped a book on his own foot. He hurt ____________________.

○ nichts ○ him ○ himself

c Sue's plane leaves in two hours. She really needs to hurry ____________________ up.

○ nichts ○ her ○ herself

d Oh, yes. Now I remember ____________________ you. You are Greg's friend, right?

○ nichts ○ me ○ myself on

e The party was so nice. I really enjoyed ____________________.

○ nichts ○ me ○ myself

f The party was so nice. I enjoyed ____________________ it very much.

○ nichts ○ me ○ myself

183

Übersetze die Pronomen in Klammern.

a Greg loves Gina. Gina loves Greg. = They love ____________________ (einander).

b Richard knows Ann. Ann knows Richard. = They know ____________________ (sich).

c I love you. You love me. = We love ____________________ (uns).

d Tom, do you love Rita? Rita, do you love you Tom? Rita and Tom, do you love

____________________ (euch)?

e I'm enjoying myself. He's enjoying himself. We're enjoying ____________________ (uns).

f Why are a – d the same, and e is different? ____________________

____

182 a her; **b** himself; **c** nichts; **d** nichts; **e** myself; **f** nichts
183 a each other; **b** each other; **c** each other; **d** each other; **e** ourselves; **f** The verbs in a – d are actions which happen mutually (auf Gegenseitigkeit), and the verb in e is reflexive.

184

Entscheide, welches Pronomen die Übersetzung aus dem Deutschen richtig vervollständigt. Kreuze an und trage es in die Lücke ein.

a Bedien' dich! = Help ________________! — you / yourself

b Er hat sich verletzt! = He hurt ________________. — him / himself

c Sie spricht mit sich selbst. = She speaks to ________________. — herself / her

d Er denkt nur an sich. = He only thinks about ________________. — him / himself

e Amüsiere dich! = Enjoy ________________! — you / yourself

f Benimm dich! = Behave ________________! — you / yourself

g Siehst du dich im Spiegel? =

Do you see ________________ in the mirror? — you / yourself

185

Welche Übersetzungen von „uns" und „euch" sind richtig? Entscheide, welche Option am besten die folgenden Sätze vervollständigt. Kreuze an und fülle die Lücke dann aus.

a Er kennt euch. = He knows ________________.

you / each other / yourselves

b Ihr kennt euch, oder? = You know ________________, don't you?

you / each other / yourself

c Kennen sie uns? = Do they know ________________?

us / ourselves / each other

d Kennen wir uns? = Do we know ________________?

us / ourselves / each other

e Wir haben uns verletzt. = We hurt ________________.

us / ourself / ourselves

184 a yourself; **b** himself; **c** herself; **d** himself; **e** yourself; **f** yourself; **g** yourself

185 a you; **b** each other; **c** us; **d** each other; **e** ourselves

186

Entscheide, welche Übersetzung der hervorgehobenen Pronomen am besten ist. Kreuze sie an und trage sie dann in die Lücke ein.

a He's a friend of ______________________. (ein Freund von mir)

○ I ○ me ○ myself ○ mine ○ my

b She's a friend of ______________________. (eine Freundin von ihm)

○ he ○ his ○ himself ○ him ○ hisself

c They are friends of ______________________. (Freunde von uns)

○ ours ○ we ○ ourselves ○ our ○ us

d They are friends of ______________________. (Freunde von dir)

○ you ○ yous ○ yourself ○ yourselves ○ yours

e He's a friend of ______________________. (ein Freund von ihr)

○ she ○ her ○ herself ○ hers ○ herselves

f He's a friend of ______________________. (ein Freund von ihnen)

○ theirs ○ they ○ themselves ○ their ○ them

187

Manche Verben sind im Deutschen reflexiv, im Englischen aber nicht. Übersetze.

a Setz dich bitte hin. = ______________________

b Schau dich an! = ______________________

c Entscheide dich, was du willst. = ______________________

d Er hat sich verletzt. = ______________________

e Ich fühle mich nicht wohl. = ______________________

f Beeilt euch! = ______________________

g Er wird sich hinlegen. = ______________________

186 a mine; **b** his; **c** ours; **d** yours; **e** hers; **f** theirs
187 a Please, sit down. **b** Look at yourself! **c** Decide what you want. **d** He hurt himself. **e** I don't feel well. **f** Hurry up! **g** He's going to lie down.

188

Vervollständige die Tabelle mit den besitzanzeigenden Pronomen.

a	me	my	mine
b	you		
c	him		
d	her		
e	it		
f	us		
g	you		
h	them		

189

Setze die Pronomen aus der Tabelle in die Lücken ein.

a That car belongs to my family. It is ____________ car. The car is ____________.

b Does that house belong to your family? Is it __________ house? Is that house ____________?

c That cat belongs to Veronica. It's __________ cat. That cat is __________.

d This video game belongs to Michael. It's __________ video game.

This video game is __________.

e This laptop belongs to me. It's __________ laptop. This laptop is ____________.

189 a our / ours; **b** your / yours; **c** her / hers; **d** his / his; **e** my / mine
188 b your / yours; **c** his / his; **d** her / hers; **e** its / its; **f** our / ours; **g** your / yours; **h** their / theirs

190

Entscheide, welches Pronomen am besten passt. Kreuze an und vervollständige die Lücken.
Tipp: *each other* kann „wir uns", „ihr euch" oder „sie sich" bedeuten!

a Tom kennt Jim. Jim kennt Tom. = They know ______________.

- they
- each other
- them

b Jill kennt Jim. Jill kennt Tom. = Jill knows ______________.

- them
- each other
- themselves

c Tom hat sich verletzt. Jim hat sich verletzt. = They hurt ______________.

- them
- each other
- themselves

d Tom liebt Jill. Jill liebt Tom. = They love ______________.

- they
- each other
- them

e Tom benimmt sich. Jim benimmt sich. = They are behaving ______________.

- them
- each other
- themselves

f How else can each other be translated into German? ______________

191

Übersetze die folgenden Sätze. Achte insbesondere auf die hervorgehobenen Satzteile.

a Ein Freund von uns hat sich verletzt. = ______________

b Kennen wir uns nicht? = ______________

c Du musst dich beeilen! = ______________

d Es gehört dir nicht. Es ist meins ! = ______________

e Sie verstehen sich . = ______________

f Ich erinnere mich nicht an diese Freundin von euch . = ______________

____

190 a each other; **b** them; **c** themselves; **d** each other; **e** themselves; **f** mit „einander"
191 a A friend of ours hurt himself. **b** Don't we know each other? **c** You have to hurry up. **d** It doesn't belong to you. It is mine! **e** They understand each other. **f** I don't remember that friend of yours.

192

Vervollständige die Tabelle mit der Form von *to be* in der entsprechenden Zeitstufe.

	Passengers	are	picked up	by taxis.
	The car		sold.	—
	It		repaired.	—
	America		discovered	by Columbus.
	The letter		delivered.	—

193

Bevor du die Form von *to be* bildest, musst du herausfinden, wer das Subjekt im Passiv ist. Unterstreiche es. Schreibe dann die Sätze im Passiv auf.

Beispiel: The teachers make plans for the class outing (= Klassenfahrt).

The plans for the class outing are made by the teachers.

a The students ask their parents for help.

b The parents hire a bus driver.

c All of them prepare material for field trips (Exkursionen).

d The students pack all kinds of clothes.

192 The car was sold. It has been repaired. America had been discovered by Columbus. The letter will be delivered.
193 a The parents are asked to help by the students. **b** A bus driver is hired by the parents. **c** Material for field trips is prepared by all of them. **d** All kinds of clothes are packed by the students.

194

Fülle die Lücken mit der Passiv-Form im *simple present*.
Tipp: Verwende das *simple present* von *to be* und das Partizip Perfekt.

a Many unusual animals ____________________ (exhibit) for the visitors in more than 400 aquariums.

b Most people ____________________ (attract) by the orcas.

c You can read articles in the newspaper about how swimmers ____________________

____________________ (attack) by sharks.

d Coral reefs all over the world ____________________ (threaten) by ignorant tourists.

e Visitors of SeaWorld ____________________ (told) a lot about the oceans and its wildlife.

f The dolphins ____________________ (train) for the shows by only a few trainers. They know them very well and don't listen to anybody else.

195

Es gibt eine ganze Menge Dinge, die Amerikaner Jahr für Jahr tun, die also immer wieder geschehen. Formuliere die Sätze um ins *simple present passive*.

Beispiel: write postcards for Christmas

Postcards are written for Christmas.

a they send Valentine's Day cards to loved ones

____

b they prepare a big turkey dinner for Thanksgiving

____

c they celebrate Independence Day on the 4th of July

____

d they hold presidential elections every four years

____

194 a are exhibited; **b** are attracted; **c** are attacked; **d** are threatened; **e** are told; **f** are trained
195 a Valentine's Day cards are sent to loved ones. **b** A big turkey dinner is prepared for Thanksgiving. **c** Independence Day is celebrated on the 4th of July. **d** Presidential elections are held every four years.

196

Tom wurde Zeuge eines Banküberfalls. Vervollständige seine Erzählung mit den Passivformen im *simple past*.
Tipp: Verwende das *simple past* von *to be* und das Partizip Perfekt.

Beispiel: A bank robbery *was watched* (watch) by Tom.

a The front door ______________________ (open) by a robber with a gun.

b The police ______________________ (call) at once by a clerk.

c The customers ______________________ (tell) to sit down on the floor.

d The clerk ______________________ (order) to open the safe.

197

Tom hat ja erst die Hälfte erzählt. Wenn du wissen willst, wie es ausging, formuliere die Sätze um ins *simple past passive*.

Beispiel: The clerk took out the money.

The money was taken out by the clerk.

a Then he gave the money to the robber.

____

b The robber put the money into a suitcase.

____

c An accomplice (= Komplize) outside the bank helped the robber to escape.

____

d But the police caught the two straightaway! (= sofort)

____

196 a was opened; **b** was called; **c** were told; **d** was ordered
197 a Then the money was given to the robber. **b** The money was put into a suitcase by the robber.
c The robber was helped to escape by an accomplice outside the bank.
d The two were caught straightaway by the police!

198

Marias Oma kommt zu Besuch! Maria und ihre Eltern sind noch hektisch bei den Vorbereitungen. Manches ist schon erledigt, einiges muss noch gemacht werden. Vervollständige die Sätze im *present perfect passive*.
Tipp: Verwende das *present perfect* von *to be* und das Partizip Perfekt.

Beispiel: The windows *have been cleaned* (clean).

a The garden ______________________ (water).

b The guestroom ______________________ (decorate) with fresh flowers.

c Dinner __________ just ______________________ (prepare).

d The carpets ______________________ (not hoover) yet.

e The car __________ already ______________________ (wash).

f Granny __________ not ______________________ (arrive) at the station yet.

g Her train ______________________ (delay)!

199

Die Kunstschule *Young Artists* organisiert eine Ausstellung mit den Bildern ihrer Schüler. Mrs Gable erzählt von den vielen Vorbereitungen, die nun aber längst abgeschlossen sind. Vervollständige die Sätze im *past perfect passive*.

Oh my god, it wasn't easy! We had to make sure everything had been done, so I went down the checklist with the students who were helping me set up:

First of all, the pictures a) ______________________ (arrange). The coffee bar b) ______________________ (prepare) for our visitors. We didn't want to charge an entrance fee, so no cashdesk c) ______________________ (set up). The wardrobe d) ______________________ (clean) by Suzy. The spotlights e) ______________________ (install), and before we let the visitors in, cakes f) ______________________ (deliver) by the bakery.

198 a has been watered; **b** has been decorated; **c** has just been prepared; **d** have not been hoovered yet; **e** has already been washed; **f** has not arrived; **g** has been delayed.
199 a) had been arranged; b) had been prepared; c) had been set up; d) had been cleaned; e) had been installed; f) had been delivered.

200

***Simple past* oder *simple present*? Setze die jeweiligen Formen von *to be* und die Partizipien richtig ein.**

a In earlier times people and products ______________________________ (transport) from one place to the other by horsecarriages.

b Today people ______________________________ (transport) by much more comfortable means of transportation.

c In earlier times overseas letters __________________ (send) by ship and took a lot of time to arrive.

d Today airmail letters __________________ (fly) from one country to another.

e In the 70s computers __________________ (use) only by a few people for work.

f Today thousands of computers __________________ (use) not only for work but also for fun by almost everybody.

201

Ihre Mutter berichtet stolz von Marias fleißiger Unterstützung. Doch was genau hat Maria zu welcher Zeit getan? Verbinde die Teilsätze miteinander.
Tipp: Achte auf die verschiedenen Signalwörter. Und: Manchmal ist es im Passiv nicht zwingend notwendig zu sagen, wer etwas getan hat! (Siehe auch Kurztest 204.)

a The shopping	i) have just been ironed by Maria.
b The windows	j) had already been washed last month.
c Dinner for the family	k) will be taken out for a walk.
d All the shirts	l) has been baked for Mum's birthday.
e A delicious cake	m) are being cleaned by her right now.
f The dog	n) was prepared by her yesterday.
g The car	o) is usually fed by Maria.
h The cat	p) is always done by Maria.

200 a were transported; **b** are transported; **c** were sent; **d** are flown; **e** were used; **f** are used
201 a+p); **b**+m); **c**+n); **d**+i); **e**+l); **f**+k); **g**+j); **h**+o)

202

Maria geht mit ihrer Klasse auf Klassenfahrt. Zuvor bespricht die Lehrerin mit ihnen die Regeln. Ergänze die Sätze mit dem Partizip Perfekt der Verben in Klammern.
Tipp: Nach den Modalverben steht *be* immer im Infinitiv.

Beispiel: All preparations *must be done* (must / do) by Thursday.

a Reservations for musicals ____________ (can / make) at the reception desk.

b The rooms ____________ (must / clean) every day.

c Breakfast ____________ (can / delivered) to your room until 11 am every day.

d Lunch ____________ (can / book) separately. The standard booking includes breakfast only.

e Soft drinks ____________ (can / purchase) at any time at the reception.

f Valuable articles ____________ (should / leave) in the hotel safe.

203

Bringe die durcheinandergeratenen Sätze in die richtige Reihenfolge.

a can / too / massages / be / booked / at the day spa

____

b the whole trip / mustn't / consumed / alcohol / during / be

____

c in a diary / written down / should / be / your memories

____

d until / at the hotel disco / can / midnight / great music / heard / be

____

202 a can be made; **b** must be cleaned; **c** can be delivered; **d** can be booked; **e** can be purchased; **f** should be left
203 a Massages can be booked at the day spa, too. **b** Alcohol mustn't be consumed during the whole trip. **c** Your memories should be written down in a diary. **d** Great music can be heard at the hotel disco until midnight.

204

Wenn es nicht ganz klar ist oder auch unwichtig, wer etwas gemacht hat, wird das Passiv ohne *by-agent* verwendet. Wenn man den Urheber der Handlung nennen kann oder sollte, verwendet man den *by-agent*. Wie würdest du bei den folgenden Sätzen verfahren?
Tipp: Einen *by-agent* kann es geben, muss es aber nicht. Meistens verwendet man ihn, wenn es wichtig ist, wer etwas getan hat oder tut.

by their owners — by consumers — by millions of people — by journalists

a New stories about the Royals are reported ______________________ almost every day.

b *Lord of the Rings* was watched ______________________.

c In Christmas time a lot of houses are decorated with lots of lights ______________________.

d In the USA a lot of plastic bags are used ______________________.

205

In welchen Sätzen sollte der hervorgehobene *by-agent* genannt werden? Unterstreiche.

a Millions of people from all countries are attracted by New York's sights every year.

b The Statue of Liberty is visited by thousands of people from many countries every single day.

c Most of the Broadway musicals are sold out by the theaters for months.

d The World Trade Center area was named "Ground Zero" by Americans after the terrorist attacks in 2001.

e The city was founded by Dutch families in the 17th century.

f The streets and buildings of New York are often used for films by film directors.

g The Empire State Building, for example, was "destroyed" by *King Kong*.

204 a by journalists; **b** by millions of people; **c** (by their owners); **d** (by consumers)
205 Der *by-agent* sollte in folgenden Sätzen stehen: a; b; e; g

206

Wenn es nicht ganz klar ist oder auch unwichtig, wer etwas gemacht hat, wird das Passiv ohne *by-agent* verwendet. Wenn man den Urheber der Handlung nennen kann oder sollte, verwendet man den *by-agent*. Formuliere die Sätze ins Passiv um.

a Levi Strauss invented the jeans.

____

b People in the USA eat a lot of fast food.

____

c Steven Spielberg produced the movie *Titanic*.

____

d J. K. Rowling wrote *Harry Potter*.

____

207

Übersetze. Entscheide, in welchen Fällen es sinnvoll ist, den *by-agent* zu setzen.
Tipp: Der *by-agent* wird verwendet, wenn es wichtig ist, wer etwas getan hat oder tut.

a SeaWorld wird jedes Jahr von vielen Menschen besucht.

____

b Es wird ein spezieller Kindertarif angeboten.

____

c In den Shops können von den Besuchern Souvenirs gekauft werden.

____

d Gerade wird eine neue Orca-Show von den Trainern entwickelt.

____

206 a Jeans were invented by Levi Strauss. **b** A lot of fast food is eaten by people in the USA. **c** The movie *Titanic* was produced by Steven Spielberg. **d** *Harry Potter* was written by J. K. Rowling.
207 a SeaWorld is visited by many people every year. **b** A special children's price is offered. **c** Souvenirs can be bought in the stores. **d** A new Orca show is being developed at the moment.

208

Oft kann man Sätze sowohl im Aktiv als auch im Passiv ausdrücken. Aktiv wird eher in der gesprochenen Sprache verwendet, Passiv im Schriftlichen. Bilde aus den Passivsätzen unten die Aktivform. Achte darauf, in der richtigen Zeit zu bleiben.
Tipp: Der *by-agent* wird zum Subjekt des Aktivsatzes!

Beispiel: A democratic state is ruled by an elected government.

An elected government rules a democratic state.

a In the 19th century, a lot of the work in factories was done by children.

____

b The Statue of Liberty was given to America by France as a sign of friendship.

____

c Many Irish were forced to emigrate to the US by a famine (= Hungersnot) in the 1840s.

____

209

Tom weiß viel über Kunst, Kultur und Technik. Manchmal gibt er ein bisschen damit an. Das Passiv klingt in diesem Fall besser, stelle daher seine Sätze zu Passivsätzen um.
Tipp: Achte auf die verschiedenen Zeiten!

a American voters	elected	J. F. Kennedy	in 1960.
b Christopher Columbus	discovered	America	in the 15th century.
c Scientists	will develop	more economical cars	soon.

208 a In the 19th century, children did a lot of the work in factories. **b** France gave the Statue of Liberty to America as a sign of friendship. **c** A famine forced many Irish to emigrate to the US in the 1840s.
209 a J. F. Kennedy was elected by American voters in 1960. **b** America was discovered by Christopher Columbus in the 15th century. **c** More economical cars will be developed by scientists soon.

210

Vervollständige die Tabelle mit der Form von *to be* in der richtigen Zeit.
Tipp: Der *by-agent* kann gesetzt werden, muss aber nicht.

	They		entertained	by some actors.
	The car		cleaned	by Tom.

211

Mrs Brown ist im Krankenhaus und hat jetzt Angst, dass es zu Hause ohne sie nicht klappt. Aber sie kann beruhigt sein, ihre Söhne kümmern sich um alles. Fülle die Lücken mit der Passivform im *present progressive*.
Tipp: Verwende das *present progressive* von *to be* und das Partizip Perfekt.

a The flowers ______________________ (water) by Glen at the moment.

b Currently the dishes ______________________ (clean) by Harry.

c And the cat ______________________ (feed) by Ian.

212

Nach ihrer Entlassung berichtet Mrs Brown ihrer Nachbarin Mrs Miller, wie sehr ihr alle geholfen haben. Schreibe ihre Sätze im *past progressive* des Passivs auf.

a The cat / take care of / by Ian.

____

b The garden / look after / by Glen.

____

c The kitchen / clean / by Harry.

____

210 They are being entertained by some actors. The car was being cleaned by Tom.
211 a are being watered; **b** are being cleaned; **c** is being fed
212 a The cat was being taken care of by Ian. **b** The garden was being looked after by Glen.
c The kitchen was being cleaned by Harry.

213

Wenn man ausdrücken möchte, was über eine Person gedacht wird oder was man von einer Person erwartet, verwendet man das *personal passive*. Bilde aus den Bruchstücken ganze Sätze.
Tipp: Im Deutschen wird das *personal passive* oft mit „man" übersetzt.

Beispiel: Tom *is said to be* (say / be) one of the best students of the school.

a Maria ______________________ (say / be) very talented at dancing.

b Today children ______________________ (expect / study) hard in order to get a good job later.

c In the 18th century, Indians ______________________ (think / be) unintelligent and uncivilized.

d This is why Indians ______________________ (expect / move) to reservations and leave the land to whites.

214

Es gibt eine Menge Vorurteile über Menschen aus bestimmten Kulturen. Auf Englisch drückt man sie mit dem *personal passive* aus. Finde eine geeignete Einleitung und bilde aus den Bruchstücken ganze Sätze.
Tipp: Verwende für die Einleitung Verben wie *say* und *think*.

a Italians / eat only pizza and spaghetti

____

b Germans / be very strict

____

c Japanese / travel a lot

____

d English people / be unable to cook.

____

213 a is said to be; **b** are expected to study; **c** were thought to be; **d** were expected to move
214 a Italians are said/thought to eat only pizza and spaghetti. **b** Germans are said/thought to be very strict. **c** Japanese are said/thought to travel a lot. **d** English people are said/thought to be unable to cook.

215

Bringe die Sätze ins Passiv. Benutze alle Formen, die du kennst: *simple present, present progressive, simple past, present perfect, past perfect* und *past progressive*. Beachte das *personal passive* und eventuelle Hilfsverben.
Tipp: Achte auf Signalwörter.

a The US ____________________ (always / think of) as the Land of Opportunity.

b A lot of problems ____________________ (create) for the American population after New York ____________________ (invade) by so many immigrants.

c Americans thought that their jobs ____________________ (take away) by all the immigrants.

d A lot of street gangs ____________________ (form) and serious fights developed between the immigrants and the American citizens of that day.

e People ____________________ (often / kill) in fights, and the police were unable to stop the violence.

f The idea for *West Side Story* ____________________ (adapt) from Shakespeare's *Romeo and Juliet* and ____________________ (base on) a real story in the US in the 1950s.

g People ____________________ (always / fascinate) by the lovestory of *Romeo and Juliet*, so this story ____________________ (integrate) into *West Side Story* by Andrew Lloyd Webber.

h After *West Side Story* ____________________ (perform) for the first time in New York, it became one of the most popular musicals ever.

i People in the audience ____________________ (force) to think about the bad situation of the immigrants and the sense of violence.

j *West Side Story* is a great example how art, entertainment and political messages ____________________ (can / integrate) successfully.

215 a has always been thought of (oder: was always thought of); **b** were created / was invaded; **c** were being taken away (oder: were taken away); **d** were formed; **e** were often killed; **f** was adapted / was based on; **g** had always been fascinated (oder: were always fascinated) / was integrated; **h** was performed; **i** were forced; **j** can be integrated.

216

Du hörst den folgenden Dialog und erzählst gleich danach einem Freund davon. Entscheide, welche Verbform in die Lücken gehört.
Tipp: Verwende hier die gleiche Zeit wie im Dialog.

Tim: Hey, they are making a movie in downtown L.A!
Carl: I know. And Julia Roberts is there too.
Tim: Who told you that?
Carl: Richard told me that she was there.
Tim: Well, I don't believe Richard, but I do want to see them making a movie while we're in the U.S.
Carl: Me too. Let's go!

a Tim says they ______________________ a movie in downtown L.A.

- made
- have made
- are making

b Carl says he already ______________________ that they are making a movie there.

- knew
- had known
- knows

c Carl also says that Julia Roberts ______________________ in downtown L.A.

- was
- has been
- is

d Tim says he ______________________ what Richard says.

- doesn't believe
- hasn't believed
- don't believe

217

Vervollständige die Tabelle unten. Pass besonders auf die hervorgehobenen Wörter auf:

a	"I am …"	
b	"We were …"	
c	"I can go today."	
d	"We will go tomorrow."	
e	"I am helping you."	

f Was ändert sich bei so einem Bericht **nicht mehr**:

- Verbzeiten (is > was)
- Zeitangaben (today > that day)
- Verbform (am > is)
- Pronomen (I > he)

216 a are making; **b** knows; **c** is; **d** doesn't believe
217 a he is; **b** they were; **c** he can go today; **d** they will go tomorrow; **e** he is helping me/us;
f Verbzeiten und Zeitangaben ändern sich nicht mehr.

218

Verändere die hervorgehobenen Pronomen so, dass die indirekte Rede stimmt.

a Greg: "**I** love **myself**." > Greg said that ______ loved ________________.

b Ann: "**I** like **you**, Greg." > Ann told Greg that ______ liked ________________.

c George: "**My** mother's name is Gina." > George said that ______ mother's name was Gina.

d Richard: "**Our** friends go to the same school **we** do." > Richard said that ____________ friends go to the same school __________ do.

e John: "Lisa, **your** mother is here." > John told Lisa that ______ was there.

f Juliet: "Romeo, where are **you**?" > Juliet asked Romeo where ______ was.

219

Im ersten Satz siehst du, was Amy gesagt hat. Schreibe darunter, wie du jemandem berichtest, was Amy gesagt hat. Fange jeden Satz mit *Amy said* ... an.
Tipp: Verwende hier das *simple past* von *to be* und die *-ing*-Form!

a Amy: "I am reading a really good book."

____

b Amy: "I am doing my homework."

____

c Amy: "Grace is coming to visit soon."

____

d Amy: "Grace and I are going to the cinema tomorrow night."

____

e Amy: "I am going to bed soon."

____

218 a he / himself; **b** she / him; **c** his; **d** their / they; **e** her; **f** he
219 a Amy said she was reading a really good book. **b** Amy said she was doing her homework.
c Amy said Grace was coming to visit soon. **d** Amy said she and Grace were going to the cinema the next night.
e Amy said she was going to bed soon.

220

Entscheide, welche Form in die Lücke gehört.
Tipp: Hier muss im *past perfect* berichtet werden, also mit *had* und *past participle*.

a "I was at school." > John said he ____________________ at school.
- had been
- was
- has been

b "I went home, too." > John said he ____________________ home, too.
- have gone
- went
- had gone

c "I had a lot of money." > John said he ____________________ a lot of money.
- had
- had had
- have had

d "It was in my rucksack." > John said that the money ____________________ in his rucksack.
- had been
- was
- has been

e "I left it in my locker." > John said he ____________________ it in his locker. (= Spint)
- left
- leaves
- had left

f "I went back to school to get it." > John said he ____________________ back to school to get it.
- went
- has gone
- had gone

221

In Spalte 1 siehst du, was Tony seiner Freundin Beth sagt. Schreib in Spalte 2 auf, wie Beth dir sagt, was Tony gesagt hat. Benutze hierbei *simple past*.
Tipp: Achte darauf, dass sich in manchen Fällen die Person ändert!

a	"I can't help you."	*Tony said that he couldn't help me.*
b	"I have no money."	Tony said that
c	"But Sue has money."	Tony said that
d	"Sue is nice."	Tony said that
e	"She can help."	Tony said that
f	"I am sure."	Tony said that

220 a had been; **b** had gone; **c** had had; **d** had been; **e** had left; **f** had gone
221 b … he had no money. **c** … Sue had money. **d** … Sue was nice. **e** … she could help. **f** … he was sure.

222

Lies den kurzen Dialog, und vervollständige die darauffolgenden Aussagen:

Tony: Hey, Sue! I just talked to Beth, and I told her that you could help us. Can you give us some money?
Sue: I **don't have** very much money right now.
Tony: Hey Beth, can you ask your parents to help you?
Beth: Well, I guess so, but my parents aren't in town at the moment. They**'re** in Europe.
Sue: But I can ask my parents!
Tony: Would you do that?
Sue: Sure! I **will ask** them when they get back home.

a Sue said that she ______________________ have very much money.

b Beth said that her parents ______________________ in Europe.

c Sue said that she ______________________ her parents for help.

223

Welche Formulierung muss in den Bericht? Kreuze an.

Tony: Hey, Sue, it is so nice that you **will ask your** parents to give Beth some money.
Beth: I **don't think** that is a good idea.
Sue: Why not? My parents **will** help **us**. They have enough money.
Beth: Sure, but that's not the point (= Darum geht's nicht.). **We need to** find another way. **I think I will give** English lessons and earn some money!

a Tony said Sue was nice because she ______________________ parents for the money.
○ wanted to ask her ○ would ask your ○ would ask her

b Beth said she ______________________ it was a good idea.
○ doesn't think ○ didn't think ○ doesn't thought

c Sue said her parents ____________ help ____________.
○ will / them ○ would / us ○ would / them

d Beth said ______________________ find another way to get money for her.
○ they will need to ○ they needed to ○ we needed to

e Beth said that ______________________ English lessons.
○ she had thought of giving ○ she thought she would give

222 a didn't have; **b** were; **c** would ask
223 a would ask her; **b** didn't think; **c** would / them; **d** they needed to; **e** she thought she would give

224

Beth erzählt Sue noch mehr von ihren Plänen, sich Geld mit Englisch-Nachhilfe zu verdienen. Sue berichtet später ihren Eltern davon.

a Beth said she ________________ (want) to give English lessons for kids, because she ________________________ (not have) any more money.

b She said that this ___________ (be) the first time that she _______________ (need) a job.

c Beth told me she ___________ (be) excited.

d I told her that I ______________________ (think) it was a great idea!

225

Wie muss die hervorgehobene Zeitangabe jeweils in der indirekten Rede lauten? Kreuze die richtige Variante an.

a Tom: "I was there **last week**." > Tom said he had been there ________________________.

- last week
- the week before
- next week

b Bob: "I will go there **next year**." > Bob said he would go there ________________________.

- in a couple of years
- next year
- the following year

c Rosa: "I will go there **tomorrow**." > Rosa said she would go there ______________________.

- the next day
- the day after tomorrow
- tomorrow

d Gina: "I'll be there **today**." > Gina said she would be there ____________________________

- tomorrow
- today
- that day

e Rich: "I'll see you **this evening**." > Rich said he would see us ________________________.

- this evening
- that evening
- the next day

f Stella: "There is a great party **tonight**!" > Stella said there was a great party ___________.

- that evening
- this night
- the next day

224 a wanted, didn't have; **b** was, needed; **c** was; **d** thought
225 a the week before; **b** the following year; **c** the next day; **d** that day; **e** that evening; **f** that evening

226

Entscheide, welche Form in die Lücke gehört.
Tipp: Bei *present perfect* muss in der indirekten Rede *past perfect* stehen, also *had* und *past participle*. Und bei *past perfect*?

a Samantha: "I have never been to Africa." > Samantha said that she …

____

b Gwen: "I have lived in this house since 1999." > Gwen said that she …

____

c Carl: "I had never seen that girl before today." > Carl said that he …

____

d John: "Before my trip to Vietnam, I had never been to Asia." > John said that he …

____

227

Vervollständige die Tabelle unten.
Tipp: Beachte die Zeiten, die Personen und die Zeitangaben!

a	"I am …"	
b	"We were …"	
c	"I can go …"	
d	"We will go …"	
e	"I will go tomorrow."	
f	"She will come here."	
g	"I am helping …"	
h	"I have had no help."	

226 a … had never been to Africa. **b** … had lived in that house since 1999. **c** … had never seen that girl before that day. **d** … had never been to Asia before his trip to Vietnam.
227 a he was … **b** they had been … **c** he could go … **d** they would go … **e** he would go the next day. **f** she would go there. **g** he was helping … **h** he had had no help.

228

Bilde aus den folgenden Verben das Gerundium durch Anhängen der *-ing*-Form und fülle dann die Lücken aus.

go   have to   iron (= bügeln)   play   eat   swim   read   pay   buy

a I like ______________________ video games.

b I hate ______________________ spinach.

c My mother hates ______________________ our clothes.

d My sister loves ______________________ new clothes.

e My father hates ______________________ bills.

f My father loves ______________________ to the lake.

g My mother loves ______________________ books.

h My sister and I don't like ______________________ go to school.

i We all love ______________________ in our pool.

229

Die *-ing*-Formen haben nicht immer die Funktion eines Verbs. Übersetze die kurzen Sätze und Satzteile und entscheide, ob es sich bei den *-ing*-Formen jeweils um ein Verb, ein Substantiv oder ein Adjektiv handelt.

a Ich bin beim Spielen. = I am ______________. ○ Verb ○ Subst. ○ Adj.

b Spielen macht Spaß. = ______________ is fun. ○ Verb ○ Subst. ○ Adj.

c die weinenden Kinder = the ______________ children ○ Verb ○ Subst. ○ Adj.

d Warum weinst du? = Why are you ______________? ○ Verb ○ Subst. ○ Adj.

e Weinen ist für Babys! = ______________ is for babies. ○ Verb ○ Subst. ○ Adj.

228 a playing; **b** eating; **c** ironing; **d** buying; **e** paying; **f** going; **g** reading; **h** having to; **i** swimming.

229 a playing, Verb; **b** Playing, Subst. **c** crying, Adj. **d** crying, Verb; **e** Crying, Subst.

230

Bilde aus den hervorgehobenen Verben das Gerundium.

My family used to live on a farm, but we live in Hamburg now. For me, a) live in a big city is a lot more fun than b) have a home in the countryside. Of course, c) play with the farm animals was fun, but now I have many new friends in Hamburg. d) Go to a big school is also better because they have many different courses. Many courses are more interesting and much more difficult than at my last school, but e) have to study harder and longer is not fun. f) Leave my old friends was difficult, but I have to say that I like my new life in the big city.

a) ______ d) ______

b) ______ e) ______

c) ______ f) ______

231

Bilde aus den folgenden Verben das Gerundium durch Anhängen der *-ing*-Form und fülle dann die Lücken aus.

study become listen ski have do hang out play be

a Skifahren macht Spaß! = ______ is fun!

b Hausaufgaben zu machen ist nicht mein Ding. = ______ homework is not my thing.

c Ihm zuzuhören ist langweilig. = ______ to him is boring.

d Der Boss zu sein ist nicht einfach. = ______ the boss is not easy.

e Spielen mit Freunden ist, was ich am meisten vermisse. = ______ with friends is what I miss the most.

f Schauspieler zu werden war immer mein Traum. = ______ an actor has always been my dream.

g Herumhängen mit Freunden ist manchmal langweilig. = ______ with friends is sometimes boring.

h Viel Geld haben ist nicht, was ich will. = ______ a lot of money is not what I want.

i Lernen macht keinen Spaß! = ______ isn't fun!

230 a) living; b) having; c) playing; d) Going; e) having to; f) Leaving
231 a Skiing; **b** Doing; **c** Listening; **d** Being; **e** Playing; **f** Becoming; **g** Hanging out; **h** Having; **i** Studying

232

Bilde aus den hervorgehobenen Verben das Gerundium.

My family and I went to the U.S. on holiday last summer. We got an upgrade (= einen Platz in einer höheren Klasse bekommen) on the way to New York and enjoyed a) **fly** in Business Class very much. We all liked b) **have** a choice of films and, of course, we liked c) **get** to sleep on a flat bed! It was not really that important, but it made us feel like VIPs – at least for a day!

Once we got to New York, though, we had a very different experience. We absolutely hated d) **go** through "Immigration" (= Passkontrolle) and "Customs" (= Zoll). The people were very rude to us, and we didn't like e) **have to** answer all those strange questions. I mean, who would like f) **be** asked whether you were a member of a terrorist organization?

Anyway, after we finally got to the hotel, we decided to forget that bad experience and to enjoy the rest of our trip. Unfortunately, that didn't last long. There were no bathrooms in our rooms, and my mother didn't like g) **share** the bathroom with complete strangers on our floor. She told the manager, and he gave us one large family suite. That was very nice!

That evening we went "out on the town" and really enjoyed h) **see** the American "way of life". Even though it had started off a bit negative, the rest of our trip to the U.S. went very well. I guess, that it's true that America is the "land of extremes", just like they say.

a) ____________________ e) ____________________

b) ____________________ f) ____________________

c) ____________________ g) ____________________

d) ____________________ h) ____________________

233

Vervollständige die folgenden Sätze mit der richtigen Verbform.
Tipp: Wenn du unsicher bist, kann dir ein Blick in den Kurztest 228 helfen!

a I enjoy (to travel) to foreign countries. ____________________

b I want (to see) more foreign countries. ____________________

c I like (to eat) food from foreign countries. ____________________

d Would you like (to visit) my grandparents? ____________________

e Do you like (to visit) your grandparents? ____________________

232 a) flying; b) having; c) getting; d) going; e) having to; f) being; g) sharing; h) seeing
233 **a** travelling; **b** to see; **c** eating, to eat; **d** to visit; **e** visiting

234

Schreibe einen kleinen Dialog zwischen Amy und James mit den vorgegebenen Wörtern. Achte besonders auf die Kombination der hervorgehobenen Satzteile.

a Amy: **would mind** / you / **help** / me / with my homework?
James: no / of course / I / **would mind** / not / **help** / you.

b James: I / **enjoyed** / **listen** / to Mr Smith's lecture / last week.
Amy: I / **didn't like** / **listen** / to it. I / **wanted** / **hear** / something more interesting.

235

Entscheide, ob hier von *go* das Gerundium oder der Infinitiv gebildet werden muss. Manchmal ist auch beides möglich.

a	I like (go)…		
b	I enjoy (go)…		
c	I stopped (go)…		
d	I want (go)…		
e	I don't mind (go)…		
f	I tried (go)…		
g	I hate (go)…		
h	I feel like (go)…		

234 a Amy: Would you mind helping me with my homework? James: No, of course, I wouldn't mind helping you.
b James: I enjoyed listening to Mr Smith's lecture last week. Amy: I didn't like listening to it. I wanted to hear something more interesting.
235 a going/to go; **b** going/–; **c** going/to go; **d** –/to go; **e** going/–; **f** going/to go; **g** going/to go; **h** going/–.

236

Entscheide, welche der beiden Verbformen jeweils passt. Kreuze an und fülle dann die Lücken damit aus.

a I'm **tired** of ______________________ talk to Jim! He just won't listen.

- try
- trying to
- trying

b I was **surprised** ______________________ him at the party.

- see
- to see
- seeing

c We were **worried** about ______________________ Jim angry.

- to make
- make
- making

d We were **interested** in ______________________ a better way to confront him.

- finding
- to find
- to finding

e We were **lucky** ______________________ Jane.

- meeting
- to meet
- meet

f She is so **good** at ______________________ people.

- to talking to
- talk
- talking to

g We are **glad** ______________________ her on our side.

- have
- having
- to have

237

Entscheide, welche Form das Verb in Klammern haben muss.

a I'm looking forward **to** ______________________ (see) you soon.

b It was wrong **to** ______________________ (speak) to him.

c We need **to** ______________________ (talk) to him as soon as possible.

d We are used **to** ______________________ (listen) to people.

e I was shocked **to** ______________________ (hear) about his problems.

f We are ready **to** ______________________ (go) home.

g I can't get used **to** ______________________ (listen) to that kind of music.

236 a trying to; **b** to see; **c** making; **d** finding; **e** to meet; **f** talking to; **g** to have
237 a seeing; **b** speak; **c** talk; **d** listening; **e** hear; **f** go; **g** listening

238

Schreibe die richtige Form des Verbs in Klammern in die Lücken.

a They were talking **about** __________ (help) us with our school project.

b I'm thinking **of** __________ (study) biology when I go to university.

c I apologize **for** __________ (be) late. We were stuck in traffic.

d Don't worry **about** __________ (go) to the new school. You'll find new friends.

e I dream **of** __________ (become) an astronaut one day.

239

Bilde aus den hervorgehobenen Verben die richtige Form. Unterstreiche anschließend, in welchen Fällen die *-ing*-Form etwas über das Verhalten anderer aussagt.
Tipp: Um das Verhalten einer anderen Person zu beschreiben, verwendet man ein Objekt + die *-ing*-Form des Verbs.

I have started a) **play** football after school. We have a new coach named Mr Jones, who is Australian, and who is very strict. He makes us run a lot to build up our muscles. Many kids on the team don't like Mr Jones b) **scream** at us. It's almost like he thinks we are in the army or something! Actually, Mr Jones was in the Australian Army when he was a young man, and I like him c) **tell** us stories about his army days. Some of the kids hate him d) **talk** about things like that, but every day I look forward to him e) **share** his memories about those times. It reminds me a little bit about the stories my grandfather told me when I was younger, but – of course – that was a very different time!

Anyway, many of the parents also worry about their kids f) **not have** enough time to do their homework. But we spend time g) **practise**, so we can get better. And Mr Jones has helped us h) **win** many matches. I like playing football, and I enjoy having Mr Jones as our coach.

a __________ **e** __________

b __________ **f** __________

c __________ **g** __________

d __________ **h** __________

239 a playing; **b** screaming; **c** telling; **d** talking; **e** sharing; **f** not having; **g** practising; **h** win/to win
238 a helping; **b** studying; **c** being; **d** going; **e** becoming

240

Alle diese Sätze kannst du im Englischen viel eleganter ohne *that* ausdrücken, und zwar mit der Konstruktion Verb + Objekt + *to*-Infinitiv. Formuliere entsprechend um.

Beispiel: I think that you should do this exercise. I want *you to do this exercise*.

a I think that Peter will win the race.

I expect ______________________________.

b I think that Mr Kenneth should get the job.

I want ______________________________.

c I hope that you will study more for your tests.

I'd like ______________________________.

d I think that the team has to fight harder.

I want ______________________________.

241

Bilde Sätze mit der Verb + Objekt + *to*-Infinitiv-Konstruktion.

a the student / the teacher / do the homework / wanted

____

b the wild dogs / the ranger / bite / expected

____

c the boys / the angry neighbour / not play soccer in his yard / told

____

d the lawyer / the client / not say anything / advised

____

240 a … Peter to win the race. **b** … Mr Kenneth to get the job. **c** … you to study more for your tests. **d** … the team to fight harder.

241 a The teacher wanted the student to do the homework. **b** The ranger expected the wild dogs to bite. **c** The angry neighbour told the boys not to play soccer in his yard. **d** The lawyer advised the client not to say anything.

242

Im Englischen darf nach *want* und *would like* kein *that* stehen! Es muss ersetzt werden durch eine Verb + Objekt + *to*-Infinitiv-Konstruktion. Die Sätze sind noch alle falsch. Kannst du sie verbessern?

a I want that you wear different clothes.

---

b Mr Timothy would like that you should come and see him.

---

c Do you want that I call him?

---

d I don't want that anybody gets injured.

243

Übersetze die Aussagen der Mutter ins Englische. Wähle hierfür geeignete Verben aus und benutze die Verb + Objekt + *to*-Infinitiv-Konstruktion.

advise – prefer – ask – expect

a Ich bevorzuge es, wenn Stefan seine Klamotten wäscht.

---

b Ich bitte Timo, das Essen zu kochen.

---

c Ich rate Fred, dass er sie dieses Mal anruft.

---

d Ich erwarte, dass ihr alle zusammenarbeitet.

---

242 a I want you to wear different clothes. **b** Mr Timothy would like you to come and see him. **c** Do you want me to call him? **d** I don't want anybody to get injured.

243 a I prefer Stefan to wash his clothes. **b** I ask Timo to cook the food. **c** I advise Fred to call her this time. **d** I expect you all/all of you to work together.

244

Peter ist ganz schön anspruchsvoll. Setze den Infinitiv des Passivs mit *to* in die Lücken ein.
Tipp: Der Infinitiv des Passivs bildet sich hier mit *(not) + to be + past participle*.

Beispiel: Peter expects (drive) *to be driven* to the studios.

a Peter hopes (know) ______________________ one day by a lot of people.

b He doesn't expect (invite) ______________________ to a lot of parties though.

c He seems (admire) ______________________ by a lot of girls already.

d He would like (employ) ______________________ by a big company.

e Peter also hopes (take out) ______________________ to dinner many times.

f He expects his book (publish) ______________________ by the end of next year.

245

Setze folgende Sätze ins Passiv. Verwende dabei den Infinitiv des Passivs mit *to*.

a "We expect you to show us the Grand Canyon."

The people expect ______________________ the Grand Canyon.

b Mrs Clark hopes that you ask her before booking the flight.

Mrs Clark hopes ______________________ before the flight is booked.

c You would like to take the tourists to the park. The tourists would like that very much.

The tourists would like ______________________ to the park.

d Megan expects you to tell her interesting facts.

Megan expects ______________________ interesting facts.

244 a to be known; **b** to be invited; **c** to be admired; **d** to be employed; **e** to be taken out; **f** to be published
245 a to be shown; **b** to be asked; **c** to be taken; **d** to be told

246

Nach Modalverben steht der Infinitiv ohne *to* - auch im Passiv. Setze die richtige Form ein.
Tipp: Denke dran, dass auch hier das *past participle* verwendet wird!

a The car can ________________________ (find) in the garage.

b The book might ________________________ (sell) in Selma's bookstore.

c The man could ________________________ (ask) about the accident.

d The house can't ________________________ (renovate) anymore.

e Mr Trevor may ________________________ (not elect) mayor.

f Ancient tools can ________________________ (discover) here.

247

Setze ins Passiv. Verwende dabei den Infinitiv ohne *to*.

a Theo may walk the dogs later on.

The dogs may ____________________ by Theo later on.

b My father might not buy another car.

Another car might ________________________ by my father.

c My professor can't accompany the group.

The group ____.

d My uncle might repair my computer.

My computer ____.

e My neighbour could water the plants in my garden.

____.

f The policeman will investigate the murder.

____.

246 a be found; **b** be sold; **c** be asked; **d** be renovated; **e** not be elected; **f** be discovered
247 a be walked; **b** not be bought; **c** can't be accompanied by my professor. **d** might be repaired by my uncle.
e The plants in my garden could be watered by my neighbour. **f** The murder will be investigated by the policeman.

248

Um zu sagen, was in der Vergangenheit hätte geschehen sollen, benutzt man den Infinitiv Perfekt. Setze die richtige Form in die folgenden Sätze ein.
Tipp: Der Infinitiv Perfekt wird mit Modalverb + *(not)* + *have* + *past particple* gebildet.

a You should ______________________ (buy) the car.

b The Parkers might ______________________ (leave) by now.

c You shouldn't ______________________ (do) this.

d Terry ______________________ (could / give) me the money.

e Jack ______________________ (must / have) the key.

249

Aus diesen Satzteilen zum Beispiel! Kannst du sie sinnvoll zusammenfügen?

a her mum / have / Tina / told / should / the bad mark / about

____

b could / sent / the referee / him / have / off the field

____

c must / the deer / been / hurt / have / badly / in the accident

____

250

Übersetze.

a Du hättest nicht dort sein sollen.

____

b Er muss betrunken gewesen sein.

____

248 a have bought; **b** have left; **c** have done; **d** could have given; **e** must have had
249 a Tina should have told her mum about the bad mark. **b** The referee could have sent him off the field. **c** The deer must have been hurt badly in the accident.
250 a You shouldn't have been there. **b** He must have been drunk.

251

Setze die Fragewörter sinngemäß ein.

when – who – whether – why – how much – what – where

a I have no idea ____________________ to ask for some money. My parents maybe?

b The student asked ____________________ to use for the kite. Paper or cardboard?

c I asked the officer ____________________ to wait. I didn't want to be in his way.

d I wasn't sure ____________________ flour to put in the cake. So I looked at the recipe.

e He just doesn't know ____________________ to stop. He can be so annoying.

f We don't know ____________________ to go to Vegas or New York. They are both such great cities!

g I wonder ____________________ he did this. There was no reason for it.

252

Die folgenden Sätze kann man kürzer schreiben. Schaffst du dies mithilfe einer Infinitivkonstruktion?

a We really didn't know what we could do.

____

b We weren't sure if we should bring a sleeping bag or not.

____

c The woman didn't remember who she should give the paperwork to.

____

d The children had no idea where they could get help.

____

251 a who; **b** what; **c** where; **d** how much; **e** when; **f** whether; **g** why
252 a We really didn't know what to do. **b** We weren't sure whether to bring a sleeping bag or not. **c** The woman didn't remember who to give the paperwork to. **d** The children had no idea where to get help.

253

In einer Bastelsendung sind viele Fragen zusammengekommen. Der Moderator gibt diese nun an den Experten weiter. Verwende die Infinitivkonstruktion!

a Woman: "Where can I find paper like that?"

This woman wants to know ______________________________.

b Man: "How many nails do I have to buy?"

The man over here would like to know ______________________________.

c A girl: "Should I use green or blue cardboard?"

This girl wants to know ______________________________.

d A boy: "What should I wear to protect my fingers?"

This boy wonders ______________________________.

254

Ergänze den Text. Setze Infinitivkonstruktionen ein, wo möglich.
Verwende *could* oder *should*, wo es nicht möglich ist.

We didn't know though where a) ______________ (get) tickets for the soccer match. So we went b) ________________ (look) for the ticket counter. A ton of people were waiting in front of the counter! They were all wondering how they c) ______________________________ (enter) quickly because the game was about to begin! When we finally got our tickets, we wondered where we d) ______________________ (find) something to eat. We expected a snackbar e) ______________ (be) around the corner. But there wasn't one. Instead, we saw the most famous player on our team! He wanted us f) ________________ (help) him. He told us what we g) ______________________ (do) and gave us his autograph quickly because the game was about to start. What a great day!

253 a where to find paper like that. **b** how many nails to buy. **c** whether to use green or blue cardboard. **d** what to wear to protect his fingers.

254 a) to get; b) to look; c) could enter; d) could find; e) to be; f) to help; g) could/should do

255

Ordne die Superlative den Sätzen sinngemäß zu.

the fastest person – the oldest man – the first man – the only one – the youngest player

a Neil Armstrong was ______________________ to walk on the moon.

b Boris Becker was ______________________ to win Wimbledon. He was 17.

c Buster Martin was ______________________ to run a marathon. He was 101 years old.

d Kevin Murphy wasn't ______________________ to swim through the Channel.

e ______________________ to run the 100 m is currently Usain Bolt from Jamaica.

256

Bilde aus den hervorgehobenen Satzteilen Sätze mit der Infinitivkonstruktion.

a Brit was very intelligent. the first / know answers

She was always ______________________.

b Emily is very sporty. the only one in family / jump 4.35 m

She is ______________________.

c My favourite teacher is Mr Brown. the best teacher / explain English grammar

He ______________________.

d They had a pool party, and I was so embarrassed. the only one / forget my swimsuit

I ______________________.

e Sorry I called you so late. the easiest way / get home

This ______________________.

255 **a** the first man; **b** the youngest player; **c** the oldest man; **d** the only one; **e** The fastest person
256 **a** the first to know the answers. **b** the only one in the family to jump 4.35 m. **c** is the best teacher to explain English grammar. **d** was the only one to forget my swimsuit. **e** was the easiest way to get home.

257

Die Bedeutung der folgenden Verben verändert sich, je nachdem, ob sie mit dem Gerundium oder dem Infinitiv verbunden werden. Ordne die Formen den richtigen Bedeutungen zu.

to go on cleaning – to go on to clean – to stop cleaning – to stop to clean –

to remember to clean – to remember cleaning

daran denken, das Auto zu putzen	sich daran erinnern, das Auto geputzt zu haben
a	**b**

als nächstes das Auto putzen	mit dem Autoputzen weitermachen
c	**d**

mit etwas anderem aufhören, um das Auto zu putzen	mit dem Autoputzen aufhören
e	**f**

258

Kreise – je nach Bedeutung – das Gerundium oder den Infinitiv ein.

a I stopped to eat / eating the sandwich. (… hörte auf, das Sandwich zu essen)

b I stopped to drop off / dropping off a letter. (… hielt an, um einen Brief einzuwerfen)

c I remember to ring / ringing the door bell. (Ich erinnere mich daran, dass …)

d Please remember to take / taking out the garbage. (Denke daran, den …)

e I'll go on to read / reading the book. (Ich werde … weiterlesen.)

f I went on to read / reading another book. (Danach las ich ein anderes Buch.)

257 a to remember to clean the car; **b** to remember cleaning the car; **c** to go on to clean the car; **d** to go on cleaning the car; **e** to stop to clean the car; **f** to stop cleaning the car

258 a eating; **b** to drop off; **c** ringing; **d** to take; **e** reading; **f** to read

259

Auch die Bedeutung der hier folgenden Verben verändert sich, je nachdem, ob sie mit dem Gerundium oder dem Infinitiv stehen. Ordne die Formen den richtigen Bedeutungen zu.

that means painting – to mean to paint – to try painting – to try to paint

not to forget painting – not to forget to paint

das bedeutet, dass gestrichen werden muss	zu streichen beabsichtigen
a	**b**

das Streichen nicht vergessen	nicht vergessen zu streichen
c	**d**

das Streichen ausprobieren	sich bemühen zu streichen
e	**f**

260

Kreise – je nach Bedeutung – das Gerundium oder den Infinitiv ein.

a I won't forget to make / making the cake. (… werde nicht vergessen, den Kuchen zu machen)

b I won't forget to make / making my first cake. (… werde nicht vergessen, wie ich …)

c I will try to ride / riding the bike. (… es mit dem Fahrradfahren versuchen.)

d I will try to ride / riding the bike. (… mich bemühen, mit dem Fahrrad zu fahren.)

e I mean to do / doing the homework again. (Ich beabsichtige, die Hausaufgaben …)

f That means to do / doing the homework again. (Das bedeutet, dass …)

259 a that means painting; **b** to mean to paint; **c** not to forget painting; **d** not to forget to paint; **e** to try painting; **f** to try to paint

260 a to make; **b** making; **c** riding; **d** to ride; **e** to do; **f** doing

261

Nach Verben der Sinneswahrnehmung kann der Infinitiv, aber auch das Partizip Präsens stehen. Entscheide dich für eine Form.
Tipp: Der Infinitiv ohne *to* folgt, wenn die Handlung vollständig wahrgenommen wurde und abgeschlossen ist. Das Partizip Präsens *(-ing)* folgt, wenn die Handlung vorübergehend war bzw. noch im Verlauf und nicht klar abgeschlossen.

a For a while I heard the baby **cry / crying**.

b I heard a car **stop / stopping** in front of my house.

c Suddenly I felt a spider **crawl / crawling** on my leg.

d Mary saw the thief **disappear / disappearing**.

e Leon noticed something **burn / burning**.

f I noticed your brother **work / working** in the garage.

g I heard him **drill / drilling**. (drill = bohren)

h I saw him **go / going** inside at 10 pm.

262

Nach Verben der Sinneswahrnehmung kann der Infinitiv aber auch das Partizip Präsens stehen. Entscheide dich für eine Form.
Tipp: Der Infinitiv ohne *to* wird verwendet, wenn mehrere Handlungen aufeinanderfolgten.

a I saw the thief **come / coming** out of the bank and **disappear / disappearing** in the dark.

b I felt a spider **bite / biting** me and **crawl / crawling** down my leg.

c I heard something **fall / falling** on the floor.

d I noticed a girl **come / coming** into the store and **steal / stealing** a bottle of perfume.

e I heard a bell **ring / ringing** far away.

f When I came in the room, I saw my cat **catch / catching** a mouse!

g I watched my neighbour **get / getting** in his car and **drive /driving** away.

h I saw the girl **walk / walking** to school.

261 a crying; **b** stop; **c** crawling; **d** disappear; **e** burning; **f** working; **g** drilling; **h** go
262 a come, disappear; **b** bite, crawl; **c** falling; **d** come, steal; **e** ringing; **f** catch; **g** get, drive; **h** walking

263

Das war etwas zu viel Grammatik für Sven. Er hat in jedem Satz einen Fehler gemacht. Finde ihn und schreibe den Satz richtig auf.

a Gerald noticed the girl to eat.

____

b I saw the dog running after the cat and then disappear.

____

c I heard the bottle falling and hit the floor.

____

d I saw the girl putting a book in her bag and walk out of the shop without paying.

____

264

Beende die Sätze mit der richtigen Form: Infinitiv oder Partizip Präsens.

a Als ich die Schule verließ bemerkte ich, wie jemand mir folgte.

When I left the school, I noticed ______________________________.

b Ich sah, wie mein Lehrer die Kreide (= chalk) festhielt und dann auf den Tisch legte.

I saw my teacher ______________________________.

c Ich hörte, wie meine Mutter mit meinem Vater sprach.

I heard my mother ______________________________.

d Ich hörte, wie er zuerst die Autotür öffnete und dann zuschlug.

I heard him first ______________________________.

e Plötzlich hörte ich, wie jemand immer wieder meinen Namen rief.

Suddenly I heard somebody ______________________________.

263 a Gerald noticed the girl eating. **b** I saw the dog run after the cat and then … **c** I heard the bottle fall and …
d I saw the girl put a book …
264 a … somebody following me. **b** … hold the chalk and then put it on the desk. **c** … talking to my father.
d … open the car door and then slam it/shut it. **e** … calling my name again and again.

265

Bei Personen kann man verschiedene Merkmale beschreiben. Ordne die Oberbegriffe den Vokabeln zu.

build – height – face – age – clothing – hair – eyes

a	tall, short, of medium height, huge
b	huge, fat, well-built, slim, skinny, thin
c	casual, messy, tidy, clean, dirty, big, small, checkered, striped, spotted
d	blue, green, bluish-green, brown, grey, bright, sleepy
e	long, short, curly, straight, bald, fair, spiky, a ponytail, bangs (AE = Pony), fringe (BE), highlights
f	round, square, oval, freckled (freckled = sommersprossig), wrinkled, suntanned, pale, scarred (= vernarbt)
g	old, young, elderly, middle-aged, teenager, baby, child, in 20s, 30s

266

Personen kann man auch nach ihrem Verhalten beschreiben. Wähle das passende Wort.

polite – bossy (= herrisch) – arrogant – cheeky – clever – old-fashioned – curious

a When you think you are better than another person, you are ______________________.

b When you tell people what to do, you are ______________________.

c When you are rude and disrespectful, you are ______________________.

d When you are very intelligent, you are ______________________.

e When you want to know everything, you are ______________________.

f When you behave in a way that isn't modern, you are ______________________.

g When you display good manners, you are ______________________.

265 a height; **b** build; **c** clothing; **d** eyes; **e** hair; **f** face; **g** age

266 a arrogant; **b** bossy; **c** cheeky; **d** clever; **e** curious; **f** old-fashioned; **g** polite

267

Beschreibe die Personen auf Englisch. Benutze die Wörter aus den Kurztests 265 und 266.

a Herr Miller ist klein, dünn, hat ein eckiges Gesicht und blau-grüne Augen.

b Frau Summer ist höflich und hat lange Haare mit Strähnchen. Sie ist neugierig!

c Cedric ist groß und in den 30ern. Er hat Sommersprossen und ist sehr intelligent.

d Herr Grohe ist mittelgroß und glatzköpfig. Er ist ein älterer Mann und altmodisch.

268

Wenn du noch genauer sein willst, kannst du zusätzlich auch Adverbien benutzen. Wähle die passenden Adverbien aus und beschreibe die Personen noch treffender auf Englisch!

extremely – quite – always – very – absolutely – often – totally

a Simon ist ein extrem großer Junge mit sehr blasser Haut.

b Herr Rogers ist oft herrisch. Aber er trägt immer gestreifte Hosen!

c Sabrina hat ganz schwarzes Haar und sie ist ziemlich arrogant.

So könnten deine Lösungen aussehen:

267 a Mr Miller is small and thin and has got a square face and bluish-green eyes. **b** Mrs Summer is polite and has got long hair with highlights. She is curious! **c** Cedric is tall and in his 30s. He has freckles and is clever. **d** Mr Grohe is of medium height and bald. He is an elderly man and old-fashioned.

268 a Simon is an extremely tall boy with very pale skin. **b** Mr Rogers is often bossy. But he always wears striped trousers! **c** Sabrina has got totally black hair and she is quite arrogant.

269

**Bei Dingen kann man ebenso verschiedene Merkmale beschreiben.
Ordne die Oberbegriffe den Vokabeln zu.**

shape – size – colour/pattern – material – condition

a	new, old, used, fresh, unopened, shiny
b	square, round, oval, triangular, cube-shaped
c	grey, green, pink, red, blue, black, white, orange, yellow, spotted, striped, checkered
d	huge, small, tiny, big, large, medium
e	metal, wood, plastic, cloth, glass, paper, stone, leather, cardboard

270

Beschreibe die folgenden Dinge auf Englisch. Benutze Wörter aus Kurztest 269.

a Die Armbanduhr ist glänzend. Sie ist aus Glas und Metall und oval.

b Der Stuhl ist würfelförmig und besteht aus Holz und Stoff.

c Das Buch ist quadratisch. Es hat einen orangefarbenen Einband.

d Das Spielbrett ist dreieckig. Es besteht aus Pappe und ist neu.

e Der Tisch ist rund und aus Stein. Der Stein ist gelb gepunktet.

269 a condition; **b** shape; **c** colour/pattern; **d** size; **e** material

270 So könnten deine Lösungen aussehen: **a** The watch is shiny. It is made of glass and metal and it is oval. **b** The chair is cube-shaped and is made of wood and cloth. **c** The book is square-shaped. It has got an orange cover. **d** The gameboard is triangular. It is made of cardboard and is new. **e** The table is round and made of stone. The stone has yellow spots.

271

Paarwörter beschreiben Dinge, die paarweise angeordnet sind und eine Einheit darstellen, zum Beispiel beim Einkaufen (*a pair of shoes*). Wenn du mehrere davon benennen willst, sind es *pairs of*. Ergänze die Lücken.

a four ____________ jeans

b three ____________ bottles

c six ____________ cherries

d five ____________ gloves

e nine ____________ cans

f one ____________ pants

g a ____________ scissors

h eleven ____________ glasses

i three ____________ sunflowers

j eight ____________ goggles

k one ____________ bread rolls

l ten ____________ shorts

272

Bei der Angleichung von Paarwörtern muss man darauf achten, welche Anzahl vor dem Nomen steht. Steht keine Anzahl davor, steht es im Plural. Setze nun *was* oder *were* richtig ein.

Beispiel: Glasses *were* … A pair of glasses *was* …

a A pair of scissors ____________ in the sink yesterday.

b Scissors ____________ also on the table.

c Shoes ____________ under the desk.

d A pair of shoes ____________ on the desk.

e Shorts ____________ all over the armchair.

f A pair of shorts ____________ all dirty.

g Socks ____________ under the bed.

h Three pairs of socks ____________ hanging from the lamp.

i Gloves ____________ on the desk.

j And one pair of gloves ____________ on the couch.

271 a – e pairs of; **f** pair of; **g** pair of; **h – j** pairs of; **k** pair of; **l** pairs of

272 a was; **b** were; **c** were; **d** was; **e** were; **f** was; **g** were; **h** were; **i** were; **j** was

273

**Kollektivnomen fassen Individuen zu einer Gruppe zusammen.
Ordne die Gruppen- oder Kollektivwörter ihren Mitgliedern zu.**

army – family – band – team – herd – crew – audience

a a child and a mother are members of a ____________

b a zebra is part of a ____________

c a sailor is part of a ____________

d a listener is part of an ____________

e a soldier is part of an ____________

f a drummer is part of a ____________

g a soccer player is part of a ____________

274

Wenn man mit dem Kollektivwort die Gruppe meint, stehen Verb und Pronomen im Singular. Meint man hingegen die einzelnen Mitglieder als Individuen, stehen Verb und Pronomen im Plural. Kannst du die Formen entsprechend einsetzen?

gets – get – its – their

a The team (Einheit) ____________ into ____________ bus.

b The team (einzelne Spieler) ____________ into ____________ cars.

puts – put – its – their

c The band (einzelne Mitglieder) ____________ away ____________ instruments.

d The band (Einheit) ____________ away ____________ instruments.

who – who – wants – want

e This is the group of tourists (Einheit) ____________ ____________ to go to Egypt.

f This is the group of tourists (einzelne Mitglieder) ____________ ____________ to go to Egypt.

273 a family; **b** herd; **c** crew; **d** audience; **e** army; **f** band; **g** team

274 a gets; its; **b** get; their; **c** put; their; **d** puts; its; **e** who; wants; **f** who; want

275

Setze die richtige(n) Form(en) des jeweiligen Worts in die Lücken ein.

Beispiel: happiness *happy* *Glück / glücklich*

a freedom ______ ______

b truth ______ ______

c death ______ ______

d fame ______ ______

e industry ______ ______

f beauty ______ ______

276

Handelt es sich um ein Nomen oder um ein Adjektiv? Ordne die Endungen richtig ein.

-less -ion -ty -ive -ment -ance -ness -ous -ence -nt

	-ful

277

Bilde aus folgenden Wörtern das Nomen und/oder das Adjektiv.

a danger ______ (Adjektiv)

b to differ ______ (Adjektiv, Nomen)

c to perform ______ (Nomen)

d to exclude ______ (Adjektiv)

e to construct ______ (Nomen)

275 a free – Freiheit / frei; **b** true – Wahrheit / wahr; **c** dead – Tod / tot; **d** famous – Berühmtheit / berühmt;
e industrial – Industrie / industriell; **f** beautiful – Schönheit / schön
276 nouns: -ion; -ty; -ment; -ance; -ness; adjectives: -less; -ive; -ous; -nt
277 a dangerous; **b** different / difference **c** performance; **d** exclusive; **e** construction

278

Ergänze die Tabelle.

beautiful	a beauty
different	b
famous	c
happy	d
healthy	e
horrible	f
violent	g
young	h

i	danger
j	industry
k	nature
l	pain
m	region
n	silence
o	south
p	truth

279

Setze die richtige(n) Form(en) des jeweiligen Worts in die Lücken ein.

a (youth) When he was ______________________, he had a lot of friends.

b (truth) It is ______________________. He always tells the ______________________.

c (famous) ______________________ is necessary for______________________ people.

d (happy) ______________________ doesn't come with money.

If you want to be ______________________, do something nice for other people!

e (silence) I love the Christmas song "______________________ Night" so much!

f (different) He has been so ______________________ lately.

g (industry) The company built its headquarters in the ______________________ area.

h (horrible) It wasn't a comedy. It was a ______________________ movie.

278 b difference; **c** fame; **d** happiness; **e** health; **f** horror; **g** violence; **h** youth; **i** dangerous; **j** industrial; **k** natural; **l** painful/-less; **m** regional; **n** silent; **o** southern; **p** true

279 a young; **b** true; truth; **c** Fame; famous; **d** Happiness; happy; **e** Silent; **f** different; **g** industrial; **h** horror

280

Ergänze die Tabelle.

to attract	a *attractive*	b *attraction*
c	dead	d
e	f	hope
to live	g	h
i	safe	j
k	real	l
to fly	m	n
o	p	surprise

281

Setze die richtige(n) Form(en) des jeweiligen Worts in die Lücken ein.

a **(attract)** She was an ____________________ girl.

b **(dead)** Mr Miller __________ yesterday.

c **(hope)** She is a ________________ case. I have no __________ at all.

d **(live)** Isn't __________ beautiful? She was found ____________!

e **(safe)** The money which he had ____________ was in the __________.

f **(real)** This is the __________ life. Don't you ________________ that?

g **(fly)** The ______________ to the moon happened. The ______________ saucer didn't.

h **(surprise)** I was ____________________ by his __________________!

280 c to die; **d** death; **e** to hope; **f** hopeful / -less; **g** alive / living; **h** life; **i** to save; **j** safety / the safe;
k to realize; **l** reality; **m** flying; **n** flight; **o** to surprise; **p** surprising / surprised
281 a attractive; **b** died; **c** hopeless; hope; **d** life; alive; **e** saved; safe; **f** real; realize; **g** flight; flying;
h surprised; surprise

282

Diese Wörter werden im Amerikanischen anders geschrieben. Weißt du wie?

a programme ______

b neighbour ______

c travelling ______

d to practise ______

e centre ______

f flavour ______

g theatre ______

h to analyse ______

i counsellor ______

j storey (= Stockwerk) ______

283

Im amerikanischen Englisch gibt es für folgende Wörter ein komplett anderes Wort. Wie lautet es jeweils?

a city centre ______

b on holiday ______

c shop ______

d chips ______

e flat ______

f underground ______

g mobile phone ______

h rubbish ______

i sweets ______

j autumn ______

284

Was Menschen sagen, lässt Rückschlüsse auf ihre Herkunft zu. Erkennst du, ob die Sprecher aus Großbritannien (BE) oder den USA (AE) kommen?

a Do you have a house? ______

b He hasn't got a car. ______

c He has gotten much better. ______

d Honey, are you home? ______

e She has got nice long hair. ______

f Dear, could you help me ? ______

g I just lost my keys! ______

h … so I go "You can do it!" ______

i That was real bad! ______

j I have already seen the film. ______

282 a program; **b** neighbor; **c** traveling; **d** to practice; **e** center; **f** flavor; **g** theater; **h** to analyze; **i** counselor; **j** story
283 a downtown; **b** on vacation; **c** store; **d** fries; **e** apartment; **f** subway; **g** cell phone; **h** garbage, trash; **i** candy; **j** fall
284 a AE; **b** BE; **c** AE; **d** AE; **e** BE; **f** BE; **g** AE; **h** AE; **i** AE; **j** BE

285

Worin liegt der Unterschied? „Übersetze" ins Britische.

a I like the color green. ______________________.

b He was traveling with her. ______________________.

c I need five meters of cloth. ______________________.

d He realized it quickly. ______________________.

e He changed the tire. ______________________.

286

Weißt du, wie es heißt? „Übersetze" ins Britische.

a I am in grade eight. ______________________.

b He took the elevator. ______________________.

c He used the sidewalk. ______________________.

d I went outside at recess. ______________________.

e I went to the bathroom. ______________________.

287

Formuliere folgende Sätze in britischem Englisch. Tipp: Beachte die Grammatik.

a He is going on vacation next fall.

____

b He doesn't have a mobile.

____

c I already saw the candy, honey.

____

285 a colour; **b** travelling; **c** metres; **d** realised; **e** tyre

286 a I am in year/class eight. **b** He took the lift. **c** He used the pavement. **d** During the break I went outside. **e** I went to the toilet.

287 a He is going on holiday(s) next autumn. **b** He hasn't got a cell phone. **c** I have already seen the sweets, dear.

288

Lies den kurzen Dialog und trage unten ein, was die hervorgehobenen Wörter jeweils auf Deutsch heißen. Tipp: Jilian spricht BE und Tony AE!

Jillian: Hi, Tony. How are you?
Tony: Well, okay I guess.
Jillian: That doesn't sound very good.
Tony: Well, you're right. I sat in something on the **subway**, and my **pants** are all dirty.
Jillian: Your **pants** are dirty? Well, that is really too much information! But why on earth would you sit down in the **subway**?
Tony: What do you mean? There are seats on the **subway**! Why wouldn't I sit down? I just didn't look where I was sitting.
Jillian: You have seats in the **subway** in San Francisco?!
Tony: Of course, we do! What do you mean? You don't have them on British subways?
Jilian: Ehm, well … no, we don't…

a subway Tony = ____________ Jillian = ____________

b pants Tony = ____________ Jillian = ____________

289

In Spalte 1 siehst du, was Tony in San Francisco sagt. Schreibe in Spalte 2 auf, wie Jillian in Oxford das wahrscheinlich sagen würde.

a	"in the hospital"	
b	"at the university"	
c	"on Grant Street"	
d	"on the weekend"	
e	"fill out the form"	
f	"Write me soon, please."	
g	"take a shower"	
h	"I just had a coffee"	
i	"He already left."	

288 a U-Bahn/Fußgängerunterführung; **b** Hose/Unterhose
289 a in hospital; **b** at university; **c** in Grant Street; **d** at the weekend; **e** to fill in the form; **f** Write to me soon, please. **g** have a shower; **h** I have / I've just had a coffee. **i** He has / He's already left.

290

Die folgenden Begriffe sind in Großbritannien üblich. Wie lauten sie in AE?

a It's on the ground floor. ______

b No, no. It's on the first floor. ______

c I need to go to the chemist's. ______

d Tom's not here. He's playing football. ______

e Please, put it in the dustbin. ______

f Where's my jumper? ______

g Have you seen my rucksack? ______

h Have you seen the town centre yet? ______

i You can park your car at the petrol station. ______

291

Kennst du die unterschiedlichen Schreibweisen der Partizipien? Trage sie in die Tabelle ein.

a	learn	*learned / learned*	*learnt / learnt*
b	spell	/	/
c	burn	/	/
d	smell	/	/
e	get	/	/
f	spill	/	/

290 a first floor; **b** second floor; **c** pharmacy; **d** soccer; **e** trash can; **f** sweater, pullover; **g** backpack; **h** downtown; **i** gas station

291 b spelled/spelled, spelt/spelt; **c** burned/burned, burnt/burnt; **d** smelled/smelled, smelt/smelt; **e** got/gotten, got/got; **f** spilled/spilled, spilt/spilt

292

Weißt du, wie diese Wörter in amerikanische und britische Englisch übersetzt werden?

a		Warteschlange	
b		Hose	
c		Handy	
d		Aufzug	
e		Kino	
f		U-Bahn	

293

Wie würdest du in den USA die hervorgehobenen Sätze verstehen?
Kreuze die richtige Alternative an.

Carl: I won the race! I got first place!
Tim: **Way to go!**

a ○ Geh' weiter! ○ Echt? ○ Gut gemacht!

Carl: My father gave me a car for my birthday!
Tim: **Get outta here!**

b ○ Geh nach Hause! ○ Echt? Das glaube ich nicht! ○ Verlass das Zimmer!

Carl: Why did Gina scream at me?
Tim: Well, **she's pissed**!

c ○ Sie ist betrunken. ○ Sie muss auf's Klo. ○ Sie ist total sauer.

Carl: Here, eat this.
Tim: **No way!** It looks disgusting!

d ○ Weit weg! ○ Auf keinen Fall! ○ Lieber nicht.

292 a line/queue; **b** pants/trousers; **c** cell/mobile; **d** elevator/lift; **e** movie theater/cinema; **f** metro/subway/Underground, Tube

293 a Gut gemacht! **b** Echt? Das glaube ich nicht! **c** Sie ist total sauer. **d** Auf keinen Fall!

294

Wie nennt man diese Lebensmittel in den USA, wie in Großbritannien? Kreuze an.

a The British say **aubergine** to a vegetable which Americans call:

- egg plant
- purple plant
- egg fruit

b Americans say **zucchini** to a vegetable which the British call:

- cucumber
- green squash
- courgette

c The British say **biscuits** to sweets which Americans call:

- cakes
- cookies
- pastries

d The British say **chips** to a snack food which Americans call:

- fish
- potato chips
- fries

e The British say **crisps** to a snack food which Americans call:

- chips
- potato fries
- crispies

295

Weißt du, was die hervorgehobenen Wörter bedeuten? Kreuze an.

a Let's **hit** the mall.

- go to
- come to
- be at

b She **was like** "I don't like you."

- loved
- wanted
- said

c I am **way** better than you! I'm the best skier here!

- very
- many
- much

d **What's up?**

- What's going on?
- Are things looking to the sky?
- How is it up there?
- Can you hear me up there?

e Bill: But, mom, I want to go with you. – Bill's mom: **Tough!** You have to stay here.

- Schäm dich!
- Schade für dich.
- Gemein!

f Hey, Tom! **Chill out!**

- Setz dich hin!
- Leg dich hin!
- Beruhige dich!

294 a egg plant; **b** courgette; **c** cookies; **d** fries; **e** chips
295 a go to; **b** said; **c** much; **d** What's going on? **e** Schade für dich. **f** Beruhige dich!

296

Lies den folgenden Dialog und entscheide, was die hervorgehobenen Ausdrücke bedeuten. Kreuze die zutreffende Variante an.

John: Hey, Will. Did you hear what Samantha said about you?
Will: **No big deal.**
John: No big deal? You don't care what she said about you?
Will: No, not really. I broke up with her, and she's angry.
John: But she's saying some really bad things about you!
Will: **So what!**
John: Okay … If you say so. I just wanted to let you know.
Will: Thanks for letting me know. Anyway, I have to go. Joanna and I are going to the movies tonight.
John: Oh, okay. **Later.**
Will: Yeah. **See ya.**

a No big deal.

- Kein großes Geld.
- Egal.

b So what!

- Na und?
- Was?

c Later.

- Es ist später passiert.
- Ciao, bis später.

d See ya.

- Tschüss.
- Ich sehe dich.

297

Wozu benutzt man diese Floskeln? Umschreibe es auf Englisch.

a "How ya doin'?"

____

b "Oh, my God!"

____

c "No way!"

____

296 a Egal. **b** Na, und? **c** Ciao, bis später. **d** Tschüss.
297 a To say „hello" to someone. **b** To show that you are surprised. **c** To show you don't believe what someone is saying – or you are shocked.

298

Weißt du, wie die Entsprechungen jeweils lauten? Kreuze an.

a In the U.S. people fill up their cars with **gas**. And people in Britain?

- oil
- petrol
- petrolio

b In the U.S. people drive between cities on **highways**. And in Britain?

- motorways
- streets
- tunnels

c In the U.S. people walk along the street on the **sidewalk**. And people in Britain?

- walkside
- pavement
- zebra crossing

d Americans call the glass in front of the driver the **windshield**. And the British?

- winding
- wind protector
- windscreen

e Americans put their suitcases in the **trunk**. And people in Britain?

- book
- boot
- suitcase box

f In the U.S. people park their cars in **parking lots**. And people in Britain?

- park cars
- car parks
- parks

g In the U.S. the engine is under the **hood**. And engines in British cars?

- bonnet
- engine covers
- engine protector

299

Wie würde man die hervorgehobenen Satzteile in amerikanischem Slang sagen?

Jillian: Hi, Tony. Where are you going?
Tony: Well, I'm **going to** go to the movie theater.
Jillian: Oh, really? I would love to see a film today.
Tony: Would you like to come with us?
Jillian: Us? Who are you going with?
Tony: I'm going with Tricia, but I'm sure she won't mind.
Jillian: Well, if you don't mind, ring her and ask. I don't want to go if she would prefer to be alone with you.
Tony: Okay, **let me** call her **really quickly**.

a I'm **going to** go = ____________________

b Okay, **let me** call = ____________________

c **really quickly** = ____________________

298 a petrol; **b** motorways; **c** pavement; **d** windscreen; **e** boot; **f** car parks; **g** bonnet
299 a gonna; **b** lemme; **c** real quick

300

... aber im Text ist etwas schiefgegangen. Finde die Gegenteile der markierten Wörter und erzähle die Geschichte neu. Nutze die Liste, um die Gegensatzpaare zu sammeln.

Most subjects at school are very difficult for him. Most of all he hates maths and English. He thinks that the school building is ugly , too. Every day he leaves school early. The worst thing is his bike that he rides to school every day. It is old and it was very cheap . All the pupils at school hate Tom's bike.

difficult	
hate	
ugly	
leave	
worst	
old	
cheap	

301

Und was ist die Meinung ihrer Mutter? Finde die Gegenteile zu den hervorgehobenen Wörtern.

a The Browns' garage is at the back ______________________ of their house.

b Tom always agrees ______________________ with his mother.

c The advantage ______________________ of a full-day school is that you don't have time for going out with friends or playing with the PC.

d The shops are open ______________________ on Christmas Day.

e The new living room table is too low ______________________.

f Your friend Susan is a very impolite ______________________ person.

300 difficult – easy; hate – love/like; ugly – beautiful; leave – arrive at; worst – best; old – new; cheap – expensive
301 a at the front; **b** disagrees; **c** disadvantage; **d** closed; **e** high; **f** polite

302

Setze die passenden Synonyme in die Lücken ein.

Nobody   Ages   at any time   prison   received

shout   In my opinion   extremely

a You can come ______________________ (whenever you are free).

b (A long time) ______________________ ago, people didn't have electricity.

c This cake is (very, very) ______________________ delicious.

d He had to go to (jail) ______________________ for drinking and driving.

e (From my point of view) ______________________ his statement is absolutely false.

f Yesterday they (got) ______________________ a parcel from Australia.

g (No one) ______________________ wants to do homework, but we all have to.

h Don't (yell) ______________________ at me!

303

Hilf Tom auch mit anderen Wörtern und ergänze die Tabelle:

a simple		
b a hard job		
c big		
d small		
e gigantic		

302 a at any time; **b** Ages; **c** extremely; **d** prison; **e** In my opinion; **f** received; **g** Nobody; **h** shout

303 a easy / einfach; **b** a difficult job / schwer, schwierig; **c** large / groß; **d** little / klein; **e** huge / riesig

304

Toms Freund Leon aus Hamburg ist zu Besuch. Leider versteht Leon nicht alles. Tom versucht, ihm die Wörter zu erklären. Schreibe Toms Erklärungen auf.

a To whisper means ______________________________

____

b Obvious means ______________________________

____

c A sunset is ______________________________

____

d The climate is ______________________________

____

e The environment is ______________________________

____

305

Tom versucht sein Bestes, um Leon alles zu erklären. Aber manchmal fehlt ihm einfach das treffende Wort. Weißt du, wie es heißt?

a There is a special word for something that is very, very big: ______________________?

b The emotion you feel when you are very happy: ______________________.

c You get this feeling when you are scared: ______________________.

d Not "citizen", but all the people who live somewhere: ______________________.

e The political organization that takes care of the state: ______________________.

304 For example: **a** To whisper means to speak very quietly or softly. **b** Obvious means something that is clear and easy to see. **c** A sunset is the time when the sun goes down. **d** The climate is the weather which is typical for a country. **e** The environment is the nature that surrounds us.
305 a huge; **b** joy; **c** fear; **d** population; **e** government

306

Wie sind Menschen so? Ihre Eigenschaften können sehr schwierig zu definieren sein, wenn man das Vokabular dazu nicht hat. Entscheide, welches der folgenden Eigenschaftswörter zu den Beschreibungen passt.

poor – odd – wise – ugly – brave – weak – hot-headed – lucky

a A person who acts strangely can be called ____________________

b A person who always wins things can be called ____________________

c A person who is intelligent can be called ____________________

d A person who hasn't got much money can be called ____________________

e A person who is not very beautiful can be called ____________________

f A person who isn't very strong can be called ____________________

g A person who loses his temper quickly can be called ____________________

h A person who isn't ever afraid can be called ____________________

307

Angenommen, du weißt das hervorgehobene Wort nicht, wie würdest du diese menschlichen Emotionen beschreiben?

a A **patient** person is someone who ____________________

____

b A **violent** person is someone who ____________________

____

c A **worried** person is someone who ____________________

d A **jealous** person is someone who ____________________

____

e A **relaxed** person is someone who ____________________

306 **a** odd; **b** lucky; **c** wise; **d** poor; **e** ugly; **f** weak; **g** hot-headed; **h** brave

307 For example: **a** … can wait for something without becoming upset. **b** … acts in a way which could hurt or kill someone. **c** … thinks about problems or unpleasant things and becomes nervous. **d** … is angry or unhappy because someone else has something they would like. **e** … is not stressed.

308

Im Englischen gibt es im Alltag viele Standardfloskeln, die mit ebensolchen Floskeln erwidert werden. Kennst du sie? Ergänze die Tabelle mit den folgenden Erwiderungen.

Never mind. / No problem. / Don't worry about it. Nice to meet you, too.

Yes, please. / No, thanks, I'm fine. You're welcome. / My pleasure.

Fine, thanks. And you?

a Here you are.	*Thank you.*
b I'm sorry. / I beg your pardon.	
c How are you?	
d Nice to meet you.	
e Would you like something to drink?	
f Thank you.	

309

Maria bittet eine Verkäuferin um Hilfe. Kreuze an, welche Sätze sie zu der Verkäuferin sagen kann oder sollte. Kannst du auch begründen, warum?

a Hey, come over! I need help!

b Get me a smaller size of this pullover.

c Excuse me, could you help me, please?

d Well, I know that you don't have it in the shop. Look for it in the stock (= Lager) then.

e Could you look for a smaller size of this pullover, please?

f Too bad it's out. But could you have a look in the stock for me, please?

308 b Never mind. (BE only)/No problem./Don't worry about it. **c** Fine, thanks. And you? **d** Nice to meet you, too.
e zustimmend: Yes, please./verneinend: No, thanks, I'm fine. **f** You're welcome./My pleasure.
309 c; e; f; Begründung: Die Formulierungen sind nicht so unhöflich wie die anderen.

310

Maria und ihre Freundinnen wollen ins Kino. Aber erst mal etwas essen! Susan geht zur Theke eines Fastfood-Restaurants und bestellt für alle. Nutze die Höflichkeitsfloskeln für ihre Bestellung.

the same to you — please — I'd like — thanks — Here you are.

Waitress: "Good evening."

a Susan: „Three hamburgers and three Cokes!"

____

Waitress: "Yes, of course. Here you are. That's four pounds, please."

b Susan puts down the money.

____

Waitress: "Thank you. Have a nice evening."

c Susan walks away.

____

311

Maria und ihre Freunde wollen den neuen Film mit Brad Pitt im Kino sehen. Vervollständige die Unterhaltung. Nutze Höflichkeitsfloskeln.

Cashier: "Good evening."

a Maria: "____________________________."

Cashier: "Yes, certainly."

b Maria: "____________________________?"

Cashier: "Yes, students pay only two pounds. Do you have your student ID, please?"

c Maria: "____________________________."

Cashier: "Thanks. That's six pounds then. Have fun!"

310 a I'd like three hamburgers and three Cokes, please. **b** Here you are. **c** Thanks, the same to you.
311 a For example: We'd like three tickets for the Brad Pitt movie, please. **b** Do you have a special price for students? **c** Yes, of course. Here you are.

312

Maria ist mit ihren Freundinnen beim Shoppen. Sie möchte einen Pulli kaufen, aber ...
Vervollständige den Dialog. Verwende dazu die Satzteile in Klammern.

Maria: "Oh, look at that pullover, isn't it great?"

a Susan (stimmt zu): "______________________________________."
(it / wonderful. / Yes / is)

Emma: "Well, yes, it's nice. But I think it's a little expensive."

b Maria (denkt das auch, will ihn aber trotzdem anprobieren): "________________________

____."
(But / right. / Yes, / I think / are / I'd like / to / you / try it on.)

Maria: "Doesn't it look great? I really love this pullover! Never mind that it's expensive!"

c Susan (findet, dass Maria der Pulli gut steht, dass er aber zu groß ist): "________________

____."
(on you. / The / looks / nice / pullover / it's too big. / But)

d Emma (findet, dass Maria die Farbe gut steht, denkt aber auch, dass sie den Pulli aber lieber kleiner nehmen sollte): "____

____."
(the color / Yes, / it / nice / looks / on you, / should get / too / you / but / a smaller size.)

Maria: "Okay, let's ask the shop assistant. Maybe they have it in a smaller size."

313

Lies dir noch einmal den fertigen Dialog zwischen Maria und ihren Freundinnen durch.
Mit welchen Wörtern werden Zustimmung und Ablehnung jeweils eingeleitet?
Trage sie hier in die Tabelle ein.

312 a Yes, it's wonderful. **b** Yes, I think you are right. But I'd like to try it on. **c** The pullover looks nice on you. But it's too big. **d** Yes, the color looks nice on you, too, but you should get a smaller size.
313 Zustimmen: Yes, ablehnen: but

314

Tom und Maria diskutieren über den Sinn von Hausaufgaben. Setze die Wörter in den Text ein. Unterstreiche Redewendungen, die sie benutzen.

This is why   for example   But   and second   because   so   first

Beispiel: Tom: "I think it's quite clear that homework is necessary."

Maria: "You may be right. a) ____________ in my opinion it's a problem b) ____________ a lot of students have other important things to do in the afternoon. Betty, c) ____________, has to look after her little sister."

Tom: "I see what you mean, but I think that her mother should do that, d) ____________ Betty could do other things."

Maria: "Well, it's true. But I'd like to make another point. e) ____________, we spend a lot of time at school already f) ____________, we need free time, too. A lot of students have special talents, but there is no time during the week. g) ____________ think that homework is too much for students!"

315

Trage die Redewendungen aus Kurztest 314 in die Tabelle ein, die Maria und Tom in der Diskussion benutzen.

314 a) But; b) because; c) for example; d) so; e) First; f) and second; g) This is why
315 Zustimmen: You may be right. / I see what you mean. / Well, it's true. widersprechen: But; eigene Meinung: I think it's quite clear; In my opinion; I'd like to make another point

316

Weißt du noch, wie man im Englischen ein Frageanhängsel bildet? Ergänze die Tabelle.
Tipp: Das an einen Satz angehängte „. . ., oder?“ darf im Englischen nicht wörtlich übersetzt werden! Man verwendet dafür die *question tags*.

A trip to downtown Chicago **can** be dangerous,	*can't it?*
You like American sweets,	
It **can't** be so difficult to learn American English,	
I **should** go to see an Indian Museum while I'm in the USA,	
The weather **couldn't** have been better,	
You **don't** like fast food,	
Girls **can** be really stressful,	
We **could** go to the cinema tonight,	

317

Marias Freunde sollen bestätigen, was sie sagt. Ergänze Marias Sätze mit den passenden *question tags*.
Tipp: Wenn kein Hilfsverb im Satz steht, dann verwende eine Form von *to do*.

a We can do the homework together, ______________________?

b It would be nice to go to school in Australia for a year, ______________________?

c We all help at the exhibition, ______________________?

d We all like Mrs Gable, ______________________?

e This ice cream doesn't taste very good, ______________________?

f Tom doesn't help us much with the project, ______________________?

316 You like American sweets, don't you? It can't be so difficult to learn American English, can it? I should go to see an Indian Museum while I'm in the USA, shouldn't I? The weather couldn't have been better, could it? You don't like fast food, do you? Girls can be really stressful, can't they? We could go to the cinema tonight, couldn't we?
317 **a** can't we? **b** wouldn't it? **c** don't we? **d** don't we? **e** does it? **f** does he?

318

Tom unterhält sich mit seiner Mutter über den Urlaub. Ergänze seine *question tags*.
Tipp: Im *simple past* ist *was/were* das Hilfsverb.

Beispiel: The holiday was great, *wasn't it?*

a The first hotel was very nice, ______________________________?

b The cowboys in the Wild West Show were really cool, ______________________________?

c The giant rollercoaster was great fun, ______________________________?

d We weren't the only ones having fun, ______________________________?

e Those holidays were the best ever, ______________________________?

f The food in that last hotel wasn't that great, ______________________________?

g You were a little nervous about the long flight, ______________________________?

319

Maria ist ziemlich vergesslich. Manchmal weiß sie nicht mehr, was sie erledigt hat und will sich vergewissern. Ergänze ihre *question tags*.
Tipp: Im *present perfect* ist *has/have* das Hilfsverb.

Beispiel: I have done my homework, *haven't I*?

a I have cleaned my room, ______________________________?

b You have given me the books, ______________________________?

c I haven't left my keys at home, ______________________________?

d You haven't tried to call me, ______________________________?

e She hasn't written me an e-mail, ______________________________?

f He has brought some more drawing paper for me, ______________________________?

g They have taken the books to the library for me, ______________________________?

318 a wasn't it? **b** weren't they? **c** wasn't it? **d** were we? **e** weren't they? **f** was it? **g** weren't you?
319 a haven't I? **b** haven't you? **c** have I? **d** have you? **e** has she? **f** hasn't he? **g** haven't they?

320

Verbinde die Sätze mit dem richtigen *question tag*.

a We can't go downtown Chicago again,
b They will visit us for one day,
c You felt sick on the ship,
d We didn't write a postcard to Maria,

e did we?
f can we?
g won't they?
h didn't you?

321

Welches Anhängsel ist richtig? Unterstreiche.

a Maria is good at dancing, but bad at school, doesn't she / isn't she / can she?

b Tom is the perfect son-in-law, isn't she / does he / isn't he?

c Mrs Brown and Mrs Miller are really curious, will they / don't they / aren't they?

d Tom couldn't be better at school, can he / is he / could he?

e She will go to YA next summer, won't she / will she / won't he?

f They should take the bus to YA, don't they / should they / shouldn't they?

322

Ergänze.

a They arrived late at the airport, ____________________?

b She hasn't finished her picture yet, ____________________?

c I could sleep at your house after the party, ____________________?

d We will go to Spain next summer, ____________________?

e The school project was a great success, ____________________?

320 a + f; b + g; c + h; d + e
321 a isn't she; **b** isn't he? **c** aren't they? **d** could he? **e** won't she? **f** shouldn't they?
322 a didn't they? **b** has she? **c** couldn't I? **d** won't we / will we not? **e** wasn't it?

323

Entscheide, welche Kombination mit *get* richtig ist für die jeweiligen Fahrzeuge.

get in   get on   get off   get out of

Beispiel: ship: *to get on a ship, to get off a ship*

a car		
b train		
c taxi		
d plane		
e bus		
f limousine		
g boat		

324

Entscheide, welche Kombination mit *get* am besten passt, um den Satz zu vervollständigen. Streiche die falschen Alternativen durch.

a What time does your plane get (to / in / at)? Would you like me to pick you up?

b What time do you normally get (on / in / up) in the morning?

c Can you help me? Can you tell me how to get (on / to / at) the police station?

d I need to get rid (on / of / at) this jacket. It's so hot today!

e I just can't get used (in / of / to) his loud singing. It drives me crazy!

f I don't like him very much. He really gets (on / of / at) my nerves.

323 a to get in, to get out of; **b** to get on, to get off; **c** to get in, to get out of; **d** to get on, to get off; **e** to get on, to get off; **f** to get in, to get out of; **g** to get on, to get off
324 a in; **b** up; **c** to; **d** of; **e** to; **f** on

325

Übersetze die Kombinationen mit *get* aus dem Kurztest 324.

a	to get in	
b	to get up	
c	to get to a place	
d	to get rid of sth	
e	to get used to sth	
f	to get on someone's nerves	

326

Entscheide, welche Kombination mit *go* richtig ist für die Bedeutung in Klammern und trage sie in die jeweilige Lücke ein.

a Ticket prices for travel have gone ___________ over the past year. (steigen)

b Those tennis shoes don't go ___________ your tennis outfit. (passen zu)

c As he was in a wheelchair, we had to wait for the escalator to go ___________ to the lobby. (hinuntergehen/-fahren)

d We didn't want to stop and decided to go ___________. (weitermachen)

327

Entscheide, welche Kombination mit *take* richtig ist für die Bedeutung in Klammern und trage sie in die jeweilige Lücke ein.

a His hobby is to go to the airport and watch planes take ___________. (abheben)

b The boys took the dog ___________ for a walk. (ausführen)

c The first thing I do when I get home is take my shoes ___________. (ausziehen)

325 a einsteigen/ankommen; **b** aufstehen; **c** zu einem Platz/Ort kommen/erreichen; **d** etwas loswerden; **e** sich an etwas gewöhnen; **f** jemandem auf die Nerven gehen
326 a up; **b** with; **c** down; **d** on
327 a off; **b** out; **c** off

328

Mit welchem Wort kann man die hervorgehobenen *phrasal verbs* ersetzen?

increase decrease match continue arrive

a	What time does your plane **get in**?	
b	Please, **go on**. Don't stop because of me.	
c	That shirt doesn't **go with** those trousers.	
d	Do economists expect prices to **go up**?	
e	Prices are so high. I hope they **go down** soon.	

329

Wähle aus, welches Verb jeweils am besten passt. Streiche die falschen durch.

a How did your exams (get / take / go)? I hope well!

b How do I (get / take / go) to the post office?

c What time does her plane (get / take / go) off?

d She talks so loud! She really (gets / takes / goes) on my nerves.

e How did this all (get / take / go) so wrong? What happened?

f If we're not careful, everything will (get / take / go) much worse.

g Don't worry. Everything is (getting / taking / going) fine.

h I don't like to (get / take / go) risks like that. That's too dangerous!

i I'm (getting / taking / going) crazy. I don't understand what's happening!

j Let's (get / take / go) turns (= abwechseln). You can go first.

328 a arrive; **b** continue; **c** match; **d** increase; **e** decrease
329 a go; **b** get; **c** take; **d** gets; **e** go; **f** get; **g** going; **h** take; **i** going; **j** take

330

Entscheide, welches der beiden Verben am besten passt und vervollständige die Sätze.
Tipp: Achte darauf, dass du die richtige Verbform verwendest! Ein Hinweis darauf steht zu deiner Sicherheit noch einmal in Klammern dahinter.

a He's ______________ a huge mistake, I'm sure. (progressive)

b May I use your phone? I need to ______________ a phone call. (infinitive)

c We really have to ______________ a choice here. (infinitive)

d Did he ______________ the dishes last night? They are not clean! (infinitive)

e He thinks he's so funny. He's always ______________ jokes, but no one ever laughs. (progressive)

f Thank you for your hard work. You have ______________ a very good job. (past participle)

g The company will ______________ an offer next week. (infinitive)

331

Entscheide, welches Verb am besten die jeweilige Übersetzung wiedergibt und trage es in die Lücke ein.

a	mir den Tag retten	to ____________ my day
b	ein Baby bekommen	to ____________ a baby
c	etwas auf den Grund gehen	to ____________ to the bottom of sth
d	ein Foto machen	to ____________ a picture
e	mir einen Gefallen tun	to ____________ me a favour
f	schiefgehen	to ____________ wrong
g	Hol' mir bitte eine Cola.	____________ me a Coke, please.
h	Du gehst mir auf die Nerven!	You ____________ on my nerves!

330 a making; **b** make; **c** make; **d** do; **e** making; **f** done; **g** make
331 a make; **b** have; **c** get; **d** take; **e** do; **f** go; **g** Get; **h** get

332

Welche Präposition gehört jeweils zum hervorgehobenen Verb? Kreuze an.

a If you want some money, you'll have to **ask** ______________ it. Don't be shy!

○ on ○ for ○ over

b What are you **waiting** ______________ ? Don't just stand there! Do it!

○ of ○ for ○ at

c I have no idea where Tom lives. I haven't **heard** ______________ him for many years.

○ of ○ for ○ from

d Have you **heard** ______________ the plane crash in India?

○ of ○ about ○ from

e Have you been **working** ______________ your homework?

○ on ○ for ○ at

f Who's **looking** ______________ the kids? Are they at home alone?

○ at ○ for ○ after

g I wish he would stop **looking** ______________ me. It makes me uncomfortable.

○ at ○ to ○ after

h Did he **apologize** ______________ what he said to you?

○ about ○ for ○ after

333

Trage die hier fehlenden Präpositionen in die Lücken ein.

a Would you stop doing that, please? I' really getting **tired** ______________ it!

b I love to watch him play. He is really **good** ______________ tennis.

c Where is she? I am really getting **worried** ______________ her.

d We're going to the concert. Tara is really **crazy** ______________ the band!

e Are you **interested** ______________ joining us? You are welcome to come along.

f I think we're too loud. They are not **used** ______________ having so much noise.

332 a for; **b** for; **c** from; **d** about; **e** on; **f** after; **g** at; **h** for
333 a of; **b** at; **c** about; **d** about; **e** in; **f** to

334

Welche Präposition gehört jeweils in die Lücke?

a Is there a **reason** ____________ this? Why would he do such a thing? (Grund für)

b What's our **plan** ____________ the next few days? (Plan für)

c Did he get an **invitation** ____________ the party? (Einladung zu)

d This is a **picture** ____________ my cat. Isn't she pretty? (Foto von)

e Our class has no **interest** ____________ that subject. (Interesse an)

f They have no **respect** ____________ their father. (Respekt vor)

g This is an **example** ____________ the wrong way to do it. (Beispiel für)

h I'm still waiting for an **answer** ____________ my letter. (Antwort auf)

335

Entscheide, welche Präposition jeweils am besten die Übersetzung richtig vervollständigt, und schreibe sie in die Lücken.

a	sich auf etwas freuen	to look forward ____________ sth
b	von jemandem weglaufen	to run away ____________ somebody
c	an etwas gewöhnt sein	to be used ____________ sth
d	in die Sterne hinaufschauen	to look up ____________ the stars
e	mit etwas weitermachen	to carry on ____________ sth
f	aus dem Weg gehen	to get out ____________ the way
g	sich an etwas gewöhnen	to get used ____________ sth
h	mit jemandem Schluss machen	to break up ____________ somebody

334 a for; **b** for; **c** to; **d** of; **e** in; **f** for; **g** of; **h** to
335 a to; **b** from; **c** to; **d** at; **e** with; **f** of; **g** to; **h** with

336

In den folgenden Sätzen fehlt jeweils die Mengenbezeichnung *some* oder *any*. Setze richtig ein.
Tipp: Bei positiven Aussagen steht *some*, bei negativen und Fragen steht *any*. Das gilt auch für die Ableitungen *somebody/someone/something* und *anybody/anyone/anything*.

a Do you have ____________ books by Dafoe?

b I'd like ____________ carrots, please.

c There aren't ____________ pencils in this box.

d Tamy likes to have ____________ coffee.

e Isn't there ____________ soda left?

f She hasn't got ____________ paint left.

g Are there ____________ steaks in the fridge?

h I need ____________ money.

i I haven't got ____________.

337

Setze in die folgenden Lücken entweder *somebody* oder *anybody* ein.

a Have you seen ______________________________ ?

b I cannot take ______________________________ with me.

c There is ______________________________ in the kitchen.

d He talked to ______________________________ I don't know.

e I'd like to take ______________________________ with me. I don't want to go on my own.

f Is there ______________________________ you can call? We need help.

g I don't want to talk to ______________________________ right now.

h Hello? Is ______________________________ here?

i I can't stand ______________________________ being around now. (stand = ertragen)

336 a any; **b** some; **c** any; **d** some; **e** any; **f** any; **g** any; **h** some; **i** any
337 a anybody; **b** anybody; **c** somebody; **d** somebody; **e** somebody; **f** anybody; **g** anybody; **h** anybody; **i** anybody

338

Setze in die folgenden Lücken *someone* oder *anyone* ein.
Tipp: Sieh im Zweifel noch einmal nach bei Kurztest 336.

a Do you know ______________________ who can do this?

b I know ______________________ who can do this.

c Please find ______________________ to do this!

d Did you see ______________________ out on the street?

e I am looking for ______________________.

f I need ______________________ to help me with this.

g Does ______________________ want to watch this?

h ______________________ called me last night. I don't know who it was.

i I don't want to see ______________________ after 9 pm.

339

Setze in die folgenden Lücken *something* oder *anything* richtig ein.

a I am sorry but we haven't got ______________________ left.

b Is there ______________________ you need?

c I need ______________________ to drink.

d Did you get ______________________ expensive?

e You can't get ______________________ here!

f I want to buy ______________________ to wear.

g Have you noticed ______________________ different?

h There is ______________________ wrong with him.

i ______________________ was missing.

338 a anyone; **b** someone; **c** someone; **d** anyone; **e** someone; **f** someone; **g** anyone; **h** Someone; **i** anyone
339 a anything; **b** anything; **c** something; **d** anything; **e** anything; **f** something; **g** anything; **h** something; **i** Something

340

Setze in die folgenden Lücken *somewhere* oder *anywhere* richtig ein.

a Is there ______________________ you want to go today?

b Jim wants to take me ______________________ nice today.

c I really don't feel like going ______________________ tonight.

d Let's go ______________________.

e I can't find the book ______________________.

f Is there ______________________ we can talk in private?

g Do you live ______________________ near Susan?

h ______________________ there is somebody for me.

341

Hast du *some* und *any* im Griff? Wo muss welche Form eingesetzt werden?

somebody (2x) – anybody (1x) – anything (1x) – somewhere (1x) –

anywhere (1x) – some (1x) – any (2x)

a I know ______________________ who can help you.

b Mary hasn't got ______________________ milk left.

c Have you seen ______________________ like this before?

d Sorry but I can't take you ______________________ tonight. My car is broken.

e Please go to the store. I need ______________________ potatoes.

f You have to have the CD ______________________! Look again!

g ______________________ stole my bike last night.

h Can ______________________ help me with this project?

i Sorry, I can't give you ______________________ flour.

340 a anywhere; **b** somewhere; **c** anywhere; **d** somewhere; **e** anywhere; **f** anywhere; **g** anywhere; **h** Somewhere

341 a somebody; **b** any; **c** anything; **d** anywhere; **e** some; **f** somewhere; **g** Somebody; **h** anybody; **i** any

342

In den folgenden Sätzen erscheinen *some* und *any* in Ausnahmen. So kann *some* auch in Fragesätzen stehen, wenn eine bejahte Antwort erwartet wird, sowie nach *where*, *when* und *how*. *Any* kann auch in bejahten Sätzen stehen, wenn es die Bedeutung „jeder beliebige" hat oder in *if*-Sätzen steht. Setze nun richtig ein.

a Would you like ____________ tea?

b You can use ____________ pen here.

c If I had ____________ money, I would give it to you.

d If ____________ of these belong to you, then take them!

e Can I have ____________ of the strawberries, please?

f You can come and see me ____________ time.

g Where can I get ____________ paper?

h When can I expect ____________ money from you?

343

Füge Formen mit *some* und *any* ein. Achte dabei auf die Ausnahmen.

any – anybody (2x) – anything – anywhere (2x) – some – something

a I can't have ______________________________ alcohol. I am too young.

b Megan could have received ______________________________ from her father.

c Would you like to watch ______________________________ film tonight?

d You can go ______________________________ you want.

e I have got ______________________________ in my hair.

f Is ______________________________ there?

g I haven't been ______________________________ lately.

h If ______________________________ sees the bank robber, then call the police.

342 a some; **b** any; **c** any; **d** any; **e** some; **f** any; **g** some; **h** some

343 a any; **b** anything; **c** some; **d** anywhere; **e** something; **f** anybody; **g** anywhere; **h** anybody

344

Bei der Verwendung von *much* und *many* muss man unterscheiden, ob die Nomen zählbar oder nicht zählbar sind. Kreuze die zählbaren Nomen an.
Tipp: Wenn du den Plural mit einem s am Ende bilden kannst, ist etwas zählbar.

a ○ milk
b ○ leaves
c ○ houses
d ○ money
e ○ time
f ○ ideas
g ○ petrol
h ○ pencils
i ○ sugar
j ○ computers
k ○ doors
l ○ work
m ○ friends
n ○ alcohol
o ○ noises (= Geräusche)
p ○ water
q ○ windows
r ○ sleep

345

Setze *much* oder *many* richtig ein.
Tipp: „Matsch und Dreck kann man nicht zählen." (Matsch = Aussprache von *much*)

a We didn't have ____________ water.

b How ____________ books has King written so far?

c ____________ children were injured.

d How ____________ sleep did you get last night?

e My neighbour has got too ____________ cats.

f That is as ____________ time as I could spend with you.

g The people didn't leave ____________ dirt.

h There is so ____________ work left!

i There were so ____________ people in the gym.

j How ____________ money do you have?

k I have eaten too ______________________________.

344 zählbare Nomen: **b** leaves; **c** houses; **f** ideas; **h** pencils; **j** computers; **k** doors; **m** friends; **o** noises; **q** windows
345 **a** much; **b** many; **c** Many; **d** much; **e** many; **f** much; **g** much; **h** much; **i** many; **j** much; **k** much

346

Übersetze die folgenden Ausdrücke. Achte dabei auf die richtige Verwendung von *much* und *many*.

a nicht viel Geld ______________________

b nicht viele Bücher ______________________

c nicht viel Benzin ______________________

d nicht viele Hemden ______________________

e nicht viel Hilfe ______________________

f nicht viele Kirchen ______________________

g nicht viel Öl ______________________

h nicht viel zu trinken ______________________

347

Verwandle die positiven Aussagen in negative und verwende dabei *much* oder *many*.

Beispiel: I have a lot of time. *I haven't got much time.*

a Daniel eats a lot of sandwiches.

____

b I have got a lot of ideas.

____

c Harry drinks lots of water.

____

d Mr Colbridge put a lot of sugar in the pudding.

____

346 a not much money; **b** not many books; **c** not much petrol/gas; **d** not many shirts; **e** not much help; **f** not many churches; **g** not much oil; **h** not much to drink

347 a Daniel doesn't eat many sandwiches. **b** I haven't got / don't have many ideas. **c** Harry doesn't drink much water. **d** Mr Colbridge didn't put much sugar in the pudding.

348

***Much* und *many* werden in verneinten Sätzen und in Fragesätzen verwendet, sowie in Verbindung mit *too, as, so* und *how*. In bejahten Sätzen werden, wenn es geht, Ausdrücke wie *a lot of* bevorzugt. Kannst du jeweils richtig einsetzen?**

a I like to eat ______________________ meat.

b Cedric doesn't like to eat ______________________ meat.

c Do you like to eat ______________________ meat?

d How ______________________ (money) does the sweatshirt cost?

e That is way too ______________________ money!

f I have ______________________ money in the bank!

g My niece draws so ______________________ pictures.

h There are ______________________ pictures on the wall.

i How ______________________ pictures do you want to draw?

349

Achte darauf, ob es sich um ein zählbare oder nicht-zählbares Nomen handelt, ob es ein bejahter oder verneinter Aussagesatz oder vielleicht auch eine Frage ist.

a Hast du viele Haustiere?

____

b Marina hat viele Spielsachen.

____

c Wie viel Benzin haben wir noch?

____

d Meine Mutter hat nicht viel Butter zu Hause.

____

348 a a lot of; **b** much; **c** much; **d** much; **e** much; **f** a lot of; **g** many; **h** a lot of / many; **i** many
349 a Do you have many pets? **b** Marina has got a lot of/many toys. **c** How much petrol (AE = gasoline) do we have left? **d** My mother doesn't have much butter at home.

350

Auch bei der Verwendung von *a little* und *a few* muss man darauf achten, ob das Nomen zählbar oder nicht zählbar ist. Setze *a little* oder *a few* vor die Nomen.
Tipp: Bei zählbaren Nomen muss *a few* gesetzt werden.

a ______________ soup
b ______________ headphones
c ______________ sheep
d ______________ powder
e ______________ clocks
f ______________ screens
g ______________ liquid
h ______________ cream
i ______________ children
j ______________ litres of oil
k ______________ women
l ______________ dirt

351

Setze *a little* oder *a few* richtig ein. Überprüfe, ob die Nomen zählbar sind oder nicht.

a He has got ______________ success.
b She needs ______________ friends.
c Eric likes to put ______________ sugar into his tea.
d There is a ______________ too much noise in the classroom.
e Can you cut me ______________ flowers from the garden?
f My mum wants ______________ support.
g He had ______________ pints of beer.
h Peter put ______________ salt on the salad.
i I need ______________ help with my homework.
j He owns ______________ houses along the west coast.
k There were ______________ people in the pool this morning.

350 a a little; **b** a few; **c** a few; **d** a little; **e** a few; **f** a few; **g** a little; **h** a little; **i** a few; **j** a few; **k** a few; **l** a little
351 a a little; **b** a few; **c** a little; **d** a little; **e** a few; **f** a little; **g** a few; **h** a little; **i** a little; **j** a few; **k** a few

352 ★★☆ Sag's positiv!

Formuliere die folgenden Aussagen so um, dass du nur *a little* oder *a few* benutzt.

Beispiel: He didn't have much money. *He only had a little money.*

a She didn't have many friends.

____

b Mr Rogers didn't perform in many plays.

____

c Mr Watson didn't drink much.

____

d They haven't eaten much bread.

____

e Mandy hasn't eaten many slices of bread.

____

353 ★★★ „Wenig" und „wenige" richtig übersetzen

Achte darauf, ob es sich um ein zählbares oder nicht-zählbares Nomen handelt.

a Er hat wenig Milch zu Hause.

____

b Mein Onkel hat gestern nur wenige Tassen Kaffee getrunken.

____

c Meine Tante trinkt nur ein wenig Kaffee.

____

352 a She only had a few friends. **b** Mr Rogers only performed in a few plays. **c** Mr Watson only drank a little. **d** They have only eaten a little bread. **e** Mandy has only eaten a few slices of bread.
353 a He has (got) little milk at home. **b** My uncle only drank a few cups of coffee yesterday. **c** My aunt only drinks a little coffee.

354

Setze in die Lücken entweder *a little / a few* oder *much / many / a lot of* ein.

a I don't have a chair. There are not very ____________________ chairs in this house.

b I cannot give you any money. I only have ____________________ coins.

c Mr Stephens hasn't watched ____________________ soccer games. He doesn't even know what "offside" means!

d Hello Mrs Heffner. Could you give me ____________________ flour, please? I ran out of it.

e Harry likes ____________________ snow. He cannot get enough of it.

f I'd like to try ____________________ soup, please.

g Do you get ____________________ sun here?

h Oh, we get ____________________ sun. Don't you see my sunburn?

i I didn't get ____________________ information from him.

j Could you give me ____________________ jars of the jam? I really like it a lot.

355

Übersetze. Verwende *a little / a few* oder *much / many / a lot of*.

a Herr Miller hat viele Kinder.

____

b Gabi kauft nicht viel Essen ein.

____

c Ich habe nur wenige Tüten zu Hause.

____

d Hat Frau Hanson viele Bücher in ihrem Regal?

____

354 a many; **b** a few; **c** many; **d** a little; **e** a lot of; **f** a little; **g** much; **h** a lot of; **i** much; **j** a few

355 a Mr Miller has (got) a lot of/many children. **b** Gabi doesn't buy much food. **c** I have (got) only a few bags at home. **d** Does Mrs Hanson have … / Has Mrs Hanson got many books in her shelf?

356

Während *every* vor Nomen im Singular „jeder/jedes“ bedeutet, steht *each* für „jeder einzelne aus einer begrenzten Anzahl“. Die Vereinzelung wird dabei besonders betont. Setze die beiden richtig ein.

a (Jedes einzelne) __________ member of the club got a membership card.

b (Jedes) __________ member had to show their membership card.

c (Jeder) __________ swimmer had to wear a swimming cap.

d (Jeder einzelne) __________ swimmer in the pool had to wear a swimming cap.

e You have to ask __________ (jedes einzelne) child.

f You have to ask __________ (jedes) child.

g You have done __________ (jede einzelne) exercise.

357

In dieser Aufgabe kommt nun *any* hinzu. *Any* bedeutet „jeder“, im Sinne von „x-beliebig“. Setze *each*, *every* und *any* richtig ein.

a Jedem kann das passieren. (Im Sinne von: egal wem)

This can happen to __________ person.

b Jedem kann das passieren. (Im Sinne von: jedem Einzelnen hier)

This can happen to __________ person in this room.

c Jedem kann das passieren. (Im Sinne von: jedem – ohne Ausnahme)

This can happen to __________ person in this world.

d He bought two games for 15 $ __________.

e He bought __________ game. (Im Sinne von: alle – ohne Ausnahme)

f He bought __________ game. (Im Sinne von: jedes Einzelne)

356 a Each; **b** Every; **c** Every; **d** Each; **e** each; **f** every; **g** each
357 a any; **b** each; **c** every; **d** each; **e** every; **f** each

358

Setze die Mengenangaben *every* und *all* richtig ein:

every + Nomen im Singular = jeder/jedes
all + Nomen im Singular = ganz
every + Grundzahlen + Nomen im Plural = alle
all + Nomen im Plural = alle
all + *the* + Nomen im Plural = alle (von einer bestimmten Anzahl)

a ____________ pupil has got homework to do. (Jeder Schüler)

b ____________ pupils have got homework to do. (Alle Schüler haben)

c ____________ the pupils in this class have got homework to do. (Alle Schüler dieser Klasse)

d He visits his mom ____________ three weeks. (alle drei Wochen)

e ____________ the players were on the field. (Alle Spieler)

359

In den folgenden Sätzen sollst du die Mengenangaben „alle" und „jeder" richtig übersetzen. In Kurztest 358 kannst du noch mal nachschauen, wann man *every* und wann man *all* nimmt.

a Er geht alle fünf Tage schwimmen.

____

b Alle Kinder mögen Eis.

____

c Beinahe jeder Sänger hat Probleme mit der Stimme.

____

d Alle Spieler des FC Liverpool waren krank.

____

e Alle Kinder (bei einer Geburtstagsfeier) wollten am Computer spielen.

____

358 a Every; **b** All; **c** All; **d** every; **e** All
359 a He goes swimming every five days. **b** All children like ice cream. **c** Almost every singer has got problems with his/her voice. **d** All players on the FC Liverpool team were sick. **e** All the children wanted to play computer games.

360

Ordne die Wörter *each, every, any* und *all* (2x) ihren Bedeutungen zu.

a jeder Junge (in allgemeiner Bedeutung)

______________ boy wants a toy truck.

b jeder einzelne Junge (aus begrenzter Anzahl)

______________ boy in here has got a toy truck.

c jeder x-beliebige Junge

______________ boy can have a toy truck.

d alle Jungen (ohne Ausnahmen)

______________ boys have toy trucks.

e alle Jungen hier (alle aus dieser Gruppe)

______________ the boys here have toy trucks.

361

Übersetze die folgenden Sätze und benutze entweder *each, every, any* oder *all*.
Im Zweifel kannst du noch einmal in den Kurztests 356 und 358 nachschauen!

a Alle Schüler dieser Schule mussten einen Test schreiben.

____

b Jeder Schüler musste einen Test schreiben.

____

c Jeder einzelne Schüler musste einen Test schreiben.

____

d Jeder Schüler hätte diesen Test schreiben können. Er war sehr einfach.

____

360 a Every; **b** Each; **c** Any; **d** All; **e** All
361 a All the students at that school had to do/take a test. **b** Every student had to write a test.
c Each student had to write a test. **d** Any student could have done/taken this test. It was very easy.

362

Ordne die Zahlwörter *both (of)*, *either* und *neither* ihren Bedeutungen zu.

der eine oder der andere / der eine wie der andere	**a**
keiner von beiden	**b**
Beide	**c**

363

Setze *both (of)*, *either* oder *neither* richtig ein.
Tipp: *Neither* = *not* + *either*. Das *not* darf aber nicht doppelt stehen!

a ____________________ of you two is going swimming. It is way too cold!

b It doesn't matter which soup you make. I like them ____________________.

c ____________________ way will take you to Munich. This one is just longer.

d I have got two cars and ____________________ works. So I have to walk.

e Jack and Sarah are ____________________ taller than you now!

f ____________________ of them has got a computer. So they cannot email you.

g Emily doesn't care about the colour. She likes ____________________ shirts a lot.

h Would you like the red purse or the green one? I don't like ____________________!

i ____________________ can tell me what happened. They didn't see the accident yesterday.

j ____________________ these nails are crooked. Give me two new ones, please.

k ____________________ pen is fine. I can write well with the blue one or the black one.

l ____________________ of us was elected. I guess people didn't have confidence in us.

362 a either; **b** neither; **c** both (of)
363 a Neither; **b** both; **c** Either; **d** neither; **e** both; **f** Neither; **g** both; **h** either; **i** Neither; **j** Both of; **k** Either; **l** Neither

364

Verbinde die Sätze mit der Konjunktion *after*.
Tipp: Der Satzteil, in dem *after* vorkommt, steht hier immer im *past perfect*.

Beispiel: She had finished cleaning. She went to the cinema.

After she had finished cleaning, she went to the cinema.

a She had finished her picture. She framed it.

____

b Tom had listened to some music. He worked at the computer.

____

c Maria started to paint a new picture. She had read a short story.

____

d They had dropped a bottle of milk. They had to clean the whole kitchen.

____

365

Vervollständige die Sätze mit den angegebenen Wörtern und *after*.

a We left for the airport, ______________________________ (we / give the key to our neighbours).

b We put the luggage in the trunk, ______________________________ (Dad / call the taxi).

c I closed the front door, ______________________________ (Mum / tell me to do so).

d I sent my friends a holiday text message, ______________________________ (we / get into the taxi).

364 a After she had finished her picture, she framed it. **b** After Tom had listened to some music, he worked at the computer. **c** Maria started to paint a new picture, after she had read a short story. **d** After they had dropped a bottle of milk, they had to clean the whole kitchen.
365 a … after we had given the key to our neighbours. **b** … after Dad had called the taxi. **c** … after Mum had told me to do so. **d** … after we had got into the taxi.

366

Verbinde die Sätze mit der Konjunktion *before*.
Tipp: Der Satzteil, in dem *before* vorkommt, steht hier im *simple past*, der andere im *past perfect*.

Beispiel: The school dance was announced. Maria had planned to go with Tom.

Before the school dance was announced, Maria had planned to go with Tom.

a She had bought a wonderful dress. She asked Tom to go with her.

____

b Tom had had a dancing lesson. He accepted Maria's invitation.

____

c They had dressed carefully. They went to the photographer.

____

d They opened the door. The headmaster (= Direktor) had told them to make sure there was enough money in the till (= Kasse).

____

367

Maria erzählt, was sie alles vor ihrer Geburtstagsfeier zu tun hatte.
Vervollständige die Sätze mit den angegebenen Wörtern und der Konjunktion *before*.
Tipp: Der Satzteil, in dem *before* vorkommt, steht auch hier immer im *simple past*.

a I had bought a lot of delicious things, ______________________________
______________________________ (I / start cooking).

b I had written about 20 invitation cards, ______________________________
______________________________ (I / decide to send invitations via email)

c Mum had helped me to decorate the table, ______________________________
______________________________ (she / leave to meet Mrs Brown).

366 a She had bought a wonderful dress before she asked Tom to go with her. **b** Tom had had a dancing lesson before he accepted Maria's invitation. **c** They had dressed carefully before they went to the photographer. **d** Before they opened the door, the headmaster had told them to make sure there was enough money in the till.
367 a … before I started cooking. **b** … before I decided to send invitations via email. **c** … before she left to meet Mrs Brown.

368

Verbinde die Sätze mit der Konjunktion *while*.

Tipp: Der Satzteil, in dem *while* vorkommt, steht im *past progressive*, der andere im *simple past*.

Beispiel: We were watching TV. Mum dropped a bottle of milk.

While we were watching TV, Mum dropped a bottle of milk.

a We were watching *Harry Potter*. Mum cleaned the kitchen.

____

b We were sitting in front of the TV. We ate crisps and popcorn.

____

c Mum went to the shop for milk. We were talking about the film.

____

d Mum returned from the shop. We were still discussing *Harry Potter*.

____

369

Wie kann man Wartezeit auf den Bus oder beim Arzt sinnvoll nutzen? Vervollständige die Sätze mit den angegebenen Wörtern und – wo nötig – mit der Konjunktion *while*.

Tipp: Der Satzteil, in dem *while* nicht vorkommt, steht im *simple present*.

a While you are waiting for the bus, ______________________________

______________________________ (you / can repeat vocabularies).

b You can watch other people, ______________________________

______________________________ (you / wait for the train).

c While you are sitting in the waiting room, ______________________________

______________________________ (you / read a book)

368 a While we were watching *Harry Potter*, Mum cleaned the kitchen. **b** While we were sitting in front of the TV, we ate crisps and popcorn. **c** Mum went to the shop for milk, while we were talking about the film. **d** Mum returned home, while we were still discussing *Harry Potter*.

369 a … you can repeat vocabularies. **b** … while you are waiting for the train. **c** … you read a book.

370

Verbinde die Sätze mit der Konjunktion *when*.

Beispiel: We were in New York. We tried a lot of American food.

When we were in New York, we tried a lot of American food.

a We visited Manhattan. We took a boat tour round the island.

____

b We went to Liberty Island. We climbed to the top of the Statue of Liberty.

____

c We travelled by bus to Boston. We watched *West Side Story* on the TV inside the bus.

____

d We were in Boston in 1999. We took a trip to Cape Cod, where the Kennedys live.

____

371

Tom überlegt, was ohne Strom alles anders war. Vervollständige die Sätze mit den angegebenen Wörtern und wo nötig mit der Konjunktion *when*.

a When people didn't have electricity ______________________________

______________________________ (they / not use refrigerators).

b Nobody watched TV or listened to the radio ______________________________

______________________________ (electricity / not be available).

c When electric lights didn't exist ______________________________

______________________________ (everybody / use candles or laterns).

370 a When we visited Manhattan, we took a boat tour round the island. **b** When we went to Liberty Island, we climbed to the top of the Statue of Liberty. **c** When we travelled by bus to Boston, we watched *West Side Story* on the TV inside the bus. **d** When we were in Boston in 1999, we took a trip to Cape Cod, where the Kennedys live.
371 a … they didn't use refrigerators. **b** … when electricity wasn't available. **c** … everybody used candles or laterns.

372

Auch im Englischen klingt es besser, wenn zwei Sätze durch Konjunktionen miteinander verbunden werden. Benutze die angegebenen Konjunktionen.

a (although) They had a lot of work to do. They went to the cinema.

____

b (and) Maria helps her mother. She does the shopping.

____

c (because) We can't pick you up at the airport. Our car is broken.

____

d (but) I like Chinese food. Today I would prefer a pizza.

____

373

Auch im gesprochenen Englisch werden oft Konjunktionen verwendet. Tom erzählt von den Urlaubsplänen seiner Familie. Setze die Konjunktionen passend in den Text ein.

although   and   because   but

a It is July now, ________________ we are just now starting to plan our summer holidays.

b At first Mum was not very excited about the idea of going away ________________ she says that it is very expensive to go on holiday with the whole family.

c ________________ Dad agreed with her, I was able to convince them to go away for a week.

d We decided on a campsite in Wales ________________ it is less expensive than a hotel, ________________ Mum was not excited about this idea either.

372 a Although they had a lot of work to do, they went to the cinema. **b** Maria helps her mother and does the shopping. **c** We can't pick you up at the airport because our car is broken. **d** I like Chinese food, but today I would prefer a pizza.
373 a and; **b** because; **c** Although; **d** because / but.

374

Verbinde jeweils die beiden Sätze unter Verwendung der angegebenen Konjunktionen.

a (or) We could go to the fun park. We could go to a museum.

____

b (so) We're going to Spain next week. We can't look after your dog. Sorry!

____

c (while) They were shopping in Dublin. They saw Paul Mc Cartney.

____

d (when) My girlfriend called me. I was watching the news.

____

375

Jonas erzählt von seinem Lieblingshobby. Setze die Konjunktionen sinngemäß in den Text ein.

or but so and while however because when that

a I started rock climbing ______________ I was ten years old.

b My parents didn't want me to go rock climbing ______________ they thought it was too dangerous.

c They thought ______________ I should join a soccer club ______________ play tennis.

d ______________ I gave them a leaflet (= Broschüre, Flyer) of a rock climbing school ______________ finally they agreed.

e At the beginning both of my parents watched me ______________ I was climbing with my teacher.

f After some lessons, ______________, they saw that it was not dangerous at all ______________ they let me go to the lessons alone.

374 a We could go to the fun park, or we could go to a museum. **b** We're going to Spain next week, so we can't look after your dog. **c** While they were shopping in Dublin, they saw Paul Mc Cartney. **d** I was watching the news when my girlfriend called me.
375 a when; **b** because; **c** that, or; **d** But, so/and; **e** while; **f** however, and/so

376

Setze die Konjunktionen in die Lücken ein.

if (2x) | as soon as | until | as long as

a Tonight we are going to the disco and I think we will stay ____________ 3 am.

b You can still win the competition, Tom ____________ you practise every day.

c Don't worry about me. I'll call you ____________ I get home.

d Please tell me by 4 pm at the latest ____________ you can help me.

e ____________ they are on time today, we'll go to the theatre.

377

In argumentativen Texten kommen häufig Konjunktionen vor. Setze richtig ein.

as long as | when | although | if | because | and

a ____________ I like dogs a lot, I wouldn't want to keep one ____________ I don't have enough time.

b ____________ I go to school, I can't take care of a dog properly (= richtig).

c ____________ I'm out of school ____________ start working, I'll decide ____________ I can keep a dog.

378

that (2x) | but | after | because

a ____________ I had talked to my parents, we decided to get a little dog.

b At first Mum thought ____________ it was a really bad idea ____________ having a dog is so much work.

c ____________ I convinced her ____________ I could learn a lot of responsibility if I had a dog to look after.

376 a until; **b** as long as; **c** as soon as; **d** if; **e** if
377 a Although; because; **b** As long as; **c** When; and; if
378 a After; **b** that; because; **c** But; that

379

Setze ein: however until when (2x) as soon as because but then

a __________ we lived in the countryside, we had an Alsatian (= BE Schäferhund, AE = German shepherd).

b __________ we had to look for new owners for him __________ we decided to move to the city. We had to give him to our friends __________ we only had a small flat in the city centre.

c Sometimes, __________, we still take care of the dog __________ our friends are on holiday.

d __________ we keep him in our flat __________ they return home.

380

Verbessere den Stil dieser Aussagen, indem du die Sätze mit passenden Konjunktionen verbindest. Tipp: Nicht alle Sätze lassen sich sinnvoll verbinden!

and so before when because therefore

a Keeping a big dog like a Husky in a small flat is a bad idea. Such big dogs need a lot of exercise and lots of space to play and run around.

____

____

b Also, Huskys are snowdogs. This is why they should only be kept in very cold regions.

____

____

c You want to have a dog? You have to go out with it three times every day at least. You should think twice about that. Then get a dog.

____

____

379 a When; **b** But; as soon as; because; **c** however; when; **d** Then; until

380 a Keeping a big dog in a small flat is a bad idea because such big dogs need … **b** Huskys are snowdogs and therefore they should only be… **c** If you want to have a dog, you have to go out with it at least three times every day. You should think twice about that before you get a dog.